WHERE ARE YOU?

WHERE ARE YOU?

Searching the Unknown to Make It Known

John Paterson

Library of Congress Control Number: 2019901313
ISBN: Hardcover   978-1-7960-0036-8
                   Softcover   978-1-7960-0035-1
                   eBook   978-1-7960-0034-4

Print information available on the last page.

Rev. date: 03/19/2019

To order additional copies of this book, contact:
Xlibris
1-800-455-039
www.Xlibris.com.au
Orders@Xlibris.com.au
790185

CONTENTS

Don Noble.

"In a culture where 'self' has become the focus, truth has been diluted and faith ridiculed, the message of 'Where Are You' is counter-cultural and confronting. For those with the courage to read it, you will be challenged, convicted, encouraged and refreshed as John shares his journey as a broken teenager, to naval officer, husband, father, counsellor and friend, and his honest 'groping' for real truth and a foundation on which to hang it. As an Australian Christian man (ACM) I found this book real and relevant to my journey through the 'mystery' that is life. John does not tell us 'how to' or that we should have all the answers; but encourages us to seek and search for, and reconsider, what has been lost and rejected by our secular humanistic society. Including many insightful quotes by well-known Christian mystics, past and present, I highly recommend this book."

Don Noble is a husband, father, grandfather, tutor, pastor 'Living Earth' home church, and CTM partner.

Jim Gallagher.

"I have known John since he came to Lismore and see him as a man of integrity and truth. Many men have found a new freedom and fulfilment through their interaction with him. He writes from his own background of brokenness and also with the precision he has found from his time in the Navy. He has found healing and wholeness in centring his life in Christ. I thoroughly recommend this book as we push into a deeper relationship with God."

Pastor Jim Gallagher is the President of Lismore Ministers Fellowship

Peter Corney.

"John's story and his personal struggle to find an authentic and genuine commitment to Christ, to face his life issues and live a life that is honest and real has produced an interesting and practical book. Any person wanting to face the inner issues that can hold any of us back spiritually and emotionally from growth in maturity will find this book challenging and helpful."

Peter Corney OAM is the Vicar emeritus at St Hilarys' Anglican Church, Kew Vic.

Nicholas Marks

We live in a time where we are seeing daily the devastating effects of placing ourselves at the centre of meaning and our version of truth. Have we lost our way and cut our anchor now finding ourselves adrift? If so, what do we do about it? John Paterson is a storyteller and a man who really knows how to navigate uncharted territory. This book is an exploration, a mapping of where we are, how we got here and in his insightful and conversational style, walking with us to embark on a journey he has taken, the journey back to the God who can be known, to life. *Where Are You? is* important, timely and a pleasure to read. I encourage you to dive into this book to join the conversation, a conversation that matters!

Nicholas Marks is the Chief Executive Officer, Australian Institute of Family Counselling

FOREWORD

By
Dr. Larry Crabb

LITTLE IS MORE difficult than discovering where we are in this unpredictable, chaotic world. And it is even more difficult and less easy to discover who we are. Too many of us have abandoned the search, and settled for a sense of who we are, where we are, and where we're headed that keeps God at a comfortable distance. When we distance ourselves from God we either forget these questions or answer them in ways that honour the values of our secular culture.

Where am I? Well, I live in Sydney or Miami or London, and I go to this job every day. Who am I? A loser if I don't make much money or fail to be recognized as someone important. A winner if I'm successful, financially comfortable, enjoy life, and have good family and friends. Where am I heading? To more chapters in my story of the good life.

If there is a God, a personal relational God, and if it's true that He created us, it's no stretch to assume not only that He must have some thoughts on His core question – where am I? – as well as the other two, but also that because He is God He would be willing to share His thoughts with us. As a friend of mine once said, "If God is speaking, the best thing we can do is listen".

John Paterson has been listening. The result is the book you are now holding: Where Are You: Searching the Unknown to Make it Known.

I'm pleased that I had a small part in his undertaking a book length project to shed light on the question everyone is, ought to be, asking. As John records in the following pages, he and his wife Susan travelled from Australia to be with me in a weeklong conference for 30 people on spiritual direction. During that week I learned that John had been a student of the seas in the Australian Navy, specializing in hydrographic surveys. In simplest language (I know no other) he searched beneath the waterline to find what lies beneath that the navigator needed to know. He wondered if searching beneath the surface of the soul to discover where we are and move forward without danger might be a worthy search. I replied, "I think you have a book in you."

And now, as a well-received Christian counsellor, he draws on his wide reading, his extensive conversations with struggling people, and his rich knowledge of Scripture to write these nine chapters. Nine chapters that will grab you with interesting, meaningful, provocative ideas designed to help us come to grips with where we are on life's journey.

From gently exposing where we are that promises trouble ahead to a well-documented understanding at where a follower of Jesus can be in God's larger story, John has done a great favour to all of us, Christian, non-Christian, seeker, complacent, to everyone with the courage to wonder where we are and to search long and hard to find out.

I know little that's more important for a human being than to get in touch with the deep thirst in every living soul, a thirst that when recognized and felt drives us away from leaking wells and towards the living water available only in Jesus. Among other virtues that make this book a worthwhile read, I came away more aware of my desire to know God and to be where He enables me to be.

A book worth reading. A man worth listening to. A message worth exploring, and heeding. Where are you? Let John accompany you on your search.

PREFACE

T HE INSPIRATION FOR this book came from Paul's address to the Athenians.

To an Unknown God

Paul then stood up in the meeting of the Areopagus and said: 'People of Athens! I see that in every way you are very religious. For as I walked around and looked carefully at your objects of worship, I even found an altar with this inscription: TO AN UNKNOWN GOD. So you are ignorant of the very thing you worship—and this is what I am going to proclaim to you.

'The God who made the world and everything in it is the Lord of heaven and earth and does not live in temples built by human hands. And he is not served by human hands, as if he needed anything. Rather, he himself gives everyone life and breath and everything else. From one man he made all the nations, that they should inhabit the whole earth; and he marked out their appointed times in history and the boundaries of their lands. God did this so that they would seek him and perhaps reach out for him and find him, though he is not far from any one of us. 'For in him we live and move and have our being.' As some of your own poets have said, 'We are his offspring.'" Therefore, since we are God's offspring, we should not think that he divine being is like gold or silver or stone—an image made by man's design and skill. (Acts 17: 22–29)

Not so long ago, I met a bloke who was suffering overwhelming pain and was in severe distress. He wasn't able to be with those he loved. He felt alone, rejected, abused, and powerless. He believed he had nothing left to give any more. He had come to the end of himself and had lost all sense of caring about anything. That was a soul whom I thought was feeling pretty close to what it must be like to be in hell. The reason I thought this was because the bottom line in this person's life was that he didn't believe God was good. Here was a person who actually believed God existed, but who did not believe that God was good and so could hardly trust Him to come through for the wretch he saw himself to be. Of course, that is not the God whom you and I know through our intimate relationship with Him, is it? Our God who we know to be perfectly loving and desiring only good for us? You and I believe this, don't we? My friend didn't. He didn't believe God was really good, and he didn't trust Him to come through with His promises. He didn't know God as He truly is, as He desires to be known, and who longs to be in relationship with us!

This book is written intentionally to Christian men and women who seek to follow the Christian God—and in the following pages, I hope to tease that out a bit more. But if you are not yet a Christian, this book might also help in a few areas. I say this because, well, we all seem to worship someone, or something, don't we? We might not like to admit it but it's true. We all hold something up to be of most worth and more valuable than anything else. Despite the *self* now being widely accepted to be the centre of the universe (which means 'everyone but me is off-centre'), all human beings need something outside of themselves to focus on, or to be distracted by, otherwise we would all either implode, or spin off into the Never Never. This is not just a matter of religion. Most Australians I have met are very religious. They (we) all worship (hold to be of most worth) *something* and seem to be pursuing *something* very religiously. It might be God (whoever we hold God to be) or something, or someone else? More likely, unconsciously or consciously, it is probably fame, power, fantasy, sexuality, riches (in various forms), glory, significance, purpose in family, work, entertainment, academia, politics and/ or religion, or some other thing—searching, longing for something—why? Do you ever wonder about what/who the *something* is?

If we could stop being so busy, seeking to be entertained and/or distracted, and instead were still just long enough (long enough at least to wonder about life, about our lives, seek some deeper meaning, and actually think about it), well then, we might actually get in touch with something that is alive and deep down inside of us. Can you sense it? It is there, if you stop still long enough and be quiet enough. This something seems to be about desire or longing for something that I want, need, should have, am entitled to, or deserve. Or is it the emptiness, the boredom, the lostness, and the loneliness that seems to bear down on us from life—life that is out of control, and that just seems to happen to us. Maybe this is the very reason we don't stop and be still? What do you think? So we remain too busy, too stressed, too tired, and too occupied with stuff that has got to be done (but doesn't satisfy) so that we don't have to feel the ache of the longing.

I know that there are things going on inside of me that I should be attending to, but not now. My life's a mess, and if I'm being honest, I know I can't fix it! So I need a distraction—perhaps something to entertain me, comfort me, make me feel good, or at least to feel like I'm alive. But, nothing too deep that requires too much reasoned thought or the examining of moral conscience—just something light, fun and with enough fantasy to let me escape a bit from life. Nothing wrong with that, is there? Yet no matter what I do, it just never seems to be enough and it never fulfils me, and so I seem to settle for some lesser thing and convince myself that it's OK—that it's good enough at least.

I believe in God. I do want to be in relationship with Him—I just don't really know how. Sometimes I wonder, *Are you really good, God? Can I really trust You?* The search for answers to these sorts of questions about my faith has taken me sixty-four years, and I'm finally beginning to believe that God *is* good—even if He and I (well, mostly me) still argue sometimes about the definition of 'goodness'. I do know there is something actually alive in me, and that *something* is telling me that I desire *it* more than anything else. It's why I am still a Christian and why I am writing this book.

In late August 2017, I was half enjoying a slow day, winter's slow growth keeping outside gardening jobs to a minimum, only one client for the week—although there were other commitments: a visit to the dentist, two coffees and conversations with mates (you know, regular blokes who help make life seem somewhat reasonable), and a trip to the vet with my ageing second best friend Honey Dog (a red kelpie just like Red Dog) for her six-monthly arthritis jab. I was catching up on some reading around the Christian journey of spiritual formation, living the Christian life, union with Christ, and communion with God—the sorts of themes I never really spent much time on the first sixty years of my life. Life to me seems to be flying by—how about you?

Anyway, I was brought suddenly to a standstill while reading Acts 17:22–31, Paul's speech to the Athenians. Verse 27 seemed to leap out of the page and grabbed my attention: '*God did this so that they would seek him and perhaps reach out (grope) for him and find him, though he is not far from any one of us.*' God did this so that we would respond to His goodness and seek

Him? He is near? And my response is . . . Of course, we all know that Paul was referring to the Unknown God—and the thought occurred to me, *Is this still the Unknown God that exists today—both within and outside the Christian faith—in our civilised, Western society of First World cultures particularly?* Of course, you may not agree, but allow me to introduce this thought a little more because it seems to be the case that many Christians I spend time with actually seem to think this way.

But first, let me backtrack a little. Allow me to briefly introduce myself. I describe myself as an ordinary bloke, although C. S. Lewis would disagree because he says there is no such thing as an ordinary person. I was raised as a country boy, growing up in a small country town in Proserpine, North Queensland and in Airlie Beach, where I gained a love for the ocean. I guess the best way to say it was that at seventeen I ran away to sea. Closer to the truth is that I joined the Navy to escape the ever-increasing fights with my father and to seek some sort of life and satisfy a sense of lostness. I was given an identity and learned about responsibility, authority, and discipline during a thirty-year career in the Navy. I am forever grateful for the safety framework the military provided during that time of my life. In 2001, I believe I heard God calling me out from my security blanket, and I left the Navy a year later.

Now I am sailing in a very different 'ship'—civilianship—and I am a self-confessed struggler, and pilgrim trying to navigate a different journey these last sixteen years, relearning life again, endeavouring to understand what it means to be an Australian Christian man (ACM). It's been a hard and sometimes lonely journey, but I haven't been alone. I know this because I have been an avid reader, student, and now call myself a friend of Larry Crabb, who is also a self-described struggler, and who, I think, is an authentic and earnest seeker after God. He and others I have read, walked with, observed, witnessed, shared with, and learned from are an inspiration and encouragement for my own walk.

So I haven't been alone, you see? But, well, let's face it; each of us has our own journey to go on, and since it is our journey, no one is going to walk it for us, though they may walk some of it with us. And for that, I am thankful to those who have companioned me. Along the way, we hope and seek to gain wisdom and knowledge so that we may choose the good way and walk it—just like Jesus did. It is our Christian faith that tells us that these character traits of wisdom and knowledge can only be found in Jesus Christ Himself. The *way*, of course, is the way of love that He showed and commanded of us. But, what does that mean today, and how do we define it? I wonder about these things still. I ponder about what God is up to. I seek to know Him more closely and intimately. I grapple with my wretchedness and how I am the 'jewel in His crown' and the 'apple of His eye'. But I know that He is close, and I know He promises that I will find Him. I know now that He is good and that His promises are true, so until He calls me home, this hope that I can walk this walk is my anchor—my strength and my courage.

Why This Book?

In our postmodern society and Western culture, God seems to be either regarded as non-existent, weak, even bad, or irrelevant in the sense that we have no real need of Him. Even from within our Christian communities, I think we seem to reinterpret Him to what best suits our purposes and fit within our cultural way of living—culture being the total way of life as a people. Various authors seem to agree that generations and societies reinterpret Christianity through their various cultures and the prevailing ideologies of the times. Where does this leave a cohesive and communal understanding of God and ourselves so that we can live and move together on this planet? Postmodernism proposes, nay, demands that there is no truth, no reference point or fixed point from which to find a starting place, and no firm foundation to build onto except what a person constructs for themselves. You just make it up as you go. But Jesus clearly asserts that He is the life, the truth, and the way, doesn't He?

If Jesus is the same yesterday, today, and tomorrow, and if God's standards don't change, what on earth is going on? How is it that we seem willing to reinterpret God so that He fits in with our culture and lifestyle, which seem to be forever changing to keep up with the values asserted by a secular humanistic society? It's creepy! It's an atheistic secular creep, with some creep behind it all. Or worse, how is it that we think we can know better, through theological studies alone, how to know God, rather than from what Jesus Himself revealed? So part of my passion for writing this book comes out of a frustration with the way the Western church in general seems to have presented Christianity. Have we got it wrong? But since I know many ministers and pastors to be fine human beings, I am reluctant to criticise and would rather be an encourager because those I talk with seem to generally agree. The other passion I bear is a compassion for those many others I have met who share my confusions, are groping to hold on to some truth, and who are striving to walk the walk that Jesus showed us.

John Calvin said that the whole of Scripture could be summed up in these two things: knowing God and knowing yourself (in relationship with God). While I do not consider myself to be a theologian and I certainly submit my views to those who are, I am a searcher and studier of the Bible and I seek to know God through how He has revealed Himself through His Word and in the person of Jesus Christ. So an authentic understanding of what Scripture is saying that sits within the larger story God is telling us about Himself and us, and how we are related, and that accords with what Jesus says is essential for me—and I continue to seek, grope, and hope to find further understanding. It is my belief that any theology about God needs to be from seeking to understand Him from how *He* has revealed Himself. That is why, for me, the truth of Scripture needs to meet two main criteria. Firstly, it is true when it is in accord with the larger story God is telling us about Himself and us and how we are related from His personal self-revelation. Secondly, it must accord with the person of Jesus Christ as He showed Himself to be and how those who were once close to Him wrote of Him.

These two criteria (and a few others that may come out later) fit in with a theology that is lived out through relationship with a God who desires to be known at the deepest of levels and who longs for us to understand who He really is so that we are drawn ever nearer towards Him in a heartfelt way. Scripture has to make sense in the larger narrative that God is telling us about Himself and where we fit in because we are really living in His story. All history is His story—and this is our time, place, and part within it. I am not one to think that God would invite us into an eternal relationship with Him without making that possible for us by giving us all we need, all the resources we require, and all the capacity necessary so as to take our place, and in every way have a role to play, so as to be living out and abundantly enjoying our relationship with Him now. The Christian journey is an interior one that is worked out into life (Philippians 2:12–13). God works deep within us to change our character so we become like Christ and invites us to respond to Him by coming to Him so as to be filled up and to take what He freely gives and pour it into His creation, a world and people who are in dire need of both His goodness and His life-giving love.

Why now? Well, take a moment to have an honest look at what is happening around you—in our society, in our communities, in our schools, churches, families, and marriages—and ask yourself if we are really OK. I leave the answer up to you; however, I will say this much: if 'love' and 'freedom' have different meanings within the Kingdom of God than in our present society, then it is no surprise to me that marriage does now as well—it didn't use to. Christians had better get used to the reality that the values of secular society and the various world cultures are different to the way of life as shown by Jesus in the Kingdom of God, and it is not OK to reinterpret Jesus so that our Christian way of life fits neatly into the world so that it is convenient and comfortable. That won't go well for us in the long term.

The need for men and women who declare themselves for Christ to live lives authentically for the Kingdom of God and be His image bearers on earth, is needed more now than ever before. Increasingly, it seems to me, that our Father as revealed by Jesus, His Son, and their relationship with the Spirit have become less known—it already seems to be the case—and God seems to be becoming more irrelevant for most people. Should we be surprised and daunted by this? Most definitely we should not. We were told in the Scriptures that this would be the case. I think as we go forward, there will be more opportunities for God's children—His called-out ones—to reflect His glory in this world and shine like stars even more brightly in the encroaching darkness. Even dim lights burn more brightly as the darkness increases.

A really important prerequisite for reading this book is to be willing to wear a particular set of glasses, with specialised lenses. These glasses view Scripture through relational lenses so as to encourage the reader to be *living out a practically authentic Christian faith through our relationships with God first and in our Christian communities.* So I am inviting you to put on a pair of specs with relational lenses because I believe that what Australian Christian men in particular are really looking for, and really need, is a way that provides the means to *be living what we say we believe,* to *be living it authentically and practically so that it is really real.* Let me tell you why. Because God is relational, and so are we! Therefore, our lives must be lived out relationally. We give glory to God and honour Him by the way we live, love, and relate—with Him first and through our relationships with each other.

A Little More About Me

Easter 1990 was a turning point in my life. My world came crumbling down. My wife of fourteen years had endured enough of my self-centredness and our lives being focused around my career, so we separated. I was 36 years old, at the pinnacle of my Navy career, and was enjoying my third straight command before being banished to Canberra and staff college in preparation for higher rank and expected promotion. Life was all about me, of course.

That might give you some indication of where I was at and what God was working on as I was brought to my knees.

I found myself confused, lost, shattered, alone, and scared—just as I had been twenty years earlier, after surviving the rage that seems to accompany teenage years. I still had no insight into the deeply embedded consequences of child sexual abuse that caused dark and angry storm clouds to often build deep inside of me. These were like extreme weather systems that I was refusing to pay attention to because I enjoyed the adrenaline and energy the storms provided—if not the darkness. It was what I needed to empower me and provide the motivation and drive necessary for me to be competitive and survive my military environment. I had thrived in the Navy because it had provided a safe and secure place to learn life disciplines, how to look after myself and to be totally in control of how to make my way in life. It also gave me an identity, social status, and a community in which to enjoy a 'good' lifestyle. This protected me for twenty years—enough time to survive the childhood abuse impact. At a particular critical and dangerous point in time, about three months after my wife had left, I cried out to God and handed myself (mostly) over to Him. But of course, you would be very aware that this was only the beginning. My self-determined defence strategies, the false idols of comfort and security, and self-constructed identity personas all had to be brought down if I was ever going to authentically walk the Christian path following Jesus.

God was gracious towards me and seemed to take the initiative in pouring Himself into me during the following year. Twelve months after being devastated by a marriage break-up, I reconfirmed my Christian faith and received the gift of my two daughters to become a full-time single parent. Nadine and Rhiannon were ten and eleven years old at the time they came to live with me. This caused a major reset in my life's course. As a single parent in the Defence Forces (although, to my everlasting gratefulness, I was well supported), the situation made me no longer post able or promotable within my specialised category.

I didn't know it at the time, but all of this (and I am including my childhood and teenage struggles), was preparing me for a new life that was yet to unfold. I threw myself into my new community of faith and a new identity as a Christian man and father. I soaked up Christian fellowship and formation programmes. I read the Bible profusely. I consumed Christian books—and I went to counselling. The husband-and-wife counselling team had started a Christian counselling training institute and they invited me to undertake training to learn the theory behind what I was experiencing in the counselling process. My Navy superiors also thought this was a good thing and wanted me to obtain counselling qualifications for the team I was working with. This set a course for a change in career, and I proceeded to head towards becoming a Navy chaplain.

Life happens, of course, and did not go the way I would have imagined or would have chosen. I guess there are not many surprises there for some readers. My father died in 1998. What a blessing to have had seven years in which to reconcile with him, and we were able to mutually express our love for each other. The next four years were some of the most healing I experienced. The girls had grown into young women. One returned to Cairns to look after her mother; the other had made friends and a life in Canberra. I went to Wollongong to live and worked at the Hydrographic Office. In Wollongong, we began a new area community as part of the Australia-wide church community I was part of. What a blessing this time was in my life. The relationships formed there retain a large part of my heart. And, I will always remember my time of healing and growth in the Wollongong community very fondly.

At some time in 2001, I received a sense of a call, which I believed to be from God, to leave the Navy—the place of my security and comfort for thirty years. This was a big thing for me because at this time, there was no sense of what I was to do. I resigned from the Navy, and the only commitment I had made was to lead a team into Russia in June 2002 under the Love for Kids Russia programme (what an honour and adventure). Then, the CEO and founder of the counselling institute where I had trained heard that I had resigned and asked me to work for them on staff—and I met Susan, who was to become my life friend and companion. Skipping right past the romantic part, we married, I stood aside from community, moved to Sydney, and joined Susan's church and counselling practice. I also took up a position as a male counsellor at St John's Counselling Service, Kings Cross, Sydney, and volunteered at Rough Edges street cafe. What a change this was from my disciplined and comfortable middle-class lifestyle.

Life was pretty good except for one major factor: Susan and I are country folk—the city life is just not in our DNA. We both sensed that to forge a life together in our committed journey towards God and draw closer to each other required a social and geographical change. We decided to leave the busy city life, but it also meant leaving the wonderful relationships we had both thrived on during our single years. After some discernment, we chose to move to

Lismore, northern rivers area, NSW in 2004, taking our counselling practice with us—and here we remain. Two big differences between a city practice and a country practice are that one is never anonymous in the community of a country town, and it is very much how you are known and who you are as a person that comes before reputation and achievement. So we networked widely and settled into the One in Christ Fellowship at the Lismore Soup Kitchen, making it our church community. This 'only by grace' church keeps me humble—which remains a necessary part of God's ongoing work in me.

It has taken me a long time to begin to understand the impact that culture (our Australian concept of men) and a secularised-humanistic and atheistic Western society has had on determining who we should be, nay, that demand who we are to be. While I have been so busy yet distracted, striving and struggling to make my way in the world ever since the day I was born, the world, particularly our Westernised society values and Australian culture, have been making their way in me. For a while there, I thought that I might be in this life struggle by myself—that I was the only one struggling with being a man, a Christian, and an Australian. However, reading the life testimonies of other faith seekers, being part of men's sharing groups, one-on-one conversations with close friends during many men's weekends, camps, retreats, and in the sanctity of the counselling relationship with many Christian men – walking with them, talking, listening and being with them in their struggles, I finally realised that I am not alone.

All of what I have written so far is to share with you that I have been on a journey, and still am. (Aren't we all?) During this journey, I have been a seeker, a struggler, and a ponderer of life and its meaning—in any order. Some of this is, of course, a consequence of the trauma I experienced, but also, some are personality traits and passions. I think the seeker aspects were further fuelled as I left the known world and security of the Navy to head in a new direction where I felt out of my depth and in uncharted waters in a new way. Allow me to present what I think is my main credential. I made a mess of life. Some days were like struggling to stay afloat after a shipwreck. Yet, in the midst of sometimes (still) feeling like I'm adrift on the sea of life, there is an anchor for my soul. So this book is my attempt to pass on what I believe to be some main factors behind why there are so many internally messed-up people and messed-up relationships *within our Christian communities*—and yet we can be secure in knowing at all times where we are in life when we measure ourselves using three known marks.

Where Are You?

Where do we seek the answers to life as Australian men? Where does the source for the vitality of life come from? And from where do we seek it? What, or more accurately, Who is the source? Paul tells us at verse 28, *'For in him we live and move and have our being.'* Do we really know this God in the intimate way we have described? Maybe we need to learn again from Jesus who God is. It seems that our knowledge of God has faded and lost the passion, colour, and wonder these (nearly) 2,000 years since Jesus revealed the truth about His Father and ours, the truth about who He is, why He did what He did, why He left us, and why He left whom He did to be with us. Our God says He is near now, with us and even in us. He desires our hearts to be for Him—as His is for us—and He wants to spend eternity with us and for us to be with Him where He is. It's all about relationship. We Christians get this, don't we?

If you are already aware of these concerns, then you might be glad to know that it makes sense. If you are already living this out in your lives, families, and relationships, then you might be encouraged further. If it's all new to you, then I encourage and invite you to stay the course. If you think it's *codswallop* and doesn't apply to you, then again I invite you to stay the course so that you might reinforce, or not, what you do believe in or add support to reasons for choosing a way that may better suit you. Or, you might want to check out what's on TV. If you are still wondering about who I am and what I'm doing writing this book, don't worry, you aren't alone—I am still working on that one too.

I am writing as one of you. I want this book to be an earnest appeal to Christian men and women to stand up and walk the walk of our Christian journey because it's a good walk! I am walking this journey more because of my failures than any success I have had in life. I have failed by human standards in school, career, marriage, as a father, and in life in general. I stand with you by the grace of God. I have a message to bring about how we struggle as Christians in our culture. I find it easier to ask your forgiveness if I offend you rather than to ask for your permission to speak this stuff. What I say will be overtly Christian in presentation because, to be truthful, it has to be—and the reality is that this is where the answer lies—and it's really important to seek the answer because so much hinges on it. So this is an exhortation for the reader to consider their standard of measurement for their faith, do you have a reference point, and how do you measure where you are at any point in your life along your chosen path? What I will describe in this book is an answer that is over 350 years old—I will attempt to present it in a different light.

Finally, I want to encourage all Christians, in these times, to stay the course and keep on keeping on.

ACKNOWLEDGEMENTS

DR LARRY CRABB has been a mentor in absentia and an encourager for me on my journey for 25 years. I have absorbed his openly honest, shared thoughts throughout most of his writings. Ten years my senior, he has been inspirational in two main ways: firstly, by being a self-confessed struggler, and secondly, by being along the road that I have chosen to travel and shining a torch as to where I am about to place my next step. Thank you, Larry and Rachel, for your relational love offered to so many so that no one should have to struggle in this life alone.

G'ma, G'pa, and my dad for sowing my childhood faith. Mum for her belief in me. To my extended family who love me and remind me from whence I came. To all those with whom I have travelled together with, and learned from, including Uncle Rob, Vince Fitzwilliam, Han De Grave, DOJCC mentors, Michael Lahiff for his non-judgemental acceptance, Frank and Lyn Toohey's unconditional love and gentle companionship, and my Wollongong brothers and sisters. John Kidson, Jim Gallagher for their welcome and fellowship in the Northern Rivers. Jim, Rob, Robert, Jeremy, Peter for mateship at men's coffee. Chris and Bruce for their peer support, friendship and fellowship. One in Christ Fellowship for their love, for allowing me to serve and for keeping me humble. Don Noble for your encouragement and for keeping me sane over ten years of weekly coffees and CTMs. And to all those whose journey I have had the privilege to be a part of, and especially with all who I have had conversations that matter—for you are a part of me, and I have learned much from you.

Rhiannon and Nadine for my father's heart and my joy, their husbands Dan and Phillip—my respect, and my grandchildren Phillip, Emily, Lachlan, William, and Riley. This is for you!

Susan Mary, my intimate companion, friend and lover—for your willingness to see the best in me.

And, to God be the glory.

INTRODUCTION

I see that in every way you are very religious. For as I walked around and looked carefully at your objects of worship, I even found an altar with this inscription: TO AN UNKNOWN GOD. (Acts 17:22, 23)

Out on the wastes of the Never Never—That's where the dead men lie!
There where the heat-waves dance forever—That's where the dead men lie!

Barcroft Henry Thomas Boake

HAVE YOU EVER tried to suggest to someone that perhaps they might be a little off the mark (a polite way of telling them they are wrong) on a certain matter: a point, topic, issue, situation, circumstance, or direction that they consider they have under control? Do you recall how it went? Did it go well? My thoughts about this are that, at its core, it's probably closely associated with the self being the centre of the universe—you know what I mean. This means that if I am the centre of the universe, then everybody, and everything else, is not only off-centre but revolving around me. Reno described our 'postmodern faith' as being that our own belief about life, ourselves, and others is more important and certain to us than anything someone else might say. He said that all authoritative claims are viewed as 'acts of violence' against a person's conscience, intellect, and will.[1] The authority of truth itself is denied, and all truth claims are relative. Isn't it odd when someone says something like that, and they want you to seriously take what they are saying to be true?

Of course, this dogmatic viewpoint serves a useful purpose in that it protects and prevents us from the need to change—certainly from the possibility that we may be wrong and need to do things differently. Try observing this yourself next time you tell someone that they are wrong, even your children, if you have any, and see how they respond. Sometimes,

I wonder whether it's true that humanity might in fact be evolving for the better, because even the worst of criminals declare, '*I haven't done anything wrong.*' Cynical? Yes, probably, yet in the truth of our faith, human beings are indeed wrong, off the mark, and remain sinful whenever we deviate from God's will or otherwise choose not to hold God as our primary reference point and follow His standards for us in all that is good and loving. The real tragedy about this is that this world really needs His standard of goodness.

If I declared that our Christian faith was under attack, especially throughout our Western societies, I do not think it would cause much surprise or dispute amongst Christians, because anyone with eyes open will see it is so. As far as Western civilised cultures and society are concerned, religion has to be kept at a safe distance from our secular life because nothing has a right to make a claim on our souls, especially Christianity. Take notice next time you see how Christian characters are portrayed in media, academia, and entertainment now. Usually you see a corrupt patriarchal system, evidenced by the abuse of power throughout the tightly defended institutions led by relationally awkward and emotionally absent men, characterised as sub-intelligent. There just seems to be something sinister about them.

But more than this, Christianity threatens our way of life in at least two other areas: it calls us to dependence, to give up control, and it promises, no, demands to make us different—to change us. Why should we do either? Well, one reason might be to acknowledge what J. L. Packer described as the 'anti-God virus' that exists in each and every one of us, and he warned that 'opposition (from the world) is strong from the outside and stronger from the inside', letting those of us who are in denial know 'There's a problem! Powerful forces that oppose God are in us from conception.'[2] If you doubt the force of this resistance, tap into what's going on for you now. Can you detect or notice any voice(s) that is resistant to what I am saying, or maybe trying to convince you otherwise? Maybe even discounting, or worse, what I am saying. Or maybe simply, 'Isn't he going on a bit?'

Why should you listen to me, especially when I know full well that some may be offended by what I write? Well, if people turned their backs on Jesus and walked away from Him angry and hating Him even though He was a man who loved perfectly, how much more is an ignorant, self-centred, foolish man like me likely to offend people? But I don't want to. I want to earnestly appeal to all those on the Christian journey, those considering it or yet to be introduced to it, to understand that the need for wisdom and knowledge is the holy grail given to us by God and can only be found in Jesus Christ. I want to ask the reader to consider where we are in this present time in reference to our Christian faith and to be brutally honest about what is going on: around us, between us, and in us. I even ask those who might think we are doing OK to rethink and reflect whether we are not repeating (once again) Jeremiah's time, declaring, *'Peace, peace, when there is no peace'* (Jeremiah 6:14, 8:9–11). Where is the peace?

It's almost fifty years since Francis Schaeffer wrote *Death in the City*. As I reflected on the message, I understood him to be saying (unlike Richard Dawkins or Friedrich Nietzsche) not that God was dead, rather than man himself is dead.[3] How is that? And, what did he mean? Schaeffer was saying that Man (Adam) was meant to remember what God had said, remember His Creator, and move into the world for God's purposes. But when man forgets who he is, and what life means, he is lost! Because man turns from God there is death in the *polis*—not a city but rather a sociological group and culture. Man himself is dead because he loses all sense of personality—and what it means to be a man.

Briefly, I understand Schaeffer to be saying (remember this was 50 years ago now) that the previous two generations in the USA had separated from God, turned from the truth of who God is and from His moral truth. The result was that the current generation whom Schaeffer was addressing, in the 1960s and 1970s no longer knew God. The consequences were disastrous, wrapped up in the 'death of man', which Schaeffer said meant that Western society had lost a sense of who they are—man had lost his personality and character but was hiding behind the bravado found in cultural images yet with no real sense of who he was. In essence, Schaeffer was saying that he considered Western society and culture to be morally dead—lost! How might we consider our Australian society is doing? And the reason Schaeffer gave was that people had become separated from humanity's primary reference point. So where might that position us now in 2018? The words of the Australian poet Barcroft Henry Thomas Boake caught my attention: *Out on the wastes of the Never Never—That's where the dead men lie!* This is not some romantic place in outback Australia. Rather, it is like being at a place in life where one is lost in a hell, never, never to be found again. Sometimes, I have felt like life was hell and that I was lost and alone, but I, for one, never, never ever want to go to a place where God cannot be found—that would really be a hell of a place.

I believe, like Schaeffer was trying to tell us, that Christians today are experiencing the consequences of the previous generations turning away from God and His moral truth, and no longer know who God truly is. I can think of three ways this has occurred, and I know there are more. Firstly, as Richard Rohr so subtly put it in his book, *The Divine Dance* (2016), the early church really focused on a search for God in the first four hundred years of our Christian heritage. This search very much centred on knowing who God was/is, and where Jesus fitted in—or was it around the other way? This led early Christians into a spiritual mystery, yet towards a more complete understanding of the three-fold way of God in the working and relating of the Father, the Son and the Spirit. These last seventeen hundred years has witnessed a reticence in the church to seek an understanding of this mystery, and the threeness of God seems to be missing in action. How can we know God when we no longer dwell on His mystery of three holy and perfectly loving persons in one common union of nature, essence, attitude, and purpose? Secondly, for most Christians, we can seem to forget how carnal we are in what the Bible often calls 'our flesh', or at the very least, our potential for it—how, from the moment we were born into this world, the world has been making its way in us. Now, while I am trying to make my way as a Christian man in this world, the world is busily, intentionally, and subtly making its way in me, and I can be totally unaware and/or in denial of this. As Larry Crabb reminds us candidly, 'Sin remains after conversion.'[4] This has a crucial impact adversely for the third point, which is knowing and responding to God in relationship, either corporately and/or individually. How are we in a relationship with God? Mostly, I think people no longer see that they need God, and in our basically secure and comfortable world, God has become irrelevant—until some 'earthquake' occurs and shatters our mostly comfortable and convenient lives.

My own experience of being with, listening, and sharing with 'earnestly seeking God' Christians has led me on a quest to seek out what this all means for us now. I see the loneliness and lostness in people. I sense their longing for *something* they deeply desire but don't know what it is. And, I see the foolish and the desperate ways they go about trying to find, fill, and satisfy these longings. We are hungry, thirsty, and foolish. It is us, human beings with a natural enmity towards God, who have set ourselves up as the reference point for what is good for us and what we need to do to gain the good life. Sensing something deep within us, a desire, a longing for something or someone to make us whole, something that will feel good and make us happy, something that will at least protect us from being hurt and feeling more pain, we go off in search of whatever we can find to satisfy the desire—futility in the end, of course. Not only the futility that is described in the book of Ecclesiastes, but also, as Socrates philosophised, *a desire by its nature cannot be satisfied*—well, at least it wouldn't be a desire anymore if it was satisfied.

So you might agree that leaves us with a fairly significant problem. But it is not a new problem. The German theologian, philosopher, and mystic, Meister Eckhart (1260–1328) told us, '*God is at home. It is we who have gone out for a walk.*' And, we have walked away from God because we were deceived about the truth that God is good. We have demanded to choose for ourselves what is good for us and have made a determination about how to get our needs met. We have decided that we will set the standards for what is the good life and will take matters into our own hands to get what we want when we want it. But, under the delusion that we can get for ourselves what God will not give us, what is it that we are really searching for?

Here is an extract of what Larry Crabb was saying in his Soul Care teaching.[5] Larry shared how he (sometimes) feels exposed and uncomfortable, yet also enticed by something.

> There's something in me that moves away (from God) and
> I know I've walked away!
>
> But, there is something more in me. I want to come home,
> and I sense that there's a way to get there. Maybe it's because
> I'm a Christian.

He offered us these three thoughts around what Meister Eckhart meant (and I am paraphrasing Crabb here).

1. Because of the Gospel, God's home is now in me! No longer does He only speak to me from the outside, but He whispers to me from His sanctuary inside of me. In some way that makes the journey to experiencing God a journey into my interior world—into my own soul—because that is where God is present. If I search deep enough, and listen quietly enough and do it prayerfully, contemplatively, respectfully—honouring Who He is and not being presumptuous—I may hear His whisper.
2. When I walk away from God, I walk away from myself—my true self. Somehow, somewhere along the holy highway, we have been very deceived. We think we need something more than God to be

whole. Yes, God is good, but not good enough for what I need. We convince ourselves we are walking towards God, following His will for us, being good Christians—and we can still be thinking wrongly. As C. S. Lewis in 'The Great Divorce' reminds us, when we hug any treasure close to our chest, other than God, we never find our way home to our true centre.

3. The only way to discover my true self is to come home to God. When we are in the midst of life's busyness, the pressure and messages of culture and society to conform and perform, when we are naturally going about life our own way and undergoing life's urgent pull to be in control, not only do we not know the way home, but we don't even seem to realise we are away. We don't understand our carnal self. We can lose all hope. We lose sight not only of who we are, but who we could become. As Christians, we can feel the tension between the flesh and the spirit and can lose the will to fight the battle.

Adrift, Alone, Lost?

Without any fixed point of reference other than the self, humanity is adrift in an ocean of postmodernism. We are at the mercy of whatever major currents and forces that may act on us to take us in whatever direction the predominant wind is blowing, to wherever principal elementary forces dictate. Foolishly, we think we are free, and in control of our own life. Humanity is adrift in a sea of insecurity and uncertainty—take an honest look. We are alone in our self-centred search for happiness and to get our needs met. Although we long for connection, this self-focus has the opposite effect. It actually disconnects and separates us. You know what I mean—you see for yourselves the amount of time people are spending on high-tech devices, trying to fill their need for connection even while they are physically present with other people. Take a look at couples out for a night together in a romantic setting, and they are on their devices. Cast away from any ties to the past and avoiding insight into the future, we are now confused and have lost sight of life having any value, purpose, or meaning other than the intensification of the present—to feel good about myself and to be happy. After all, God loves me, so He wants me to be happy, doesn't He?

What and where is our reference point? What is the standard of measurement for what is really good and what makes us truly happy? How do we know love? How do we know where we are and where we are going?

Are you feeling adrift, lost, and alone? Or are you anchored in the hope of your faith based on the promises of a loving God, secure in who you are, confident that you know where you are positioned, certain of the direction you are heading and assured of your destination? These are some of the questions I have asked in my own life, and I have had the privilege to search for the answers, journeying alongside others during conversations that matter, about the really important things of life. We need to ask these questions and search for the answers when navigating through the oceans of life, especially when seas are rough and the wind is blowing a hoolie. When we are cold, wet, homesick, and looking for a safe and secure passage home through the storms, that's when we need the assurance that we are well placed to know where we are and how to find our way home. Ah, yes, I remember those navy days at sea well.

What I found—more like rediscovered, uncovered, and/or found to be true—is that the answers to these vital questions all hinge on one essential foundation: a solid, unchanging, accurately positioned reference point. What I mean by a reference point is some immovable, fixed-in-position mark that is accurate to the highest quality standard and known to be true. It is a known point from which all other positions and measurements can be made so the one navigating can confidently (sometimes courageously) proceed into the unknown. From eternity past to eternity future, we have this reference point that is set apart, perfectly good, and whose quality gives, measures, and provides authenticity to all other things—and wants to be our known centre. He is our strong and loving God.

Nearly ten years ago, in an attempt to address the confusion and lostness in men, I put together a men's programme called 'A Few Good Men' (AFGM), which I presented to various church communities in the northern rivers. While the theme about men's identity seemed to meet most men where they were at, there also seemed to be something missing—something more foundational. I had based the talks in AFGM on the assumption that Christian men knew God. I am not speaking theologically, because most Christian men appear to know about the Christian God from some theological perspective—although not much about the triune God. I mean *know* Him relationally. I had been asking men in conversations, 'Who do you think you are?' This is a fairly blunt question for us blokes. When I was at school in the 1960s and 1970s, those were fighting words. However, in this context, the question seemed to hit the spot from where frequently came the response 'I don't know.'

Friends, please stay with me now as I blunder with words and invite you to think with me about the importance of what I conclude is going on. Firstly, I want to acknowledge the privilege and sacredness of being with another person who trusts the companion listener with their inner journey—the real story about their lives that really matters to them. While we understand that every individual is unique, there are some common themes that appear to be familiarly integrated within human beings' (people's) lives and, I will say, within gender. Identity—that sense of who one is, who one is meant to be and wants to be—is one such common theme and very important to men in particular. I can express this more confidently about what it means to be a man because of my familiarity with men's struggles, rather than the inner sanctum of women's lives, which I am told about and honour, but understand little. So when a man replies to the question, 'Who do you think you are?' with an 'I don't know!', then I believe it is sending a message, or at least flagging that all is not well within the heart and soul of that person.

I think it is safely accurate to say that in the countries across what we call the Westernised world, it is the predominant culture (total way of life of a people) along with the main nationalistic themes which play major roles in determining what is a man's identity—what it means to be a man, and what he should be. When a man becomes a Christian, these strong influences do not go away, but at the same time, a heart conversion turns a man towards wanting to follow Christ as both the model for manhood and in the way he should go. So a dualism is set up. Let me say as respectfully and as strongly as I can, it won't work—and it never will! 'What?' you may ask. Well, that a Christian man cannot take his identity as a man from the cultural voices and nationalistic themes that tell a man what it means to be a man in his home country and, at the same time, live as a Christian man following Jesus living now in the Kingdom of God. Here is my summary point. If you want to know who you are, then you have to go to the father heart of the Creator God who made you. Your identity can only be found in Him, and through your continued search for how you are related to Him. Paraphrasing Larry Crabb in his books *The Silence of Adam* and *Men of Courage*, if you want to be manly, you first have to be godly—and that, my friends, will be a lifelong journey seeking and reaching out to our true Father.

It took me another two years after first presenting AFGM to realise that I needed to be asking a different question up front—one that gave the other questions a reference point: 'Who is God?', 'Who is He to you?', and 'What is He like?' In different yet familiar ways, the responses have added a new dimension to what was beginning to be revealed about how God is known. Let me say this much—I have yet to receive a response that suggests a personally known, relational God. There is little indication that God is known as a perfectly holy and loving community, always giving and pouring out who they are, and inviting a response. Neither have I received a sense of an understanding, when a person shares where they are at, that they really believe it is God who takes the initiative in loving us first, and desires only good for us, to the extent that He is willing to extend unmerited grace towards us, at great cost to Himself, so as to be in relationship with us. Listening deeper, I hear nothing that gives me confidence that they conceived that their God wanted to be known intimately, wanted to be our first love and known as the source of such goodness, to the extent that we would surrender, trust, and obey Him willingly for our very own life's sake. Does what I have shared here make you wonder why God is not known in such a way?

If it is true that when I received Christ (you may have a different way of expressing this) at my conversion, I received His Spirit (and I believe it is indeed true), then my 'new' heart is now Christ's heart in me. At the deepest part of me, in my heart and soul, my spiritual being, I now desire the same things Christ desires: to glorify God in all things, to seek His will, and to will the good of others before my own self (now that's real love). I long to worship Him, and I long to be with Him. If I follow this 'new' heart and not default to my naturally inclined 'old' heart, nor selfishly position myself as the centre of the universe, then I will also discover the wisdom and knowledge I need to navigate this life with certain and assured passage into the next. This comes with no great theological revelation, it simply puts Jesus' offer of eternal life into a practical, lived-out perspective now. But, oh how I believe it would make such a difference in the world, and in our relationships, if we actually lived this way. How different a light in which the Christian church might be seen. How differently would Christians flavour the values and lived-out purpose of what it really means to be fully human. I was recently both deeply moved and quite disturbed when I read Dorothy Sayers' view about what she described as God's three greatest humiliations. The first was when God became a human being. The second was when He was hung on a cross. And the third is His church. A friend reminded me recently, sadly, the watching world judges God Himself by the lives and actions of those who bear His name. I wondered what on earth we are doing for heaven's sake, and it made me want to be a better man.

Just recently, I thought I had uncovered a mystery all by myself. I thought that I had an original thought—only to discover that John Owen had already said it 350 years ago (as I said, it's all out there). And before then, Jesus had revealed it nearly 2,000 years ago to the rich young man when He said, as recorded in the synoptic gospels, that if we want to find eternal life, then we choose and accept God's standards for what is good and use these standards for living out our lives in relationship with Him and others. This is the good life now, when we learn to love with a better love fleshed out more by Larry Crabb in his book, *A Different Kind of Happiness*, a love as was reshaped from the old way into a new way, completely fulfilling the old command by Jesus commanding us anew—His called-out ones—to love one another. We experience eternal life now, to the full, as we follow Jesus home, getting 'nearer to thee' as we come to know God and Jesus more and more each day (John 17:3).

The insights gifted to me from conversations that really matter have certainly made me wonder about a number of things (including writing this book). I am grateful for attending Ian Robinson's presentation 'Makes You Wonder' for the insight into the question *'Why are you still a Christian?'* When we reflected and shared on this in session, my immediate and honest response was as Peter replied to Jesus—which, paraphrased, was 'Where would I go? I'm snookered!' But, at a much deeper level there was more: 'There's something inside of me, and I'm not sure what it is, but I know it's something about God and that He and His promises are true.' Now that I'm writing this I think I am closer to knowing what the something is—as much as I can grasp it anyway, at this time in my spiritual formation journey.

I believe the something inside of me is what God has put there as desire, longing, thirst, hunger, emptiness, loneliness, futility, and more—but put there as a secret for me to search for and, with the love and mercy that accompanies a 'carrot and stick' approach (that's what came to mind) entices me to search for it, grope for it, knowing that I will find it because I sense how close I am, and this is leading me home, to the very centre of Himself. The something is both the desire above all else to find God and be with Him forever and an unsatisfied appetite that keeps me searching—longingly unsatisfied until I am finally with Him forever. Even though I am still in this world, He gives me little tantalising tastes of a delicious honey carrot that looks and smells so good that when I reach out, I can almost touch it and taste it.

Yet sometimes, it can seem buried deep down inside of me, often covered in so much muck, that I lose a sense of it, naturally reverting to self-management strategies to control my life and overcome my fears again. But I know it's there—and I find myself turning to it yet again. I sense it almost like a homing beacon that is tuned to a specific frequency, picking up messages from three distinct sources that are essential for finding my way home. When used all together, they tell me exactly where I am on my journey at any given time. All I need to do is to tune in to them. The main one is the predominant source on which the others depend for their true accuracy even though they are nevertheless essential in themselves to the overall determining of where I am. It is to know God first and foremost as He truly is by His self-revelation, fully in Jesus, and as he reveals Himself and relates personally to each of us. Then, we discover and come to know, understand, and believe who we are when we find God as He truly is. Thirdly, as we discover and uncover these first two essential criteria, we understand how they are related to each other and how we are related to God.

None of this is new, as I hope to show you. I think John Owen, in his great work *Communion with God*, really said it well when he described the sum of all true wisdom and knowledge under the three main headings:

a. The knowledge of God, His nature and His properties
b. The knowledge of ourselves *in reference to the will of God concerning us* (emphasis mine)
c. The ability to walk in communion with God.[6]

My inspiration for writing this book has come from Acts 17:22–31, which was quoted at the beginning of this book. When I read how Paul described the 'unknown' God, I wondered whether there needs to be a resetting of how we see God today in line with Paul's description, closely aligned to what John Owen considered, and how I think Jesus meant in His prayer in the Gospel of John (also called the Fourth Gospel) chapter 17. Please bear in mind that I am not suggesting the reader does not know God. Rather, I will be earnestly appealing to restore God to the place of most worth in our lives because we all need Him as our primary source of reference, and that we have and can easily stray away from the source, sometimes without conscious awareness. There is a very real need to restore and reset God as the mark and standard for our lives.

I am grateful to Larry Crabb for encouraging me to tell this story through my experience in the Navy as a hydrographic surveyor. Larry's inspiration came with his fascination with the concept of hydrographic surveying and charting and said to me that I had a story to tell. So I will use the metaphor of carrying out hydrographic surveys for describing the search for something— for the purpose of making what is unknown known—mostly in uncharted waters. In the case of hydrographic surveys, it is so that seagoing vessels may seek and choose safe passage while navigating where they need to go. This metaphor will assist me in explaining, describing, and helping to put down on paper the thoughts I have on this matter and, hopefully, give the reader a little taste and understanding about life at sea, undertaking hydrographic surveys.

The absolute dependence on the primary, first-order known point, and the primacy of three as being required to attain both accuracy and precision for positioning, will become clearer. If there is one outcome from this book that I would like to leave the reader with, it is a sense of being able to know where they are, in a fuller way than a simple theological answer like 'being positioned in Christ'. While this is indeed true, sometimes the answer is not so well understood and can be more a deflection and defensive response than a genuine and personally insightful answer. It can be the sort of response that we give when the self has assumed centre position and we are protecting ourselves from the threat that we might be off course and need to change direction. I will exhort you to select a given starting point—a reference point, if you will—and to choose a primary known fixed point, a solid foundation on which to live your life, and not on the shifting sands of self-centredness. A known position provides a sense of assurance, certainty, and security that, when used alongside two other valuable and measured marks that are linked to this primary point, we can know where we are at all times on our faith journey. We are then able to better pass through the unknown waters of life—even in stormy weather, rough and dangerous seas, and uncharted waters, with a hope based on the true positioning of the chart maker, so that our way home is confidently experienced as well as certain and assured. I hope to encourage and exhort the reader that this is true for them, as it is for me.

Notes on Introduction

1. R. R. Reno, *In the Ruins of the Church* (2002), 36–39.
2. Cited in Crabb, *Fully Alive* (2013), 158–160.
3. Francis Schaeffer, *Death in the City* (1969), 16–25.
4. Crabb, (2013), 177.
5. University Global Net Online, Soul Care Units, SC 204, Lesson 1: Supernatural Community.
6. John Owen, *Communion with God* (2007).

CHAPTER ONE

Making the Unknown Known

So you are ignorant of the very thing you worship—and this is what I am going to proclaim to you. (Acts 17:23)

If there was a controlling power outside the universe, it could not show itself to us as one of the facts inside the universe . . . The only way in which we could expect it to show itself would be inside ourselves as an influence or a command trying to get us to behave in a certain way. And that is just what we do find inside ourselves. Surely this ought to arouse our suspicions? (C. S. Lewis, *Mere Christianity*)

The next step is always the most important one. (A Spiritual Guide)

Giving Attention to the Next Step

WHEN I WAS discharged from the Navy, after spending twenty-eight of my thirty-year career in the Hydrographic Service, I had no idea what I would be doing next. I have since learned that the next step is always the most important one, but at that time, March 2002, I packed up the car and left Wollongong in New South Wales, where I was living, and headed for the shores of Lake Alexandria to discern what my future might be—and I hoped that God would make it very clear. I was also looking forward to seeking some practical and respectful wisdom from Rob Paterson, my dad's last surviving sibling, and Australia's first lay-ordained Lutheran pastor. Uncle Rob lived with his wife Eunice south of Adelaide, South Australia, in close proximity to the beautiful wine region of McLaren Vale, noted for its full-bodied reds. The three-week sabbatical was refreshing and rewarding as I enjoyed the serenity of the countryside, the companionship of extended family, and the fruit of the winemakers' labour around Langhorne Creek, Currency Creek, and later, McLaren Vale—but I hadn't heard a whisper from God. I really wanted to hear from Him because I had only recently met Susan, after having been on my own for five years, and I needed to be sure about the next step.

On the return journey to Wollongong, some things about what the next step might be became a little clearer, as is usually the case when eyes become wide open. I was regularly in contact with Susan by phone, and on one occasion, I was telling Susan that I had a good quantity of decent wines with me—but I had nowhere to store them. When she responded that there was an ideal cellaring place underneath the stairs of her inner-Sydney terrace cottage, suddenly she had my full attention. With apologies to the romantics among the readers, I am not wanting to make this into what could be a long story. Anyway, as our relationship progressed, it turned out that Susan had established a counselling practice in Newtown, Sydney, along with two other partners, and one partner had recently left, so Susan and the remaining partner invited me to become part of Connect Counselling. Also, Susan was a friend of Margaret Lawton, who headed up the counselling services at St. John's Anglican Church, King's Cross, and they were looking for a male counsellor. Part of the outreach by St. John's to the King's Cross area was Rough Edges street cafe, so I began counselling and became a volunteer simultaneously. Within a month of returning from a very short sabbatical, I was counselling professionally and received a phone call from the CEO of the counselling institute where I had trained, asking me to come on staff. So the direction I was to head seemed set, and as I stepped towards a counselling career and away from the protected and disciplined life in the Navy, I didn't realise then that it would be another fifteen years before I would be able to understand and figure out where I was at.

Curt Thompson, in his book *Anatomy of the Soul*, describes surprising connections between how our minds work and spiritual practices that can transform our life and relationships. He describes attention as being like the 'ignition key of the mind'.[1] Imagine the disciples when they saw Jesus approach them, walking across the water. I wonder how that got them thinking. Thompson was pointing out how important paying attention is to what the mind is actually attending to. This is metacognition, a capacity that God has given human beings that His other creatures don't have—we can think about what we are thinking about. Yet, most of us live most of the time not paying attention to what is most important for our lives. It seems we would rather seek comforting distractions that entertain us, excite us, and enable us to fantasise about what we think is the good life and how we can achieve it. But we remain tuned out and unaware that our brains are not being formed or exercised to attend to what is necessary to have life to the full and to participate fully in our primary relationships, and to attend to the things in life that really matter.

This really begs the question 'What *are* our minds actually paying attention to?' Believe me when I say that after listening to men, in particular, confess their thoughts, you don't really want to know. How can we then not conform to the thinking patterns of the world and its attitudes to God? For example, who said pain and suffering were bad for us? Now, I'm a fair-weather sailor. I don't like rough seas and stormy weather. I like smooth sailing. Yet, I cast my eyes over the OT, and I tend to agree with C. S. Lewis' *The Problem of Pain*: "it is His [God's] megaphone to rouse a deaf world." Someone has sold us a dummy, slipped us a pass while we were distracted, and we have fallen for yet another deception. With a good dose of Australian apathy, we seem to shrug off concerns that should have our attention, with a 'she'll be right, mate' attitude. Along with other enticing attractions to whatever distracts and/or entertains us, we go on searching for the good life or the next thing on our agenda. But how do we hear from God about what we really need if we are not tuned in and paying attention—especially amidst the noise and busyness of everyday life? Hopefully, if you are still reading this, I have your attention—so just for a moment more, allow me to venture into the metaphor of surveying.

Casting Our Minds Over Something

Literally, when we survey something, we let the eyes pass over what it is we need to attend to. In the metaphor of life as a journey, we are letting the eyes of our mind cast over something that is important to us so we can figure out the direction, course to steer, safe passage, and so on that we need to take so as to proceed through life relatively safely and well. Imagine Moses as he stood casting his eyes over the Red Sea, then turning around to regard the approaching Egyptian army—the situation probably demanded his undivided attention, and he knew what his next step needed to be. We cast our mind over something and then collect, usually by measurement, the facts needed to determine a position, a value—some criteria that enables us to declare where we are in relation to this something—with some level of confidence. It surely requires that we pay attention to our thinking so that we can show, in some way, that what was previously unknown is now known. We need to go in search of what we are looking for, seek it out earnestly, and hope to find whatever it is that is valuable, and that we consider is worth all the effort—like a pearl of great price (Matt.13:46).

Unlike life, planning for a survey involves communicating with the Hydrographer of the Navy about the next survey: where it will be, what the purpose is, how long we have got, and what priorities he might suggest—remembering that a suggestion given by a higher authority is actually a direction. Next, the charge surveyor, usually the commanding officer (CO) receives all the detailed information and instructions that are required to carry out the survey. At the ship (sharp) end, we, the ship's company (including the hydrographic specialists) were kept at the level of readiness—training, knowledge, and expertise—necessary to fulfil the instructions and conduct the survey operations. On reflection, maybe that's closer to life than I originally thought—especially when the hydrographer was viewed almost on a level with God. But maybe in life, the initial wondering and questioning comes out of that depth level *in* us—the deepest parts—where, if I try to sound it out, only the slightest indication of an echo tells us that there might be something there. It can be so deep that we are left with something like a prompting, almost an intuition that there is more to me, and we are more, and there it is again (can you sense it?), something in us that confirms that this is true but, as yet, is unknown.

You might be relieved to know that I will not be philosophising on the questions of epistemology and existential ontology, such as how do I know, what is true, where do I come from, where am I going, who am I, what's of value? These are important questions that rise out of the depths of human beings who take the time to consider these matters—I just won't be going into the philosophic background, only pointing to them being there. Yet, if we really pay attention to these questions and search within ourselves for the answers, at some point, we come to understand that the answers don't seem to come from out there but rather from a resonance deep within us—but it's not us. Neither can we know who we are as persons in isolation from others. These are big issues for us in these postmodernist times, especially so when the strongest and loudest voices are proclaiming that the self is the centre of the universe.

This line of thinking then leads one to ask the big question about God—and now I am not referring to the Hydrographer of the Navy, Chief of Navy, or Chief of Australian Defence Force. Does God exist? If God does exist, what's He like? Is He good? If God is good, will He be good to me, and for me? Will He be good enough? How do I get to know this God? As I do get to know Him further, what is my response to be? What I am trying to do in this book is provide a picture of what the survey planning might need to be as we set off now to cast our mind over something and begin to gather information so we can measure the facts of our survey. And all this is just preplanning—we are not at the area to be surveyed yet.

What Are We Surveying?

We know much more about the oceans now than we ever used to, especially so with the advances made with sonar technology, underwater cameras, active and passive listening instruments, and the like. As an aside, it is interesting that the research in imaging and ultrasound technology for medical research have paved the way for much of these underwater advancements. There are deepwater multibeam sonars, either mounted on the ship's hull or better-performing towed sonars that can 'fly' deeper under the surface behind the ship. Both manned and unmanned submersibles can dive into the deep ocean trenches and are able to provide images never seen before. Scientists, oceanographers, and hydrographers are gaining knowledge exponentially about the oceans. However, there is much about the oceans, and especially the deepest parts, that we still know very little about—yet we know much more about the deep oceans than we do about the supernatural God, naturally. Knowing little about the oceans and knowing that dangerous creatures that attack humans live there don't stop us from going for a swim, having a surf, enjoying recreational boating, fishing for pleasure or for a living, travelling on, or going to work in whatever vessel or seagoing field one is involved in. So why should we avoid enjoying God's invitations, and thus be prevented from diving into the joyful hopes of His promises, or the deepest parts of Himself that He wants to reveal to us?

There is one very important qualification that I need to make before going any further, and that is, we can only know God as He reveals Himself. In a hydrographic survey, the surveyor ventures into the geophysical reality that is, so he can find and measure what is revealed. He then presents that information in a way that seafarers can understand. In somewhat the same way, those on a journey with God can search for Him, reaching out towards everything He has revealed so that we can know Him as He shows Himself to us. It is probably Theology 101, but we do this from the evidence and visible wonder of His Creation and from His Spirit-inspired Word handed down through His body, the church. The Scriptures of the Old Testament (or Bible, if you prefer) record the relationship of God with His people and point to the coming of Jesus Christ. The Gospels and New Testament writings narrate the reality of Jesus' life when He was here with us, through the testimony of eye witnesses, and through personal encounters, such as Paul, along with the life of the early Christians. In my understanding, while God may continue to reveal Himself in personal encounters, these are wonderfully special, and true, when they align with the evidence of Scripture and Jesus' life.

There is *something* alive in us that desires to know God in a deeper, fuller, and more intimate way. This *something* deep down inside of me wants me to live life fully. I want to. It seems to whisper to me, or is it just an echo of something lost? It makes me wonder about what it is. It stirs, frustrates, saddens, gladdens, and sometimes, excites or frightens me. What is it? C. S. Lewis seemed to know about it. He seemed to be pointing out in his classic *Mere Christianity* that it was (almost) out of reach, yet it's there, present with us and even in us. Something beyond, something that exists deep inside of us as a force—we just know it's there. Francis Collins, in his book *The Language of God*, agreed with Lewis, both of them saying that it is a force for the good— altruistic love at its essence. Yes, I long for that. We know it exists because in our heart of hearts, in the very depths of our being, there is the hunger and desire to know love—to be loved and to love.

John Eldredge also wrote about this desire. Since he has already described it, I do not need to go on about it, but I will mention this much: Eldredge described the desire as a secret set within our hearts and said, 'It is the desire for life as it was meant to be.' He also lamented that it would be 'the greatest human tragedy . . . to give up the search' for it. He quoted Gerald May in *The Awakened Heart*:[2]

> There is a desire within each of us, in the deep centre of ourselves that we call our heart. We were born with it, it is never completely satisfied, and it never dies. We are often unaware of it, but it is always awake . . . Our true identity, our reason for being, is to be found in this desire.

Imagine if we just left it there—aware of something and responding, 'Yeah, whatever—she'll be right, mate.' Dag Hammarskjold seemed to be content in his final writings:

I don't know Who—or what—put the question. I don't know when it was put. I don't even remember answering. But at some moment I did answer 'Yes' to Someone—or Something—and from that hour I was certain that existence is meaningful and that, therefore, my life, in self-surrender, had a goal.[3]

He discovered that existence is meaningful and his life had a goal, and that someone or something was behind it all—and then he died. Wonderful—but did he miss something? What about being in an intimate relationship with that great Someone, having a friend and companion on the journey and being encouraged, inspired, and strengthened by a mate along the way? What about knowing and imagining where you were going and being able to live fully alive while on the way there, until you arrived? It is one thing to have a life and live it—it is another thing altogether to know that it is for eternity, and you can live it abundantly now.

Leanne Payne agreed with John Gaynor Banks' *The Master and the Disciple*[4] and linked that something in the very core of our centre with God.

There is a centre in every man in which and through which God works. To that Centre He speaks; through that Centre He acts. When man discovers his own divine Centre, he stands at the gateway to a powerful living.

If Lewis, Crabb, Eldredge, May, Payne, Banks, and many more than I can reference are all saying this, then it is good enough for me because I also read it in God's Word. Larry Crabb gave insight to what really gets in the way of our knowing what it is we are looking for, because as we seek it, we can tend to take such a shallow look. He says that when we look just beneath the surface of what is happening in our lives, we find that something is wrong.[5] That something has been lost, distorted, and destroyed! Something good that God put inside of us—he put it there for a reason, and Jesus entices us to get in touch with it especially when we are too blind to see it—'*otherwise it remains unreleased in most men*'.[6] In every believer, it is there—much deeper than we seem prepared to search.

So we have to go deep. Deep down inside of us, something is alive, and it has great power. I long to be as one with this force and desire to know it more intimately—yet I so often seem to get it all mixed up in the mess of my life, especially when I get in touch with how shallow I can be and how much I seem to live life on the surface. How about you? Then we can often be told that our desires for fulfilment, our longing for something more, and our hunger and thirst are wrong or misplaced. No, our desires and deep longing and wanting more are not wrong. Misdirected, maybe, and the solutions we arrive at to satisfy and fulfil them mostly are the wrong object, wrong target, and too shallow a level. The one thing that we can certainly be assured of as being really, really wrong is when we deny God as our first thing desire.

My earnest hope and appeal are that none of us would miss the greatest treasure ever to be discovered and that it would never lie concealed deep inside our souls. Most of you reading this would already know that denial is not only a river in Africa—denial is real. Denial is a defence mechanism designed to protect us from overwhelming shame, stress, anxiety, fear, and any emotional or psychological trauma that would cause us pain and suffering. It serves a useful purpose, but not when it would keep us from living life to the full, with relationships that were like *apples of gold in a silver setting* (Proverbs 25:11) and would prevent us from knowing who is at the deepest centre of our great longings.

If you have read any of the writings around the spiritual mystic St John of the Cross (1542–1591), particularly noted for his writings *Flame* and *The Dark Night of the Soul*, you would know that he did not have any doubts in declaring aloud, 'The centre of the soul is God.' God wants to be known because God wants to be found by us (Acts 17:27): *God did this so that they would seek him and perhaps reach out for him and find him, though he is not far from any one of us.* Yet, here lies a caution: while I believe it is true that God is in us at our very deepest core, we are not Him. When someone asks the question 'Who is it inside you?', if you answer, 'I am', that is true—but it is the great I AM who tells me who I am, who is in me through His Spirit, and I need to be able to identify and know the difference.

If we sound the depths of ourselves, we will discover deep longings. As Iain Matthews asks in his *Soundings from St John of the Cross: The Impact of God*, '*What makes you think your longings are God's longings?*'[7] How do we know? While this matter is not the focus of this book, one way to differentiate between God's longings and ours is to get in touch with the battle going on inside between what the Bible describes as the *flesh* and the *spirit*. It is true that the desire to relate deeply—to be known, explored, discovered, and enjoyed—is in us. This is because we are created in God's image and likeness.[8] Since God is spirit, and human beings are material in form (our body), our image and likeness to God have a spiritual nature, and our spiritual nature has the capacity to relate with God and others at a deep level.[9] It also makes sense that along with the desires for relating, God would also give us all the capacities we need so as to relate well—and that's what we want more than anything and long for so deeply: to love and be loved well.

Dwight Edwards, in his book *Revolution Within*, points this out well and quotes Teilhard de Chardin, 'We are not human beings having a spiritual experience; we are spiritual beings having an earthly experience.' As such, we are *relational* (able to consciously communicate and relate with God and others), *volitional* (able to freely exercise our will and make choices), *rational* (able to think and reason), and yes, my fellow brothers, *emotional* (able to feel with love, empathy, and compassion and to express ourselves through our feelings). What Paul is saying in Romans 5:5 was discerned by church leadership in depth at the Council of Trent (1545–63) and expressed so beautifully when they spoke of faith, hope, and love as gifts of God, given at conversion, by which God, dwelling in the soul of a Christian, takes us into His own inner life. The life that is going on inside of you and me, right at this minute, has from eternity past and will into eternity future—from everlasting to everlasting—long to be with God. It's where we are meant to be and will be someday—and that is something.

The Purpose of the Survey

Back into survey mode, having cast our eyes over what we were wondering about and having discovered it to be God, where does that leave us? Who is God to you? When Paul stood up in the Areopagus and cast his eyes over the crowd, he was determined to make the unknown known. I believe it would be an utter falsehood to think that a person can become a Christian believer and, all of a sudden, know all there is to know about God, such that the search to know Him fully is completely over. Our life just doesn't work like that, and Scripture backs it up. Knowing God is a lifelong learning quest. It is a spiritual journey over mountains and down valleys, across plains and deserts, through fair weather and foul, through trouble and times of peace. We long for the superhighway that Isaiah promised (Isa. 11:16; 19:23; 35:8), many lanes and unlimited speed, but we often find ourselves stumbling on rocky narrow paths that lead close to dangerous precipices. We search for Him, we reach, grope, and find Him, then He seems to disappear, only to reappear again—and so it goes. Yet, He is always with us—nearby—at home, waiting for us. We are the ones who go walkabout.

While I think it is vital to keep the soul alive with hope and keep our destination in mind as we continue to journey homeward, it is also important to be mindful of how we are growing spiritually. As we get to know God more each day on our way, we get to know ourselves; and as we understand ourselves more, we understand God a little more—and so we grow as we go. We do not define God; rather, we search for the reality that is and discover what is to be found, and then present this in a way for our own sure passage of understanding and offer it to other fellow journeyers who also want to navigate well through the uncharted waters of this life. We are to start with who God is. We are to cast our minds over what He reveals to us, and we keep reaching for what He shows of Himself until we find Him. When we find Him, then we find who we are and how we are related—and then we can know exactly where we are.

A Reference Point

Let me tell you why I strongly oppose the central reliance on the self as being our reference point. Sanders views the focus on self as a real issue in Christian ethics. He wrote, '*Human beings require a context of meaning and hope that is based outside self and is set in larger commons—i.e. God, nation, family, or a purpose that transcends self.*'[10] John Paul II took this idea and expanded its flaws and dangers further as he wrote:

> A conscience formed by opinion is pure illusion. It is a conscience fallen captive to our opinion and to our determination to defend and justify our own feelings and their worth. It refuses to submit to the judgment of any other, or the command of any authority whatsoever. This so-called conscience attempts to set itself up as the (sole) judge of good and evil (right or wrong) and to shape the law, the moral world, religion, and even God Himself, according to its whim. It would rob God of His right to condemn and punish.
>
> But despite its apparent power, the conscience formed by opinion remains weak in its individualism. It is unable to

resist the pressures of its intellectual environment, the media, and the crowds to whom it instinctively looks for support and protection from the inner voice. It allows itself to be drawn into agitated discussions about freedom, conscience, and peace (tolerance), which end in divided opinions, turmoil of hearts, inner emptiness, and dissatisfaction.[11]

Postmodernism is correct about one thing: no one individual holds all truth. Truth itself is outside of human beings altogether unless access is made to the truth through the Spirit of God. Yet, altogether, within the whole body of believers lies a truth that God has revealed to humankind. It is not in one particular church or one particular denomination or any specific unique community. If any think so, then they can be certain of one thing only: they are naively off the mark. But together, through all the different forms and among the various traditions, within the diversity of Christian faiths seeking understanding lies a common unity that contains the very truth itself—and it is available through Jesus Christ our Lord, and by His Spirit, who is in all of us believers together as His body. All of us are to keep searching and reaching for this truth and never think we are the only ones holding on to it with our closed, possessive, and threatened hands. There is a determined drive, among the worldly non-believers, to erase from the human record the very truth of human history—that Jesus was born a man, walked this earth, lived, died, and rose again. We must passionately stand our ground together, celebrating our unity in diversity (Ephesians 6:13) and not be moved by anti-God agendas that are out to change history, distort reality, and alter the meaning of the things that God has given to humanity.

Reference points are vital in every area of life. Before the coming of satellite navigation, sailors depended on heavenly bodies: the sun and stars and lighthouses and beacons as their reference points. Without such help to chart the direction and course of passage, ships could go off course and get lost on the high seas, or damaged when running aground, or worse, shipwrecked, sunk, and never found again. If markers and reference points are so vital in everyday aspects of life, how much more so are they vital in those areas that affect our eternal destiny? Lately, I have been reminded of one such reference point that seems to have lost its place as the most vital datum. Maybe it is embedded in me by the strong faith passed on by my Lutheran grandmother and assuredly reinforced by Billy Graham's constant response, 'The Bible says . . .' But, what I know, and believe, despite so-called intellectual theological analysis, once again referenced to human intellect, is that I hold Scripture to be both sacred and the Spirit-communicated Word of God to us. It too has to be searched, groped for, and the Spirit's truth found through the eyes of faith, hope, and love. As I write this, I am aware of a large open Bible safely locked in a beautiful display case in a Biblical Research Institute of the church. It is a 1770 edition of a German Bible translated by Martin Luther—the year James Cook surveyed Australia's east coast.

If you have ever looked along the coastline, particularly on headlands and prominent places, you might have noticed triangulation stations—surveyors call them trig points. They are usually marked by a black round top over a solid fixed structure. I chose to take a photo of the one at Cape Byron for the cover of this book. These are known points that have been thoroughly surveyed and accurately placed in position. The coordinates of these trig points are accurately known within very precise parameters. Depending on the survey parameters, they are given quality standards so as to be designated as first-, second-, and third-order stations. Generally, hydrographic surveys were to achieve third-order quality standard because this was what technology could reliably achieve for measurements being made at sea during the early 1970s to mid-1990s. Of course, we always strived for best practice and to achieve the highest quality that we could, depending on the purpose for the survey. To ensure that these trig points remained exactly in position, they consisted of a bronze plaque, uniquely marked for individual identification, and were hard set in concrete so that they would not move.

At the close of this first chapter, let me draw attention to what we are about so far. Whether on land, on the sea, or in the air, if we are on a journey towards some destination, we need a way of determining where we are. Before we know where we are, we need known points from which to measure our position. These known points are interconnected and provide rigour and coverage over our entire area and are all known accurately because they all start from one designated point—an accepted and established datum. We need to have a basis for all that we will be surveying, some point that is a starting point from which all measurements are made for determining our known world. From this starting point, we can begin to cast our mind's eye over what we need to make known. The datum will provide a model to best fit what we know to be true of the earth (and our lives on it). It is this datum that we need to define well and have total confidence in, so come with me now as we choose our datum.

Notes on Chapter One

1. Curt Thompson, *Anatomy of the Soul* (2010), 51.
2. John Eldredge, *Desire* (2007), 1–2.
3. Cited in May, *The Dark Night of the Soul* (2004), 5.
4. Cited in Payne, *Crisis in Masculinity* (1995), 15.
5. Larry Crabb, *Inside Out* (1988), 29.
6. Crabb, *The Silence of Adam* (1995), 42.
7. Iain Matthews, *The Impact of God* (1995, 2010), 44.
8. Dr Larry Crabb describes these desires at length in several of his books and what he teaches.
9. For more reading about this, I recommend Dr Crabb, Timothy Jennings, and Curt Thompson, who write on the way our God-created minds work in relationships.
10. Randolph Sanders, *Christian Counseling Ethics* (1997), 17.
11. John Paul II, *Veritatis Splendor and the Renewal of Moral Theology* (1999), 45–46.

CHAPTER TWO

Missing the Mark?

The God who made the world and everything in it is the
Lord of heaven and earth and does not live in temples built
by human hands. (Acts 17:24)

I've found it! (Baby Huey)

A S THE NAVIGATING officer, I had the job of getting us to the
survey grounds, carefully navigating the ship through charted and
uncharted waters during the survey, and bringing us back home safely into
the arms of our loved ones. I also had the responsibility to see to it that the
ship was where the CO wanted it to be, when he wanted to be there. On
receiving our survey instructions, we would cast our minds over the planning,
say our goodbyes for three months, and make passage to the survey grounds.
The CO is also the charge surveyor (in charge of the survey), and on one
particular survey, he had directed me to have us at a pre-planned place on the
survey grounds, called Saturday Island, by first light. Situated on a prominent
point of the island was our main, first-order trig station, which was to be our
primary known point on which survey control and positioning would rely.
Our first task was to recover the mark—locate it, identify it, clear the site,
and prepare to carry out further survey observations to establish positional
control across the survey area.

We arrived off the island in the early hours of the morning as planned
and brought the ship to short-stay anchor, because we were not expecting to
be there for long. The task was to simply recover the primary reference point,
erect the fixing system over the mark, and head off to the other two sites where
we would undertake the same process of establishing control over the other
two known marks. At first light, the shore party, whose job it was to locate

the trig point and establish the station, set off in the ship's boat. In charge of this team was the first lieutenant, who is second in command to the CO and usually the next most experienced surveyor. Since the first lieutenant did not keep night watches, he was the freshest among the survey officers and the most experienced for this important task. The plan was to send in the best team, get the job done quickly, and return to the ship as soon as possible (i.e. ASAP).

By midmorning, we hadn't heard a word from the shore party. The CO and I were on the bridge, the CO was smoking heavily, and I was becoming more anxious by the hour—when, thankfully, the radio crackled into voice and broke the silence. '*Flinders* [the name of our ship], this is shore party.' The CO allowed me to take the call, and it was the first lieutenant informing the CO that they were having trouble locating the mark—the detailed station description didn't seem to fit in with the actual terrain, and things weren't making sense. The CO grunted something about telling them to do the best they could and that he was wanting to get to the next place before dark—we were in uncharted waters and, as yet, unfamiliar with navigational dangers in the area. Prudence demanded that we make passage through the area in daylight hours.

Two more hours went past, and it was closing in on lunchtime when the radio crackled alive again: '*Flinders*, this is shore party.' This time, the CO beat me to the radio, but while he was trying to digest that the first lieutenant had said that they were still looking for the mark, all of us on the bridge heard a loud and excited voice somewhere in the radio background, yelling, 'I've found it, I've found it!' Now, I won't repeat what we heard come over the airwaves via channel 12 that morning, but safe to say that it would not have passed radio protocol. As the first lieutenant was recalling later, he turned around in the direction of the voice and saw a likeable, strongly built young survey sailor, affectionately nicknamed Baby Huey because of his strength and enthusiasm, standing some twenty metres away from the first lieutenant, with a look of personal achievement lighting up his excited face, and in his hands, he was holding up the supposedly immovable brass reference mark.

GDA datum

How do we know where we are for certain? Turn on the 'permission to turn on the location' field of a smartphone, and it will tell you where you are right now on the map grid that it has been programmed to use. Everything on the map grid is referenced to itself—but is it really where you are? Give me a chart, and I'll take you where you want to go by sea. Give me a map, and I'll navigate you around the countryside. I don't need a Navman or smartphone to tell me where I am because I'm a navigator. But have you ever noticed that your subjective experience of where you are and your actual position relative to other 'real' objects can be different from the map? When you use a map or chart, whether it is in material form or digitally presented on a screen, every map has a datum to refer all positions to, and to best fit the reality on the ground—which is rarely ever flat or perfectly round. If the datum the map or device is using is not a good fit, if geophysical forces such as gravity and magnetics have not been taken into consideration, and if the timing device has any error, this can confuse and adversely impact measuring instruments. The upshot of all this is that the given position is not a true position because both the map and your measuring instruments are erroneous—and you are not really where you think you are.[1]

The datum in use for Australia is currently the Geocentric Datum of Australia (usually referred to as GDA94, or just GDA), which is the starting point for the coordinate system in Australia, approved by the appropriate Australian authority, and is based on 1994 survey control values.[2] That is, it's a system of latitudes and longitudes, or east and north coordinates which we can use to locate the position of objects on a map system for Australia. GDA is compatible with modern positioning techniques such as the global positioning system or GPS uses. Forty years ago, the first SATNAV I saw that was used for finding our position was bigger than a fridge, and we had to punch holes in cards to program it—now we hold these small miracle gadgets in our hands. All positions are accurately known on the map system in use when referenced to this fixed datum, and fixed known points—the trig points positioned around Australia—are integrated into a rigorous control network using GDA94 as the datum. What I am saying here, at least in layman's terms, is that none of us would know where we were on the earth's surface, with any degree of accuracy, without having an authorised, accepted, and known datum as a reference point that best fits where we are on this earth—we would just be out there.

What we now take for granted to give us a position, we can hold in our hands. Yet, this technological advancement didn't just appear. Smartphones and iPhones have a history of evolving over time. There were many technological reiterations—failures and successes over time—to arrive at the amazing capability they now demonstrate. They were founded on knowledge handed down through years of authoritative research based on proven science and dedicated application to technological principles. Human beings progress in a similar way. How else would we know that what we know is true? Of course, this is the dilemma of our postmodern times where it is claimed that there is no authority or historical record that is acceptable or meaningful to us now—even scientifically based research can be disregarded in favour of a self-constructed narrative. There is no reference point for morality or spiritual belief except the individual's self-determined interpretation and self-constructed view of how they know that what they know is true and right for them. We simply are, don't you see? We are where we are—that's all that matters—because we are the centre of our universe. No need for a moral compass or for anything else to tell me where I am standing at the moment, no need for a reference point outside of myself that would define my position, because I have determined that I will hold all that is true to me, in my own hands.

What we hold in our own hands we can confidently, and proudly, proclaim to be our truth and declare, 'I've found it!' The loudest voice wins, of course. But unfortunately, we remain ungrounded and are not referenced to anything other than those things that have a connection to our self. So, although human beings are demanding their independence and their right for self-determination, they also seem to be demanding that their needs be met (by whoever) and are dealing with a higher-than-ever anxiety about feeling disconnected. Doesn't it make you wonder at the priority, importance, time, and resources we place on being connected? And we seem to be surprised that we, increasingly it appears, are feeling lost, disconnected, uncertain, and insecure. This is not how we are meant to be. We are meant to know in space and time exactly where we are, who we are, and how we are all connected and positioned—with God-determined accuracy (GDA).

How do we know?

There is much that has been written by credible authors about how we know what we know—our epistemology. So there is no need for me to go into this subject at any depth and confuse you or myself further. But in order to provide context and continuity to my main theme here, allow me to make this point. Fundamentally, if the self is the centre of our world, and we no longer accept any external datum or reference point, then we have separated ourselves from what is the only true fixed and known datum. This leaves us without a reason, let alone a framework, in which to even formulate the questions of epistemology (how do I know) and existential ontology (to be or not to be), let alone search for the answers. We hear much spoken about 'what it means to be human' and 'human rights', which I assume are human-constructed questions referenced around something. But I do not know what the something is, other than what God has given us. What do I mean?

A human being would not know they were human beings if they didn't have someone else or some other thing to reference themselves by. There are many examples of this, like Rudyard Kipling's *Jungle Book*, where Mowgli thought he was a wolf until he was shown and told otherwise. Most readers might have heard Edgar Rice Burroughs' story of Tarzan, a human raised by apes, who therefore considered himself to be a white ape. We all need someone and some truth outside of ourselves to truly know who and what we are. Descartes exclaimed the now famous quote, '*I think therefore I am,*' without acknowledging any of the sources of information external to himself that had become embodied within him through the information, and messages in various forms that he had received since the time he was born. All human beings need a reference point to know who they are. Every living thing needs a reference point to distinguish itself from another. Every moving thing needs a still reference point to indicate it is moving. Every material thing in physics and science needs a reference point from which to describe it—such as an authority, principle, theory, or person behind it. Without a reference point we are disconnected, out there, and unidentifiable.

So I earnestly appeal to all of us living in these postmodernist times to understand that a self-constructed narrative of what we desire our lives to look like is subjective only. It has no reference point other than the self. This encouraged worldview holds the belief that what we know and hold to be true comes from personal experience only—and from the ideas we choose to believe are true. How is it so? How do you know that is true—who said? Since the time we were born, the messages of this world have been making their way in us—all we have done is to agree with and select the voices which we admire and the messages that suit our choice of the way we believe we can make life work so that it will go well. But follow the messages back to the source and see what foundation these are based on, and you will see whether you are standing on shaky ground—or sinking sand.

How did the self become its own reference point?

Let's take a few minutes to cast our minds back and look at how we arrived at the illusion of the self being our centre. Maybe a better heading would be 'How did we get here?' Let's start back at the Dark Ages. I had always considered the Dark Ages to be a time of reversion to anarchy and paganism, after the light of Christianity had been distorted and dimmed, and that the Middle Ages were pretty much irrelevant, until recently reading the excellent historical background in both Rod Dreher's book *The Benedict Option* and Gerald Sitter's book *Water from a Deep Well*. These periods of history were actually times of *intense faith and spirituality*[3] and, sadly, a time since when there has been a transition away from the Christian faith, and a reversion over time to paganism—a humanistic natural world without God. Just take a look at what we are worshipping in society—our festivals and community events—is it just having a good time, simply good fun?

What human history presents as progress is not necessarily progression towards better outcomes for humanity—and yet, it projects that illusion. From the Middle Ages, and through the Renaissance period, human beings can be seen turning towards the natural world to find fulfilment of their felt needs, and seeking satisfaction of their felt senses through the pleasures and delights of art, literature, leisure, and the pursuit of happiness. Nothing wrong with this on a surface level, but there are consequences for humanity at a deeper level. The Renaissance was a rebirth and a beginning of a new era where the focus of the individual shifted from the glory of God to the glory of man.[4] If we take just a minute to think about this rebirth, we might reconsider it to be a resurrection of a different sort, or a reversion to how people were when Jesus came to earth—or even further back to what happened in that beautiful original garden called Eden. The direction this force of movement took, the weight of it, the constant speed it progressed without turning from its course can be likened to a huge ocean bulk carrier.

The main reason hydrographic surveys are so important, especially around the north and eastern coasts of Australia, is that ships are so big these days and their keels are so deep that passage through the shallow waters around northern Australia and within the inner Great Barrier Reef, off the east coast rely on accurate and detailed charts. Literally, the bottom of the ship can be less than a foot off the seabed in some places, and ships have to stop and wait until the incoming tide gives them sufficient depth under the keel to make safe passage through these areas (e.g. Gannet Passage approaching

Torres Strait from the west). When one of these ships is underway through the narrow passages and confined waters of the numerous reefs and islands, nothing had better get in the way of these huge vessels, or there would be absolute disaster caused to the reef and marine ecosystems—and human life. Think of a huge passenger liner called the MV (MV meaning either motor vessel, or in this instance, man-made values) *Individualism* making its determined progress in a sea of societies, heading in a certain direction with considerable momentum behind it, and unwilling to change its course. Here is a metaphor for how difficult it is to stop the human progress towards 'myself, I, me' being the obvious port of arrival of a people determined to make their own way in the world.

Maybe history blemished the truth by calling the Renaissance a rebirth. It is better described as a turning away from and a turning back to—a turning away from Christian moral values, and a turning back to the glorious civilisations that Rome and Greece had established by the turn of history, 1 BC to 1 AD. People during the Renaissance were escaping the authoritarian rule, decay, and corruption that had crept into the church. At the same time, there was a new-found freedom to seek pleasure and entertainment, pursue individual knowledge through literature—which had become readily available with the advent of the printing press—and to admire and enjoy the human intellect rising above what was becoming a powerless faith, as science and materialism overtook a superstitious spirituality. The natural and material worlds were much preferred to the supernatural ascetical world—to a lifestyle characterised by abstinence from sensual pleasures, often for the purpose of pursuing spiritual goals naturally.

Can you imagine what the pushback of the church looked like as all this was unfolding? The more independence and freedom the individual enjoyed within a changing society, the more the church endeavoured to exert its authority and tighten restrictions of the expression of these new-found freedoms. The church's control over the people was being threatened, so it tightened the screws around moralism, taxes and tithes, and church attendance and made them out to be proper signs of salvation. At the same time, more liberalised sections of the Christian church were distancing themselves from a centralised church authority, and the clergy themselves were also enjoying these new-found freedoms and privileges. What this did was to highlight hypocrisy in the lifestyle of (some) religious clergy, which in turn began to reinforce a growing belief among the people that there was no enticement, empowerment, or possibility of ever being able to practice what was preached about the Gospel, insofar as being able to live out the Gospel as an authentic Christian way of life was concerned. Society and the church were ripe to go their separate ways, and individuals rejoiced in a new-found freedom, which was interpreted as being free to do whatever they chose to do—which we know doesn't actually make us free but rather takes us into bondage, in the end.

As we continue to cast our minds over the metaphor of the MV *Individualism* determinedly making passage under the delusion of being called progress, we can begin to gain insight as to what is happening within society over time. Should we be surprised where we have come to? The church had encountered a reformation, but it too was influenced by the philosophies of the times permeating our now civilised, enlightened, and secularly educated Western societies. Individualism, humanism, materialism, hedonism, and might I suggest, paganism—and there are more—crept into our lives as subtly as the emperor parading his new clothes. These isms became the prisms that distorted, deflected, disguised, and diminished the light of truth into various assortments, shapes, and colours. The great protest against the Catholic Church had shattered unity, and Scripture alone was regarded as the proper authority for a believer's life. Within a church that was splitting apart, disunity, fragmentation, and disputes became more frequent and intense as questions arose as to whose interpretation of Scripture was now the true one. A common unity was being lost among the people of God because there was no one point of reference to unite them. Even a common belief in Jesus as the Christ didn't seem to be unifying enough.

Politics, society, and culture separated from the church, which became no longer trusted as the deposit of all truth, the holder of morality, or the guide for how people should live. The individual was free to separate the moral life taught by the church from what was determined as acceptable by society's norms. People were ready to embrace the next great adventure on the sea voyage of human progress—but where were they headed? I became aware of an example today when I was reminded how people often say with worldly wisdom, 'It's not about the destination, it's about the journey.' No, and again, *no*! Sure, if a person has no faith in an eternal future and believes that this life is all there is, then they wouldn't be very enticed by their future—they are just dead, and they revert to the nothingness that they believe they came from, by chance. So, obviously, having a good time and seeking the world's presentation of what a good life looks like is what life is all about.

Hell no, not for me—our life is all about an eternal destiny. To be all together in our eternal Father's home, with Jesus, in the midst of what's going on between the Father, Jesus, and the Holy Spirit. That is the abundant life—life to the full—lived in the real hope of God's promise now, because of our destination. So-called enlightened individuals who hold their own truth, their own reference point in their own hands claim independence and pursue their 'human rights'—their self-declared entitlements—with the age-old human demand for self-determination and embrace individualism as progress into a modern and new exciting age. They have removed from their minds any right to external claim on their lives and shut down from learning the lessons to be seen in human history. They hold a distorted self-truth made up of contaminated worldly ingredients, and they have no known source of truth. Cut off from the truth known to be God's truth, they are cut off from the source of real life and real love. When everyone on the MV *Individualism* is moving together (and no one knows they are moving), they cannot see the reality that their world is crumbling around them.

Science is now hailed king, when for centuries, Jesus reigned and had been called Lord—now no one and nothing is to lord it over the individual. No one wanted to believe Copernicus when he timidly—well, it could have cost him his head—yet courageously declared that our earth (we) was not the centre of the universe, and that actually we revolve around the sun. People were sceptical at first yet had to finally agree that the earth was round (or oval, although the real shape is geoidal) after Magellan, Diaz, Columbus, and others pushed over the edge and didn't fall off. Of course, we would have admitted knowing that apples fall from trees; still it was great that Isaac Newtown could explain to us that this is true through physics. Science grew—I cannot do justice to its many forms, but I do acknowledge the great advances in medical achievements through biology, chemistry, physics, and more. As science opened up new frontiers of discoveries, it pushed past the boundaries previously ordained as belonging to God only and filled the gaps which had been declared His to fill, watering down an already weakening faith in the real Gospel message. There was little, if any, need to reference our mighty Creator at all now—whether it was about the world, or creatures, or ourselves, the jewel in His crown and the apple of His eye.

Science became humankind's new religion, and knowledge became the new way to worship. This progression and shift in focus—from glorifying God to seeking the glory of man—had (has) a life-changing impact on us as human beings, particularly when people are describing what it means to be fully human and are determining human rights in the absence of human responsibilities. Science is now acknowledged by those who don't believe in God—and maybe by some who do—to be the source of all that is factual, real, and therefore, true. Science is seen as holding the answers to the questions of epistemology and to all questions regarding the advent of the world and all life forms—humans just haven't discovered those answers as yet, but they will, or so they believe. Allow me a little leeway here as I loosely combine and describe epistemology within an existential ontology. How do I know (what is true). Moreover, how do I know that what I know, is true? Let's take it further. Where do I come from? Where am I going? What has value? Who am I? How do I know? What does it mean to be human, to exist and to live a good life?

As we seek the answers to these questions and the unknown equations of life, while making passage on this monolith ship of individualism, where do we find ourselves going? The individual determines what is true—for oneself. The United States of America, as a leader in the values of a Westernised society, have a profound and major influence on this progress. The authors of the Declaration of Independence—that great document of identity for its people—declared the rights of individuals to life, liberty, and the pursuit of happiness. The greatest goal of humankind is to be happy! And, of course, we will be the ones who determine what happiness is to be for us. Going to God to find happiness appears to be out of our frame of reference now. Human beings seem to be content with second-best happiness and seek it in far too shallow waters, I think. If you want to follow this theme more, Larry Crabb pursues this in depth in his book *A Different Kind of Happiness.*

Yet there has been one movement that has rejected science as god—the Romantics have brought into our recipe for life their main ingredients, prizing emotion, individual expressiveness, nature, and personal freedom as their demigods. I agree with whoever stated that a system is perfectly designed to achieve the outcomes it receives (the author of the quote is disputed). What we seem to hold to be of most worth as human beings are feeling happy, demanding the right to be whoever we want to be, and entitlement to say and do whatever I like. But wait, there's more, the father of Romanticism, Jean-Jacques Rousseau (1712–1778) advanced the idea that man is born naturally good but becomes corrupted by society.[5] That's right; Rousseau would say we are all victims. Our ship has actually turned into a shipwreck—this momentum we call human progress has been underway since the fourteenth century, some 600 years—never altering course, and in the past 300 years has increasingly been picking up speed, exponentially so in the last century. The writer, theologian, and mystic Thomas Merton (1915–1968, so young) reminded us in his book *The Wisdom of the Desert* that the early Christians fled into the desert in order to draw near to God. He said that they saw society as a shipwreck from which every single man had to swim for his life. Saying further that to let oneself 'drift along, passively accepting the tenets and values of what they knew as society, was purely and simply a disaster'.[6] According to Dreher (who I have quoted a few times and is worth reading to get an expanded understanding of this 'progressive' movement), the myth of humanity evolving to higher levels of civilisations and 'becoming better' was shattered in the previous century, beginning in 1914 with the evil of WWI. But, what do you think? Will our ship berth gracefully at the Port of Nirvana? Is it heading towards a catastrophic disaster? Or is it shipwrecked already?

I would challenge those who still believe in a progressive humanity and a civilised society relying on the evolving goodness of its people. Technology is advancing at an exponential rate and seems to be the engine powering our ship—and people are supposed to steer ships. So who is leading what? Human beings have not evolved to the extent where human nature becomes good. Surely, that myth has proven to be false. I remember studying the novel *Lord of the Flies* by William Golding for my year 12 at high school. It was a shock to my teenage idealism and the values of the 1960s—which still echo in popular culture—to be confronted with the realisation of what human nature could turn into when the boundaries and rules of a civilised society break down. I have not found any reason to disagree with Golding in the (almost) fifty years since understanding more of what he was saying, nor has it contradicted the Bible (as far as I know) except by omitting to acknowledge the power of God's grace.

Pascal likened it to people being on board a ship, where everyone is moving together, so no one knows that they are moving—sounds like the ship could be the MV *Individualism* making passage through civilisation under the command of postmodernism, yet this was a similar case 2,000 years ago. I am suggesting that what was happening in society back then in the biblical time of Jesus is being repeated now. Two great civilisations had integrated: one of political domination and power, the other of art, literature, and hedonistic culture. Both were pursuing the good life—both were pluralistic in their religious outlooks, worshipping gods, idols, and whatever they held up to be of most worth. This was a Greco-Roman-governed world, surrounded by paganism (the tribal cults outside the walls of Roman influence) and was positioned within the dominant religious culture of the Jews, whose total way of life was ruled by the privileged priesthood and the observance of the Law. Out of this setting rose a man who stood still in the midst of the power, corruption, and decadence—and everyone suddenly became aware that they were moving, so they killed Him. Are we really enlightened 2,000 years later? Don't we realise that Jesus Christ, the one we worship, is asking us to do that now? This is our time to stand firm and to be courageously strong and loving.

Is the church exempt from what has been described in those previous paragraphs—the movement away from what Jesus was showing the people of God and the retarded human tendency to be attracted to the force of self-determination and choose for themselves what is good? How is Scripture interpreted now? Which denomination holds all the truth? Which version of the Bible is closest to the mark? How has the church dealt grace out freely? How has authority and control been demonstrated? Since our Lord only gave us one commandment, how are we going in following (just) that one? How are you going with it? We seem to be busy. Great structures, strategies, and fantastic programmes and methods of performing the Christian life and achieving sanctification are being produced, continually improved, promoted, and advertised. The church seems willing to tolerate most things except a selected few behaviours that are highlighted and subjected to special treatment and control so as to take the focus off how poorly we actually live, love, and relate. Jesus only commanded one thing from His called-out ones—to love one another! Because we can't (or won't) do this one thing, we spend our time, effort, and resources on the things we can do and control. Has the church stood still as our Lord did in His time? Since we are His body now, will we? Or has the church taken up passage on our worldly ship, content to move along with society and culture and the other passengers? Does the global church, which represents the whole body of Christ, have a single main reference point? If so, how are we to describe it?

Missing the Mark

I want to invite you to think with me through this next paragraph as I am grappling with this as I write. Even so, C. S. Lewis does it much better and at more length, and *Mere Christianity* should be foundational reading on this matter. If something can indeed come out of nothing, then there is a force that already exists. I imagine that in creating the universe, there would have been a really big bang. Louie Giglio says that we can look out into the far reaches of the universe, and it seems like it's an infinite expanse of mystery and wonder. Yet Louie himself had to admit it is indeed indescribable! Say we were to call this powerful creative force God, then wouldn't that inspire us to want to know this God? What would we imagine this God to be like? If you follow that through to its logical conclusion, I suggest you would end up summarising as C. S. Lewis did in *The Great Miracle*:

> The Christian story is precisely the story of one grand miracle, the Christian assertion being that what is beyond all space and time, which is uncreated, eternal, came into Nature, into human nature, descended into His own universe, and rose again, bringing Nature up with Him. It is precisely one great miracle. If you take that away there is nothing specifically Christian left. There may be many admirable human things which Christianity shares with all other systems in the world, but there would be nothing specifically Christian.

You and I are part of this miracle story. In fact, you and I are a miracle! All I can say to that, with grateful humility is 'Thank You, God.' Out of the Gospels of Matthew, Mark, Luke, and John came eyewitness accounts of God's full and final revelation of Himself, and to the New Testament writers (Paul, the apostles, the disciples, and the early Christian converts, brothers and sisters of the faith, who believed it worthy to die for), I say, 'Thank you.' To the fathers of the Church, from the desert fathers, and from Augustine, Aquinas, Luther, Calvin, the Wesley brothers, down through the times and from all that has been written since, until now, we must respond with 'Thank you.' We stand on the shoulders of giants of the faith. To the many apologists for Christianity, who shared their faith to those who started out as atheists or agnostics, wanting to prove that God did not exist, and who became staunch believers when they examined the evidence for their faith, courageously sharing their stories, changing direction, and then standing still against the moving ship, I say, 'Thank you.' To all who have gone before, including those who died because of their unswerving faith, I say, 'Thank you.' And, I ask this question, 'How did they know that what they discovered was true?' They cast their eyes and minds over the evidence, searching for it, relying on a particular datum described with GDA—the accuracy of the Scriptures as inspired by the Spirit of God—to reveal God as He desires to be known. Our history is His story, and if we are humble enough and open to God's revelation of Himself, we will indeed be enlightened—that is His promise.

How embedded and embodied within people of our enlightened, Westernised society has the search for individual determinism become? Has the Gospel been contaminated and God's Word been distorted to the point that His truth is subjective? Is God's truth recoverable? Does anyone care? Do we now realise that we have lost the original mark established with GDA? These are only a few of the questions that lie underneath the uncertainty, confusion, and lostness I hear expressed through conversations that really matter about our faith. There has already been (although yet to be fully felt) fallout from our human foolishness and prideful determination of our human independence throughout our Westernised societies. Some of this fallout includes things like how the meaning of words have been changed to move the definition of love, freedom, human responsibility, marriage, and sexuality to new definitions contrary to God's mark. Even the value of human significance and dignity has been turned into a human rights charter. Yet, despite the demand for independence and the absolute right to self-determination, I still don't know what the secular humanistic reference point is—other than the self.

Even the search for meaning itself seems no longer to have any relevance. I realise that there are more areas of fallout, and I am not wanting to disregard any important matter—my intent is to make the point that there are consequences for removing the mark, for not having a place from which to start, and increasingly so—a subject too huge for this book. But the most arrogant distortion, deception, and destructive movement that has taken Christ out of Christianity is in the area of the study of God—what we call theology. It is the proposition that we can know God intellectually and study Him through the eyes of science, and not through the eyes of faith. Anslem (1033–1109) told us all those years ago that seeking God, reaching for Him, and having confidence that we will find Him is our *faith seeking understanding*. Or have we forgotten that only the Son and the Spirit know God?

As we conclude this chapter, let us look at the proposition Francis Schaeffer was making in his book *Death in the City*. Christians are familiar with the words 'reformation' and 'revival', and Schaeffer was saying that we tend to think of them in contrast to one another. He said, '*But this is a mistake. Both words are related to the word "restore".*' He concluded his proposition by saying, '*We need to be those who know the reality of both reformation and revival, so that this poor dark world may have an exhibition of a portion of the church restored to both pure doctrine and Spirit-filled living.*[7] We need to restore a God-determined reference point so that we can know that our understanding of God, and us as His dependents, is good and true, and one that provides us human beings with a standard which we will live by—because we can, because we must.

No, I do not believe Nietzsche was correct. We didn't kill God—because we cannot—but we have allowed Him to become unknown (again). We have failed Him once again as His people. He only asks that we love Him (back) and glorify His name—represent Him to the world by being His presence in the world and by showing all of His creation His goodness. We do not have to be concerned to defend Him. We do not have to be concerned to prove He exists—not if I understand the first two chapters of the Book of Romans correctly. We who are God's people, who love Him first and believe in His goodness, have to show that to the world. What does the world see when it looks at your life? Do you know God with a confident conviction so that your lived-out happiness is a beacon to the world? When Larry Crabb looked deeply at this, he discovered more than just himself: *'I discover within me a strangely unshakable conviction that this Ultimate Person is, in fact, the God of the Bible, the God revealed in Jesus Christ, someone thoroughly good, relentlessly moral, unstoppably powerful, unimaginably loving, and determined to display His highest virtues by making me extremely happy.'*[8] Do we show this to the world?

To believe in God is to be living as it is true—and we do this when we love Him as our first love and then love others. Yes indeed, the Word must be spoken, but we, the church, are mistaken if we think the world is listening. First, we must get the world's attention by being salt and light in the way we live, love, and relate in this world. So let us now reset the mark, making God our first and primary known point, and His Word as the only true and acceptable reference point from which we can truly know Him. It is a delusion for human beings to think that they can be their own reference point. Let's go and reset our primary mark known with GDA.

Notes on Chapter Two

1. The first official national Australian geodetic datum was AGD 66. This was selected to best fit Australia onto a grid system from a transfer from Universal Transverse Mercator projections. In our then two-dimensional world, AGD66 was a real position at latitude 25

degrees 56' 54.551.5" south and longitude 133 degrees 12' 30.0771" east. It was known as the Johnston Geodetic Station, approx. 300 km south of Alice Springs near the national highway. When AGD84 and subsequently GDA94 updated this Australian datum, it required an approximate 200-metre shift—depending on where you were.

2. As I write, Australia is transitioning to GDA 2020.
3. R. Dreher, *The Benedict Option* (2017), 28.
4. Ibid., 30.
5. Ibid., 38.
6. Cited in Eldredge, *Desire* (2000, 2007), 206.
7. Francis Schaeffer, *Death in the City* (1969), 9.
8. Larry Crabb, *Finding God* (1993), 156.

CHAPTER THREE

Restoring the Mark

And He is not served by human hands, as if He needed anything. Rather, He Himself gives everyone life and breath and everything else. (Acts 17:25)

When the foundations are being destroyed, what can the righteous do? (Psalm 11:3)

And after you have done everything, to stand. (Ephesians 6:13)

WHENEVER I HAVE felt that it seems to be me against the world, I've often wondered what General Custer might have felt at the battle of Little Big Horn. Or like David was feeling when he expressed himself in Psalm 11:3, and then I read verse 4. It's rather eerie thinking about God casting His eyes over us, observing us to see how we are observing Him. I wonder if this is a bit like what Baby Huey might have felt when he saw the look on the face of the first lieutenant and heard him express his total dissatisfaction with Baby Huey's well-intentioned efforts to recover the mark. Back on board the ship, facing up to the CO was no picnic for him either, yet much good came out of that survey for Baby Huey. He spent many hours on survey tasks ashore, gaining a lot of experience as a survey assistant. He learned so much about the importance of fixed reference marks during the remainder of the survey—how to reset them both in terms of repositioning and how to manufacture solid concrete foundations so that they couldn't be removed. In the end, he turned out to be someone you wanted on your team. As it was, this particular trig station was the main control point for the survey, so we spent the next few days restoring the mark and resetting it to the original position. Where it was known with GDA, of course.

I wonder what Paul might have been experiencing as he stood before the Athenians at the Areopagus. Maybe a bit like David or Custer or Baby Huey? We know that he was distressed over the number of idols he saw and how the people had given themselves over to them. John Stott, in his book *The Message of Acts*, indicates it's like they were swamped by their idols. I can vouch that it's no fun being in a swamped boat at the mercy of nature's elements, but I wonder what Stott meant? He is saying that they were under them, and their behaviours were very religious.[1] Sounds to me much like twenty-first-century Australia as we worship our cultural idols—the myths of nationalism, finance, entertainment, leisure, sports, gambling, the races, footy, having a few drinks and partying, all in the pursuit of happiness and having a good time. Not that there is anything wrong with having a good time, by the way—in a healthy context. Stott describes an idol as anything that we put ahead of God—even little things, even church, religion, and Christian service. Now, that should grab our attention.

> Any person or thing that occupies the place which God should occupy is an idol. Covetousness is idolatry. Ideologies can be idolatries. So can fame, wealth, power, sex, food, alcohol and other drugs (legal or not) parents, spouse, children and friends, work, recreation, television and possessions, even church, religion and Christian service.[2]

Paul was provoked to anger, and he tried to reason with the Epicureans, who saw God as remote and having no interest in humans, and with the Stoic philosophers, who saw the world as determined by fate and humans had to pursue a life of self-sufficiency. At least they seemed willing to hear Paul out—which is more than what I observe from increasingly anti-Christian and militant voices within our Western society seem prepared to do, even as they demand more tolerance and talk of sharing the love around.

A summary of Paul's five main points as seen by John Stott is

1. *God is the creator of the universe (v. 24).* Since He is both personal creator and personal Lord of everything He has made, it is absolutely ludicrous to think that human beings can interpret, limit, shape, contain, or manipulate Him in any way.

2. *God is the sustainer of life (v. 25)*. He who supplies our every need and sustains us does not need us. We are totally dependent on Him.

3. *God rules the universe with His created order—material, natural, spiritual, and moral (vs. 26, 27, 28a)*. God has determined the boundaries and times of human history (where and when they live), His purpose being that we would come to know Him by seeking Him—reaching, groping, and fumbling as a blind man does, explains Stott (ibid., 286). For it is not God who is distant from us, but rather, we who are far from Him because we are seeking after idols so as to enjoy a good life apart from God. Yet He wants to be found, known, and enjoyed.

4. *God is our Father (v. 28b, 29)*. Our Christian faith tells us that God is the Father of those who are in Christ by adoption and grace. However, in terms of creation, God is also the Father of humankind, as we are all His creatures. We are not only dependent on Him but also requiring of Him to reveal who He is to us. Nothing in our own imagination, creativity, fantasy, or self-knowledge can conjure up who God is without Him allowing us to graciously know Him through His self-revelation.

5. *God is the sole author, arbitrator, and judge of His own creation (v. 30, 31)*. Paul tells us that ignorance is not an excuse because God has fully revealed Himself to us through His natural order and revealed the truth that human beings suppress. And, He commands us to repent—turn to Him, change our minds about how we think life should be like, and accept God's calling of us home, to Himself. And He has shown us that our way home is through Jesus.[3]

Paul's Challenge to Us

Nothing that has been stated in the five points mentioned above is new. Paul saw all of this in his time, and he felt distressed and provoked to anger about how far off the mark the Greeks were—so he spoke it out. How is this going for us? Anyone feeling distressed enough to speak it out? Is God still unknown today—both within the church and among non-believers—and what might be the reasons? All of what has been said is in the Gospel about Jesus Christ, and since I could not say it better than John Stott, here is how he answers these questions.

Many people are rejecting the Gospel today not because they perceive it to be false (as such), but because they perceive it to be trivial. People are looking for an integrated world-view which makes sense of all their experience. We learn from Paul that we cannot preach the gospel of Jesus without the doctrine of God, or the Cross without the Creation, or salvation without judgement. Today's world needs a bigger gospel, the full gospel of Scripture—'the whole purpose of God'.[4]

When Stott says 'trivial', I understand him to be saying something similar to what C. S. Lewis was saying in *Mere Christianity* when he wrote, '*Christianity has nothing to say—as far as I know—to those who haven't done anything wrong and don't think they need forgiveness.*' It seems like people don't think they need God and are therefore unwilling to give any thought, consideration, time, or resource capacity towards choosing for Him or against Him—they simply do not care. Or if they did want Him on religious grounds, they want Him to be comforting and convenient. But thankfully, Christianity has everything wonderful to say to those whose lives are a mess—like me and many others I know, but not everyone. Somehow we have to be able to show a little kindness (we often sing 'Try a Little Kindness' at our church service in the Lismore Soup Kitchen) and say to a brother carrying a heavy load and a sister that has fallen by the way, 'Hey, you're going the wrong way.' And whenever we find ourselves going down the wrong road, we need to stop, turn around, go back to where we made the bad decision, and make a good one. To keep going down the wrong road is utter foolishness, but that's what we do. Scott Peck must have heard about our Australian cultural apathy when he said, '*Most Western people were just spiritually lazy. And when we are lazy, we stay on the path we are already on, even if it is going nowhere.*'[5]

Me? A sinner? Do we still talk like that today? How are we to see that the condition that humanity is in today remains the same until we accept that apart from God, we are lost and we need to be restored. Yes, all of us (Rom. 3:23, 24), and until we do, we remain under the influence of the lie that we can make life work apart from God. A distressed confidante shared with me that the head of training for their 'Christian' organisation and her supervisor both gathered around her and told her that repentance was an early Christian thing but was no longer necessary now. Do they read the Bible? But this is foolishness (Luke 12:13–21). So we need to understand from whence this *foolishness* comes (Gen. 6:5–6, 8:21, Psalm 51:5, 58:3). For example, we might agree, 'Yes, God loves me, and He is good—but I will define what is good for me.' I tried this tack for many years and (slowly) learned that because He loved me so much, God did it His way to bring me closer to Him, and because I didn't cooperate, I called it pain and suffering. God's megaphone got my attention. Our foolishness comes from the way we look at things. Self-interest is not wrong; rather, we just have a wrong understanding about it. If we were truly interested in ourselves, we would love God and respond to His precepts. Neither is seeking happiness wrong, if we understand that true happiness comes when we obey God, love Him first and then others. If only we understood what Augustine meant when he said, '*Love God and do what you want.*'

Our modern life with its instantaneous amenities, globalised markets, and massive economic system promises nothing less than constant and immediate satisfaction of all our desires and needs. And we don't have to choose because the voices of academia and the media tell us what we will love and enjoy. There appears to be nothing beyond our entitlement, or our ability to attain whatever we want. John Eldredge captures this sense well in what I think is an appropriate new philosophic word—*whateverism*. Certainly, there seems to be nothing to restrain or rein in our desires and block us from getting whatever we want, whenever we want it—and that is our deserved right anyway! Somehow this sentence that Larry Crabb wrote in his book *66 Love Letters* captures the theme of our time, '*Our quick-fix, feel-better, make-life-work-for-us, we-want-it-now-and-we're-entitled-to-have-it-now culture has wrenched our understanding of the Christian story into something that is not—and never was.*'[6]

If I said to you, 'I know what is really wrong with you and what you really need,' how might you respond? And if I said that I could fix whatever is wrong with you and that all you needed was radical, open-heart surgery, and by the way, I scheduled you in for 9:30 a.m. tomorrow, would you trust me? Wouldn't you want to be really convinced, both that I was a good surgeon and that you really needed the surgery? I think a large missing piece of the way Christianity is portrayed today is just how good we believe God is and how much we need God—especially since we have been made dependent on Him. In his book *Post-God Nation*, author Roy Williams viewed our Western society's prosperity as a major blockage to our need for God. Why?

We are really pretty well off—perhaps too well off? Consider our health system, education, welfare, workers' pay conditions, etc. in Western, First

World countries. Sort of secure and reasonably comfortable, aren't we? Yes, I know that there are struggling and hurting people in our societies too, but compared to what I observe in Third World nations and across our globe, Western societies generally have a comfortable and convenient lifestyle—you may not agree. Anyway, just keep me comfortable, well fed, and entertained, and I am fairly satisfied and happy. Just leave me be. I have the right to make my own choices and determine what I need and do. I have decided that God's role is to be convenient and cooperative to the way my life should go. I would add to that, a postmodernist view of a *sense of entitlement* cultivated by a society and culture that places self as centre, and glorifies individualism and independence, are necessary character qualities. But in my determination to author and narrate my own story, where have I put God's story? And who am I—really?

It is true, of course—our right to make our own choices. It's true because that is how God willed it from the beginning. It is also true that the love and dignity God gives to us, and the great respect He has towards us, is to allow us to take the responsibility for the consequences of our choices. There is of course another way of life that is connected to an ancient book, and that promises to lift this life to another level. This is truly the good life, and we can live it to the full now. It is the path mapped out on a blueprint for humankind by the one who loves us beyond measure—an unfathomable love. It involves self-sacrifice and hardships and hard work. It requires self-denial, self-abasement, and an other-centred mindset—much like being part of a crew on a survey ship, miles from home, united by a common vision and a love for adventure. Although our allegiance was to our naval commanders and naval regulations, this other good life is radically Christ-centred and deeply rooted in His Word. This, and no other path, leads to living life fully alive now, and everlasting happiness in the souls of human beings because of the hope we've been given through the promise of our destination. Now that is indeed good!

The Universe Needs a Known God

I hear Paul saying to us today, the God who created us knew that His creation is dependent on His goodness—needs His goodness. Human beings were created by God and were given the responsibility to keep watch over His creation and to reflect God's goodness into the world they were put in—principally by being a worshipful, loving community of people. God made people to be like Him and gave them every capacity to relate like Him—as the Father, Son, and the Spirit relate with each other. We are the *apple of His eye* and the *jewel in the crown* of His creation. All of this was God's good gifts of dignity and privilege to us, and not because He needs us, rather as an invitation to a place of honour to participate in abundant life and enjoy life with Him—in relationship with Him and with all He created. And all we need do is respond to His givingness and outpoured love. Knowing this, how could we not love Him back?

But real love does not force itself on another. God's love involves free will so that people can freely choose to accept God's giving of Himself or reject Him. Fortunately for us, our choice of relationship with God does not rely either on our faithfulness to Him or on how good we are; it relies and depends on God's faithfulness to us, His goodness, His love, His mercy, His graciousness, His promises, compassion, and generosity, which are *for* us. This is God's attitude towards us, to which He invites our yes response. Time and time again, we see humankind's (our) unfaithful response to God, our rejection of Him and His goodness, and our seeking after our own good apart from God, believing that we can attain it ourselves—and it is foolishness. Time and time again, we see God calling us back to Himself, forgiving us when we accept being found by Him and lavishing on us His grace and mercy without measure—always providing us with the resources and means to overcome any mountain-like obstacle that might prevent us coming to Him through faith. He empowers us to live the life that He knows we really long for, to the standard of goodness that He knows we need, because He knows that it is this life that reflects His glory into His Creation. Not (primarily) for our sake (Ezekiel 20:9; 36:22) but because He knows that all of creation desires to see God's goodness—which it desperately longs for and surely needs. But we have to know, believe, and trust Him to know that we need Him.

We Need His Goodness

Albeit with variously different influences, experiences, sociopolitical-cultural-economic circumstances and environmental conditions, every man has most likely faced the fork in the road on the way to finding God. One fork is signposted 'I am in control—I'll do whatever I need to do to get what I want'; the other is signposted with 'I AM is in control—grace, mercy, and love available. Trust Me and surrender to Me.' Which one do I take? Well, I have learned in my life to trust no one, and in my culture to never surrender.

It has taken me a very long time to venture the other highway. Which fork did you take, and which road are you walking?

I invite you to take an opportunity here to reflect on any areas of life or any course of action that you may be on so as to consider where you might be situated, and ask yourself, 'Who is in control?' What are God's purposes for me, and what may it mean to respond to His will, His way, for His purposes? Of the two ways we fail to know God in these times, the first is that we don't take the time or space to listen to God and do what is necessary to hear Him over and above our own chatter. We have to know Him to trust Him, and we have to believe in His goodness to even want to want to do His will His way. Second, we are far too busy, distracted, and entertaining all sorts of things that—though they may be important in the here and now—are other than those that are essential to know Him, to know who we are according to His will for us and how He desires to be in communion with us. What do you think will be most telling for your life in the long run?

If it is necessary, I encourage us all to consider where we may need to restore the mark, to reset our standards to GDA, by plumb bobbing over God's reference position, where He sets His standards for what is good and true. Let us strive against the tendency to seek our own version of what we hold to be good. I will expand on this more in the following chapter. Honestly, have a good look at what's going on in our lives, our marriages, families, communities, societies, our countries, and the world. We are God's image bearers. When we say that we worship Him, we are claiming to hold God up to be of most worth. We are God's presence on earth. We respond to God's love for us by loving Him back in the way we live, love others, and relate. Let's return to God and His ways. Let's restore the mark to His standards of goodness. Let's restart and reset off in the footsteps of His Son. Christianity is about getting a new start. When we set out having restored and reset ourselves to God's standard, we take His goodness into the world, keeping our eyes on Him as the pioneer and perfector of our faith.

It is foolishness to claim that we are independent beings—we are dependent on God to meet our needs. We must stand still against the prevailing currents and forces of societal and cultural movements that veer us away from God's way, and represent Christ, the very embodiment of truth itself, to the world in our time; otherwise we too are complicit in losing or moving the reference point. If we are not plumb bobbed exactly over His mark, then all of what we do from this point will continue to be in error and off-centre. And then the further we move away from His standards, the more distortion creeps in wherever we are, wherever we go, and in whatever we do.

Two critical areas that I think require our full attention in these present times are moral integrity and trust. These are critical factors when carrying out hydrographic surveys, to keep the ship safe at all times throughout the uncharted and sometimes very dangerous waters around northern Australia. Running the ship aground can spoil your whole day. If the integrity of establishing positional control over the uncharted waters of the survey area was diligently set up, with a strong focus on accuracy and quality, then there was confidence in believing and relying on our systems to provide good positions. This confidence was essential especially when we had to passage overnight or when the weather closed in or whenever visibility was reduced. We needed to place trust in the positional systems we had established so we could rely on the accuracy they provided for knowing where we were across the survey area, to keep the ship and us safe.

As it is for surveying at sea, so it is with relationships—to keep them safe too. Trust and integrity are crucial factors for healthy and safe relationships, especially in troublesome times—which are now. Marriages, families, and communities are being ripped apart by betrayal, violence, and hate-filled attitudes and behaviours to one another—all motivated by a self-centredness to make our own life go well. Do you see what is happening? When self is the centre and it's all about 'me', then there is little if any consideration of 'other'—not God and not those whom we say we love. We make it God's role, and the role of those who we say we love, to be available to us and for us, specifically to make us feel safe, secure, and loved—and they had better do their job well, or else. No, we are not naturally good—surely the evidence is there for even the most optimistic believer in human goodness to acknowledge that human beings are going the wrong way. We need something other than ourselves to be good. We need God's goodness.

The Importance of Moral Integrity

I am not going to pick on any particular sporting code or team—but I could. Australians used to be known around the world for their sportsmanship, having a fair go, and being good honest blokes—true to some stated or unstated code of honour. Where has it gone? What is going on? Whatever it is, it seems to be driven by a desire to win at all costs and a willingness to do whatever it takes to achieve that goal—including unsportsmanlike behaviours. But let's not just pick on our sporting teams. What about our politics, our churches, our banks and financial institutions, our legal and prison systems, aged care, child care, the bureaucracy and corporate sectors in general that are under some inquiry, Royal commission, investigation, or review. It's costing the taxpayers a fortune. What has happened to the moral fabric of our nation?

I know as a man that there is something inside me that admires qualities of honour, courage, and standing up for what is good and true. I believe this to be so as part of what it means to be a man, whether there is a belief in God or not. It's in our masculine DNA. Have you noticed a subtle creep in culture that, almost as soon as we try to encourage these qualities, there is a strong cultural resistance that tries to bring them down, in the guise of being 'over the top', being 'on our high horse' or 'full of ourselves'. But no, I shout, these are good God-given character qualities that help define what it means to be a man. So what happens in us men when we don't live by our own values and codes that we know are right and good? Well, the duplicity sets up a dualism, believing one thing and doing the opposite, and duplicity rips apart integrity—so what on earth are we doing to our manhood?

Having moral integrity means being integrated as a person in body, soul, and spirit—as a whole person—in what we value as good, right, and true. What I value, believe, think about, I say and so I do—in word, thought, and deed. Why is this so important to men in particular, and why is moral integrity so important to God—who is the authentic and original standard for all that is good and true? God wants our holiness—to be set apart from the world for Him—to show the world His glory through us in how we live, and love Him first then others. Of course, that is primary, and God also wants our holiness because of His love for us and desire for our ultimate good. Let me explain this further.

When I say one thing and do another, you can legitimately call me a hypocrite. When I have certain beliefs and values but don't live them out, I am duplicitous and dumb, because duplicity rips apart the very quality I value highly—integrity, which I want to honour. I become fragmented to the core of myself. I become confused, and cranky with myself, and project this onto others, because I lose a sense of who I am and what I stand for. I value honour and integrity—so why do I not stand up with courage and strength for what is good and right in God's sight and in my heart?

Something inside of me comes to my defence. You have to admit, we have a very competent defence attorney at times. 'Oh, it's not so bad—no big thing really. Compare yourself with others, John, and you're doing OK—you're fine. Give yourself a break.' And my heart hardens a little more against God, and I tell Him to give me a fair go and then I let Him know He is an impossible taskmaster and judge. But the tension doesn't go away—there's that persistent niggle that tells me that I really ought to move towards what is good. There's a battle going on. 'Well, that's the final straw, God, fair dinkum, what else do I need to do to please you?' Metaphorically, I shake my fist at God—and I rebel further. Oh, I like that rebel in me, don't you? We Aussies admire the rebel—particularly against any authority figure. Finally, 'OK, God, I don't believe that you are on my side or that You will come through for me on this, so I will do it myself.' And then we discover that we have become separated from God and separated from our true self.

God does not want us to be rebelling and separating ourselves—cutting ourselves off from Him—because He knows that it will not go well for us when we do. Because He loves us so much, He wants our utmost good. So He earnestly invites, appeals, urges, prompts, and prods us to live a life of moral integrity. He knows that what is wrong in us is moral depravity, a heart inclined to desire, know, love, and enjoy someone or something more (other) than Himself. The battle that is being fought for the truth is happening in our hearts, and it is for our very souls. The starting point is that we acknowledge that humans need a source—a good source—to define the standard for what is honest, good, and true, and then to trust God that His attitude towards us *is* His goodwill for us.

There are other sources external to us, of course. Thomas à Kempis was around the same age as our current senior cricketers (don't mention the cricket) when he learned that *the enemy outside is sooner conquered if the man inside is not in ruins*—and that was 600 years ago. I find this to be so with the many men I have been with, who come with shattered lives and shattered dreams; they are a mess internally, and yet, they seem unable or unwilling to be able to stand for what is good and true. Why is that? These are well-intentioned men who want to be good husbands, fathers, sons, brothers, and mates. They seem vaguely aware that there is a force deep within them that desires the good—that values integrity, honour, truth, and doing the good and right thing. But when they try, and try so hard, they fail—and it all becomes too hard. They are unable to live up to what they say they value most and hold to be of most worth—unable by themselves, I mean.

Unwillingness might be a strong word, and it needs to be because human beings are wounded, wilful, and wicked—WWW—interestingly, it's all over the Internet? I know that some of us—although we would agree theologically that sin remains after conversion and the Spirit can be quenched—actually live lives avoiding thinking about these things. We easily seem to forget what is crouching around in our culture seeking to devour us (Gen. 4:6–7; 1 Peter 5:8). Yet, most men I talk with also grew up learning to never take your eye off the ball. All of us have the potential (still) to behave in a way which prevents God's will and guidance getting through to us. This is our unwillingness to actually receive and accept it. J. I. Packer, in his classic book *Knowing God* (1973), pointed out six ways our unwillingness interferes with God's will for us.[7]

1. Our unwillingness to think and reason—calling it our spirit telling us to do/not do something without checking with reason and God's Word
2. Our unwillingness to count the cost or to look at the consequences of our actions
3. Our unwillingness to listen, hear, or take advice—Proverbs 12:15 tells us, 'The way of the foolish is right in his own eyes.'
4. Our unwillingness to be real and honest, and take a good, long, hard look at ourselves, looking at our feelings without being governed by them because of self-deception, self-defence, and denial
5. Our unwillingness to take personal responsibility and therefore blaming others (including God) for our plight, and
6. Our unwillingness to wait—demanding instant gratification now

Something is wrong! Something has been corrupted. Augustine saw our (human) problem being less about that we behave wrongly, and more about us being drawn to love wrongly.[8] He argued that we are always motivated by love—which is why Adam and Eve disobeyed God. They sinned because they loved (and chose) something else other than Him. Martin Luther went on to describe this further as human beings turning love inwards. And the consequences were . . . are . . . (fill in the blank yourself) broken relationships, including separation from God. Take a look at the time, effort, and resources we are spending on love and on trying to be connected. We hate being disconnected—especially through abandonment, betrayal, and rejection—because we were designed for love: to receive love and to give love. So when our love is rejected, this hurts so much that we never want to feel that kind of hurt ever again. So we harden our hearts and vow never to let anyone ever hurt us like that again. Trust has been shattered, and real intimacy—what we so desperately long for—is no longer possible with anyone, including God. So we are not together. We demanded our independence and the right to do our own thing, and now we are isolated and disconnected. Nothing much is integrated about us at all; rather, we are shattered, confused, and lost, having trust for no one—not God or people or ourselves.

Trust

Every one of us is looking for someone they can trust. Why is that so? Human nature could be summed up in the following three ways. People seem to have a desire for goodness. However, they seem to be incapable of doing the good that they desire, yet they expect others to do good to them. We know that we are flawed. While there seems to be a ready willingness to admit that we (may) have made a mistake, have you noticed how quickly this declaration is followed by a refusal to take any responsibility or admit that the person has done anything wrong? Yes, it's OK for us to make mistakes because we understand that we don't do the good we want. We fill in any the gaps or pauses in our declaration with 'I'm only human' (what does that mean?), 'Nobody's perfect,' 'Can't be right all the time,' 'I'm not that bad'—which seem to roll off the tongue far too quickly and easily. Is anyone sincere? Do people want my good? Do I trust them to be genuine? What's wrong is actually about broken trust, and that hits us all deep inside the heart. But since broken trust (soon to become distrust) masquerades as righteous anger, we don't actually get to take a look at what is really going on inside ourselves.

Every man is looking to someone to verify that what they sense inside of them can actually be achieved or attained—to live life fully, being loved and loving and enjoying it abundantly. Every boy is looking for a role model—someone other than those who have let them down, and other than themselves because lostness, confusion, and fear all need reassurance that 'I am OK.' What is it that entices us to watch virtual reality lives through the scenes on TV and related media? What is so missing from our lives that we are so empty and needing to comfort and compare our own lives to others, or worse, live our lives through others? Andy Warhol first expressed the idea that there are fifteen minutes of fame for each of us in this life—is that it? Is that why we are so enticed? We are too easily satisfied with much too small of an enticement, I think. What do you think? I am curious. The capacity and resources are available for all of us to live a full, rich, and rewarding life and live it abundantly. We are not ordinary people—there are no such people, says C. S. Lewis, and especially so for those who follow an extraordinary God. 'I'm only human,' indeed. Jesus was the only fully human being—to be fully human is to be like Jesus—and that is just what God wants us to be. And that's what He's doing.

Why don't we passionately seek the abundant life that Jesus offers? Is it because we still believe the lie that we can achieve the good life ourselves, apart from God? Worldly voices tell us not to accept or allow mention of the Christian God as our Father, and/or Jesus to be the source of what is good and true inside us, because human beings are good—it's the human spirit. Yet, I know that is not true for me, and from what I hear from mature and honest folks, it is not true for them either. Therefore, we need some heroes. There must be a reference point for us in our heroes. It is sadly the case that Australian culture hero-worships sports people. Time and time and time again, these imperfect and 'only' human beings fail to live up to the hopes, expectations, and dreams of our need for them to do so. Everything inside of us that is let down and betrayed grieves again and again, until we no longer believe that these wonderful, desirable traits of honour, courage, and truth do really mean anything, let alone that they are true codes that can be lived by. It is understandable that lost, lonely, scared, and confused people turn to cultural mantras such as 'look after yourself, no one else will', 'you can have what you want,' and 'do whatever it takes to get it.'

Trust is an essential element for healthy and secure relationships. It is a close relation of integrity. Trust is also the most fragile of relational qualities because it is the easiest to crumble and be destroyed, and the most difficult to repair and build up. I know for me that trust was shattered deeply through the childhood sexual abuse done to me by trusted friends of my family. I fully understand the horrendous consequences on relationships that betrayal and broken trust cause, setting up that insidious relational barrier of distrust within those of us who have been affected by this awful enemy of relational wholeness and intimacy. I have insight now because I can look into the wake of the hurt and the pain of damaged relationships in my own life.

It may be easy to agree with me about how we have experienced the disintegration of trust in society—but what about within the church? I will share with you two recent examples I heard about how broken trust brings about isolation within the Christian community. The first story is of a pastor who is dealing with issues around complex grief and trauma. Whether you wish to use language around healing or therapy isn't the point—the point is that the well-being of this person needed a safe and healing community where the person would be loved, accepted, and able to share their hurt and pain with safe and trusted people. Instead, the person felt isolated and alone—and trust in his community as a safe and healing place was shattered. The second story is of a young husband and father who struggles with sensitive issues around being different from other men in both our Australian culture and within his Christian community. His experience of being different presents (at least) two major relational obstacles for this person. First, he wonders about and questions his own capacity to be a 'real' man and raise his son, and secondly, he and his family feel alone in their heartfelt attempts to live an authentic Christian life following Jesus and belonging totally to God.

If the Christian community—the church—was functioning as it ought, I would be out of a job. I don't know if I'm much good as a counsellor—others can best answer that—but it seems I am a safe person that people can trust with their life stories that would otherwise remain untold. And in the sanctity of the counselling room and the sacredness of the relationship, it is a privilege to walk alongside people for a while so they don't have to struggle alone. No one should have to face the difficulties of their life feeling alone and isolated. The issue is around being able to truly trust others with what we are truly struggling with. What's going on in Christ's church?

C. S. Lewis gave us an insight into our problem with trust in his autobiography, *Surprised by Joy*. Lewis is saying that the desire for *joy*—like *goodness* and like *love*—is not to be found turned inwards to itself but to its object. The value lay in what *joy* was desiring, which was clearly not a state of mind, emotion, or body feeling at all. Lewis received his answer from God: 'I Myself am your want of—something other.' We have to wake up to our need to restore some standard of goodness outside of humanity, or (yours to fill in again).

We are made by love, with love, for love, to love, and trust is an essential element for us to fully participate and enjoy an intimate and fully healthy relationship. Larry Crabb says this well: *We were made by a relational God who defines Himself as 'Love' to enjoy relationship, firstly with Him and then with others. So we were designed to love—given the capacities to receive love from God (fulfilled), and then give it to others (joy). When we do this our soul is healthy and we are living according to design.*[9] This is truly the good life, and it is life to the fullest. If you are anything like me (and I believe you are in many ways), then how is it that we so quickly forget that it's God's full intention and promise to bring us to the fullness of life (Jn. 10:10)? Don't we believe Him? Will we trust Him? Crabb subtitled the chapter on Exodus in his book *66 Love Letters* as 'You Must Know Me to Trust Me'. That's what it is all about.

Restore to First Order

Francis Collins headed up the Genome Project that cracked the human genome code. You could say that he understands our DNA. In his book *The Language of God*, he said about us, *'we humans seem to possess a deep-seated longing to find the truth, even though that longing is easily suppressed by the mundane details of daily life'*.[10] Even though love has been distorted to a Hollywood version, it is surely mentioned enough for anyone to understand that we long for it. If you look closely enough people seem to admire a sense of goodness—we really like being good. Wouldn't it be wonderful to be good and loved—or maybe, to be loved really good. It is the definition of goodness that we seem to quarrel over as we appear to have different understandings of it. People desire the good life, a happy life, good health, enough money to live well in the society and culture they are in. Most would agree that this is their goal. None of this is necessarily bad, but is it first-order good?

For Christians, wisdom invites us to be very wary of seeking the good life apart from God—particularly to the extent that one might be comfortable and satisfied with this life. Christians also ought to be cautious of the potential to exhibit a false confidence. While we can be so busy in ministry, performing good works and achieving wonderful things for God, and think we are making good progress through life, we can be unaware of the world making its way in us. The subtle creep and deception of our postmodernist society permeates throughout our culture—which is a human construct of what we think the good life looks like—and it becomes our total way of life, whether we are conscious of it or not. And we can find ourselves way off the mark God set. Matthew Henry, that great commentator, was aware of this over three hundred years ago. Here is a commentary he gave on Acts 17:22–31: *'And are there not many now called Christians, who are zealous in their devotions, yet the great object of their worship is to them an unknown God?'* What do you think of that statement?

Christianity has never been a modern success story, says Francis Schaeffer.[11] Christian living has historically been weakest in times of prosperity—and strongest during times of struggle and adversity for the people of God. We are warned by Jeremiah (Jeremiah 6:14; 8:9–11) that even those who believe in God and who profess that all is fine—because God loves me—are blinded by the lie. All is not OK—yet God continues to love us. One example is how Christians today are told that they are supposed to be tolerant, so we stay quiet so as not to cause disruption in society—did Jesus? He gave us a higher calling—to love people, not tolerate them. And it is foolish to think that you will not be put down and persecuted if you speak out against the voices of society and culture—so what are we avoiding? Over time, our Creator—the one who gave us breath—has been denied, not listened to, not sought out, not followed, not obeyed, not believed, and not loved (Lewis, Schaeffer, Bonhoeffer, Willard, Crabb, et al.). Since He has determined our *appointed times in history* and where we live, we can be grateful that He should bother with us at all—yet He continues to woo us to Himself. Are we able to admit that we need God, and fall on our knees in awe at what He has done—and offer Him true worship—with all of ourselves?

We were made to be dependent on God and interdependent with our brothers and sisters in Christ so that we are encouraged and strengthened by others as we travel together. Yet human nature by its very essence will demand independence, the right to meet its own needs, to control, manipulate, and do whatever is necessary to get what it wants. And, we will continue to do that until we arrive at a place where our lives and dreams are shattered – until we lose our way, until life becomes a mess and we realise we can't fix it. Then we have an opportunity to cry out from our hearts and God promises to hear us – then His Emmanuel agenda kicks in, His plan to be with us, and His provision through His body – the community of God's people - the means to ensure that no one should have to face their struggles in this life alone.

John Eldredge says that '*At its core Christianity begins with an invitation to desire.*'[12] I have discussed previously that this desire has been put in us by God so that we would seek to know Him, and when we truly know Him, we will see His goodness, and we will really trust Him. Only then—when we trust Him—will we come to Him and surrender. And we will remain hungry and thirsty, because God is using our hunger and thirst to bring us to Himself—but we must understand that it is hunger and thirst for God, not someone or something else. Because it is hunger and thirst for God that will sustain us more than the experience of God, and any other 'good' thing in this earthly life! If an experience is what you are after, it will come and go. Experiences wilt and wane and are emotionally based. Feelings provide a reasonable weather report on what is going on inside of us and colour our world—sometimes they're great, sometimes not so good, sometimes they're awful. But it is our reasoned faith response—based on the knowledge of God

WHERE ARE YOU?

through His Word and self-revelation—that is the promise and the hope of our reality and redemption. Desiring God before all else, wanting to know Him intimately, more deeply and lovingly—this is what will sustain us in this life, until we are home with Him forever.

This is first-order good. Francis Schaeffer stipulated that the restoring of what was necessary for humankind must be from the perspective of the Word of God.[13] So our next step will be seeking to establish a positional system that will tell us where we are at all times. First, we will need to plumb-bob ourselves over the primary known mark, which has been restored to its original position, and reset firmly and accurately in the place where it belongs. Then we will establish the position of the other two marks relative to our primary known point so that they can also be known with relation to our GDA reference point.

Come with me now as we undertake some triangulation.

Notes on Chapter Three

1. John Stott, *The Message of Acts* (1990), 277.
2. Ibid., 291.
3. Ibid., 285–287.
4. Ibid., 290.
5. Cited in Richard Rohr, *Falling Upward* (2011), ix.
6. Larry Crabb, *66 Love Letters* (2009), xxiii.
7. J. I. Packer, *Knowing God* (1973), 266–268.
8. Reeves M., *Delighting in the Trinity* (2012), 67.
9. Larry Crabb, *SoulTalk* (2003), 124.
10. Francis Collins, *The Language of God* (2006), 7.
11. Francis Schaeffer, *Death in the City* (1969), 65.
12. John Eldredge, *Desire* (2000, 2007), 35.
13. Schaeffer (1969), 28.

CHAPTER FOUR

Establishing Our Position

From one man He made all the nations, that they should inhabit the whole earth; and He marked out their appointed times in history and the boundaries of their lands. (Acts 17:26)

The whole tenor of human life is affected by whether human beings regard themselves as supreme beings in the universe or acknowledge a super-human being whom they conceive of as an object of fear or love, a force to be defied or a Lord to be obeyed. (Paul E. Little)[1]

But if serving the Lord seems undesirable to you, then choose for yourselves this day whom you will serve, whether the gods your ancestors served beyond the Euphrates, or the gods of the Amorites, in whose land you are living. But as for me and my household, we will serve the Lord. (Joshua 24:15)

Triangulation

TRIANGULATION CAN BE a scary word for those who don't like maths, but I really enjoyed it. Angles, three sides, cosines, sines, and tangents—I remember them well. And that was before calculators and computers existed. Remember the Log Tables—maybe not? When I first entered the Navy, I was pleasantly surprised that my enjoyment of mathematics continued, especially solving relative velocity problems on the radar, which was fundamental for manoeuvring in high-volume shipping situations and when in a convoy with other naval vessels. Also, I really enjoyed taking astro (star) sights and navigating by the heavenly bodies when we were days out to sea and out of sight of any land. We had to get up early in crisp clear mornings, before morning civil twilight, and shoot up our stars before they disappeared with the sunrise. I found it fascinating. But when I became a hydrographic surveyor, trigonometry came into its own and was the perfect solution to accurately establishing position—relative to GDA, of course.

Surveying (at least thirty-five years ago) was all about trigonometry—measuring the angle between sides and measuring the length of the side—and solving the position of a point relative to the primary reference mark. It's very simple really, but I'll refresh your memory just in case. The internal angles of any triangle add up to 180 degrees. So it's simply a matter of knowing two internal angles, and you know that the third interior angle must sum to 180. All we need is the sine, cosine, and tangent equations—and problem solved. And the perfect triangle for me was always the equilateral triangle, where all the sides were of equal length and all the angles met at 60 degrees. If I added the word 'holy' to the perfect triangle, you would know where I was leading!

I am continually amazed at just how many different ways triangles seem to appear in life. For me, the most important triangle depicts the Trinitarian God—the *trias* and/or *triad* that Ignatius of Antioch, Polycarp and Irenaeus wrote about and the *trinitatus* that Tertullian and Origen explored further. As I alluded to in the previous paragraph, I imagine the three persons of God forming an equilateral triangle. All three sides are equal in length, and they meet at an equal angle of intersection. Therefore, their size and relationship with each other are all equal—Father, Son, and Spirit. Other triangles of note are God, human beings, and creation; God, man, and woman; Christ, husband, and wife; and many more, I imagine, throughout biology, chemistry, physics, and nature. When I first undertook studies in counselling for couples, it was suggested that man and woman were God's foundational and smallest community. I have come to believe differently now, because two could not be a God-made community. Have you observed two people in love—to the exclusion of everything and everyone else? And some of you might be thinking, 'But Scripture says it's whenever two or three are gathered.' Yes, and if there are two people, there's also God with them—that's three at least. God is not exclusive. So for me, God's intentional foundational community is three—Christ, man, and woman. Of course, I am not ruling out a community of more than three—and singles are included—because when by themselves they have Jesus with them and the Spirit. Over time, I have witnessed again and again that couples who kept their eyes on Jesus to meet their primary needs seemed to think that counselling was helpful to them. Those couples who looked to each other to meet their needs didn't seem to think I was much help at all.

But we are getting ahead of ourselves; first we need to go back and accept our datum for this book—one that meets GDA standard. Over the coming chapters, our aim is to come up with a way of determining our position wherever we are in life while we are seeking to know God, ourselves, and how we are related. So what will be our reference point? On what foundation will we stand that meets GDA quality? What will be our datum—our starting point? We have determined that this point must be the best fit for our time and space. I know that I stand on the shoulders of the giants of our faith, so if we are going to cast our minds over the most assured and certain way of knowing God and thereby also know who we really are (more later), then our reference point must be God, and our datum must be the Bible—also referred to as Scripture and God's Word. I invite you now to think with me as we intentionally choose our starting point.

I understand that there are four main accepted ways of knowing God: through His Creation, from His Word recorded in Scripture (the Bible), through the life account and recorded words of Jesus, and through experiential knowledge—with the caveat that experiential knowledge aligns with the other three ways of knowing. The Bible then meets all our GDA requirements (reinforcing this to mean God-determined accuracy) for our datum point. Quoting Jerimiah 8:9, John Owen, in his book *Communion with God*, said, *'It is untrue, false, to claim wisdom outside of God's revelation of Himself in His Word and fully, in the person of Jesus Christ.'*[2] How would we otherwise know that what we know about God is true?

We know that it is true that we can know God through His Creation because the Bible says (Psalm 19:1; Romans 1:18–25). How do we know that Scripture is a way to know God? The Bible says (Roman 16:25, 26). Most significantly, Jesus Himself referenced Scripture: when confronted by Satan in the desert He responded, 'It is written . . .' (Matthew 5:18; John 10:35). How do we know that we can know God by knowing Jesus? The Bible says (John 14:7–9; 1 John 5:20). How do we know that we can know God relationally? The Bible says (John 10:14, 17:3). As Christians (or believers), we know all this is true because of God in us—and the Spirit of God knows our Father God and His Son Jesus, who is also God. Yet it is up to God whether He will reveal Himself to a hard, blocked, and cold heart—or not. The Bible says! You may wish to follow this up by reading the first two chapters of Romans.

God in Us is the Proof of God

Most men with whom I have had the privilege to share deeply those things which really matter have passed through a sort of life transition barrier—usually somewhere between the ages of 36 and 42 years, but not necessarily—where in their earlier years, they believed that they were ten feet tall and bulletproof. Beyond these years, most admit that they are not in control of much at all—and never really were, except for their choices. These men wisely no longer trust themselves to get life right all the time and have learned other ways of discerning how to make decisions and life choices that don't all rely on them having to be in control. As we share together our hopes and goals of our journey, a common desire to know God more deeply and intimately seems to offer reassurance to each other that we are not alone on our journeys. These are the conversations that really matter because faith is empowered, hope is strengthened, and Christian love stirs us on, in the knowledge that whatever the circumstance or situation, God holds open the door of hope—and nothing can take away from us the freedom to choose this hope. Men who go through this life transition experience quite a significant shift, and it's more than the label 'midlife crisis'—it's more like a second-half-of-life movement. Richard Rohr writes well about this movement in his book *Falling Upward*.

It was very much this experience and significant shift that occurred in my life as well. Those who learn from their failures and come to accept their inadequacies as opportunities to seek a source of reference other than themselves seem to mature and grow more peacefully than those who keep fighting for control. There is a certain sense within us all to worship something (what we hold up to be of most value or to be of most worth) and our choice is critical for life—as the Paul Little quote at the beginning of this chapter said, the whole tenor of human life is affected. Oswald Chambers put it this way: 'Our knowledge of God affects our behaviour.' Those like Augustine, Francis of Assisi, C. S. Lewis, Dr Francis Collins, and many others seem to find confidence, assurance, and certainty in God and His promises of Who He is, what His purposes are, and where we fit in to the larger story He is telling.

We have all heard it said that life is a journey—and by now we ought to realise that it is an inner journey, not an exterior one. Well, there seem to be particular waypoints along the path our inner journey wends, and Paul's earnest appeal to seek God and reach for Him (I like the translation 'grope' because it sits well with my bungling, fumbling, and struggling) becomes real.

Sometimes we do this consciously, and at other times, it happens unconsciously and obscurely. I understand this is what John of the Cross is indicating in *The Dark Night of the Soul*—the Spanish word that John used for 'dark' comes from the word *obscura*.[3] Yet there still seems to be some sense of our hearts yearning, and (maybe) praying the prayer *'Teach me Your way, Lord . . . Give me an undivided heart!'* (Psalm 86:11). Something tells us that we have grown weary and sick of our duplicity—and the desire to honour what is good and true sits courageously alongside a power within to change and reshape what love really means. These are the real things that matter and can become the real drivers for our search for God and ourselves. God put this in our hearts when He gave us the same heart as Jesus, and this was His original intention. We are made to be men of courage and honour who seek what is true and good, who are to remember where this comes from and move into the world and our life situations with the purposes of God. We now have a lion's heart. You see, men are meant to do good stuff—that's what women like about us.

A. B. Bruce made the statement 'What tells ultimately is, not what is without a man, but what is within.' It's more about who we are as men than what we do. In his apologetic *Mere Christianity*, C. S. Lewis advocated that the proof that God exists lies in the existence of the *law of human nature*, the *law of right and wrong*, the *law of good behaviour*, the *moral law* as a force and/or influence that exists inside us. It is a real law, which we did not invent and which we know we ought to obey. And that is just what we do find inside ourselves (Romans 2:12–16), written on our hearts! Read how Dr Francis Collins describes what it was like for him in his book *The Language of God*.

> A burden lifted. This was true north. And the compass pointed not at self-glorification, or at materialism, or even at medical science—instead it pointed at the goodness that we all hope desperately to find within ourselves and others. I also saw more clearly than ever before the author of that goodness and truth, the real True North, God Himself, revealing His holy nature by the way in which He has written this desire to seek goodness in all of our hearts.[4]

I like the analogy of 'true north'. Anyone who has navigated the oceans knows that there is a difference between magnetic north and how true north is calculated. Usually there are two main errors. The first is variation which is like a worldly correction—mainly due to the magnetic signature in the area, and that needs to be applied to the magnetic compass reading to find true north. The second is deviation, which is the error caused in the compass by the corruption of the platform the compass is in. Imagine the errors in our hearts due to the world's and our own flaws. Yes, we surely need to know true north—that's where Jesus is. Let us prove it together! We agree that God is good! We agree that God is love! Therefore, God is interested in right conduct with mercy and love—in fair play, unselfishness, courage, good faith, honesty, and truthfulness. It's in the heart, this moral sense of goodness, to do what is honourable, good, and true, with willingness, courage, and strength—you can sense it, can't you? It's there, but we need to know our true centre.

My purpose for re-enforcing the importance of God in us is to highlight this as the principle means for interpreting Scripture.[5] For Augustine, theology was the study of God, and I think him fortunate that he did not have the various avenues to study from, that abound now. In any case there is a widely accepted view amongst biblical scholars that Anslem's definition of theology is better stated. It is *faith seeking understanding*—which I think incorporates Augustine's belief that faith must be present in theologians if they want to study God. This is what I was referring to earlier in this paragraph. Only the Spirit in us can authenticate God and interpret His Word. The reason for this is that God cannot be known outside of the way He reveals Himself. Is this what we are afraid of—God in us? Paul knew it—this mystery (Col.1:26, 27). Is this our fear—to search into my heart and not only find the real me, but also encounter the power and truth of a loving Father God, who says to trust Him and surrender your control?

What Is Love?

As I continue the analogy of setting up for a survey, it is important to stress that survey observations and positioning are all about defined accuracies, standards, and quality. So as we continue to go forward, there are two qualities that I would like to present at this point in the book—some more later. Since I am going to be writing a fair bit about love in the coming chapters, I think it's time to clarify what I will be writing about. Love means so many different things to so many different people that I often wonder if we know what we are talking about at all. This is why I want to address it up front. I don't know what the word 'love' touches in you, but it's a huge and important point because on one hand, we Christians acknowledge love to be who God is, and on the other hand, we seem to reduce love down to some sort of base human feeling level—but that is not what God's love for us is like. Brennan Manning declares, '*Human love will always be a faint shadow of God's love.*'[6]

We hear so much about love, but I am sure it is human love that we are referring to—a distorted and counterfeit version of what I understand is God's *agape* love for us. The subject of different loves has been covered by other authors, and notably C. S. Lewis in his book *The Four Loves*—which I commend to you. The other three are *eros* (romance), *phileo* (brotherly, sisterly friendship), and *storge* (affection for a child or pet). God's *agape* love for us is His benevolence, His kindness and caring attitude towards us. Because this bears God's nature about who He is, it is His unconditional gift to us. Another way to describe God's love is His charity—His way of offering His goodness to us. But before I go on, allow me to tell you what I am not talking about when I mention love.

When I mention love, I am meaning it to be God's love and therefore Christian love as an attitude: towards God as a whole being and to the Father, Jesus, and the Spirit personally, towards each other in the body of Christ (the church), and that which we ought to extend to our neighbour. I am not referring to love in the sense of being in love, in a romantic attraction way, or as physical sexual desire—as when our hormones and chemistry are all over the place. That would be the Hollywood definition, and more closely resembles lust. *Eros* does reflect the metaphor of God wooing us and the church as the bride, but this is not God's *agape* love. And I am not referring to my love of ice cream or sliding down a 1.5-metre wave in a beautiful surf break or any other thrill. Nor am I referring to the great affection I have for my 14-year-old red kelpie-collie blue cross dog.

In fact, I am not talking about love as the world knows and portrays it at all—especially Hollywood. So this is important. If you continue to read on, I urge you to fight against any paradigm that would view love other than the agape, other-centred, selfless, sacrificial love as displayed by Jesus, which defines God's relational attitude, care, and affection *for us* and is *poured out* to us in a strong, kind, faithful, gracious way—always giving, full of goodwill, and other-orientated. Yet it is not sentimental or full of human emotion and definitely not weak. I like to think of God's love as His attitude of givingness of His goodness to us. I agree fully that God has and displays emotions, and I offer to you that His emotions differ from human beings' in the context that His are not tainted by fear, the trauma of past hurts and painful suffering, or foolish sinful behaviour, anything affected by shame or guilt, or self-centredness. God is somehow other wired when it comes to the way He expresses His pure emotions.

This is not a new discovery. Martin Luther (early 1500s) made the point that human love differed from God's love.

> The love of God does not find, but creates, that which is
> pleasing to it . . . Rather than seeking its own good, the love
> of God flows forth and bestows good.

'Flows forth' from what—who? Augustine, some 1,100 years before Luther, probably got close to describing God's love when he was trying to explain the Trinity as it was known by then and couldn't quite do it. The closest he got was to explain it being like love. Then he realised that he could reverse this description when the closest he got to explaining love was by arriving at the Trinity. How so? Well, it was because of the word *perichoresis*. This is the word the early church theologians came up with to describe the indwelling relationship of the Three Persons towards one another, and what is going on between them. Their relationship displays real holy and perfect love, and it flows between them always giving, always outpouring towards the other, never holding anything back; and being openly invited and fully received by the other, almost like in a *circle dance*, and then flowing out from God into creation—and into us.

Dallas Willard defined love as '*willing the good of another, it is not willing the good of "self" through another*'—and then doing something about it. Luther went on to describe human love as being the opposite of God's love. He said that human love is orientated towards something that is inherently good in which self-love defines the content and the object of the love. Men and women love something that they believe they can enjoy. In other words, they get something out of it for themselves, which is true but can also be a deadly sin, says Luther, depending on the motive—whether it is other-centred or whether it seeks something for itself.

Of course, Jesus' definition of love is even clearer (John 15:12–14): 'This is My commandment, that you love one another, *just as I have loved you*. Greater love has no one than this, that one lay down his life for his friends. You are My friends if you do what I command you.' When I read Jesus' words, they seem very clear—and it makes me wonder what it is that we don't seem to understand about Jesus' one commandment. I think we might agree that loving like Jesus does not come naturally—which is why we need His help.

Actually, what comes naturally is doing good and loving others so that we get something out of it. So if love is wanting the good of another, whose definition of good is to be used?

God's Goodness Is the Standard

If God's goodness is to be our standard, let us look at the example Jesus gave when interacting with the young man in the following Bible verses: Mark 10:17–22; Matthew 19:16–21; Luke 18:18–25. These passages tell us the story 'The Rich Young Man'—where there is an opportunity for the young man to reset his life for the kingdom of God. He is offered a restart of life from God's divine perspective. He has a chance to restore his life of worldliness to one which he was intended for in the kingdom of God—to eternal life with God.

More and more, I am concerned that there are those who, like the young man in the story, seek Jesus out for eternal life (salvation) and yet miss what Jesus is actually trying to tell them about the necessary response. I see and hear that there are those who believe that God is kind, gracious, and merciful—much like a grandfather figure—and so He forgives us because He loves us. His main purpose appears to be that He wants us to be happy. Well, all of that is true—but that's not the complete picture of what God is about in His larger story. That sounds more like the story we would like for our own lives. If we left it at that place, we are usually far away from the mark that God has set as the standard for both His love and goodness. God's love is behind His desire for us to accept His goodness. Do you think the conversation was as hard for Jesus as it was for the young man? Jesus is very clear in His interaction with the young man, and I think Jesus is making three distinct points about the young man's question about inheriting eternal life.

Point 1: Only God is the standard for what is good.

Point 2: If you want to know the standard to live a good life, then live and relate to God first, then others as per the Commandments (the first half are towards God and the second half to others), and this response is to be an internal heart response—it is not about performance.

Point 3: God invites us to come over to His side and follow His ways, and this is for our good—it is what is best for us, it is what we need, all this because of His love for us. He is clear that His kingdom is not of this world—it is not only different from our world's view; it is also set apart from the world's standards, especially those within a culture that emanates from a humanistic and secular western society, from a people who do not accept God.

Jesus told us this at the beginning of His ministry and again as He departed. He asked us to change our thinking, change our ways, turn back from whatever direction we were heading, and follow Him because His kingdom is near (Matt. 4:17–20). He does this not from any position of authority or desire to exert control over us, but from the understanding that we belong with Him in God's kingdom. Jesus announced how wonderful God's kingdom is by describing how blissful it is for all those who can enter the kingdom. He told us that our ultimate well-being and distinctive spiritual joy will abound because we will share in the salvation available through an eternal relationship with Him and be with Him (Matt. 5:3–12). And we whom He has called are to be living this life now because God wants us to be flavouring this world, preserving His standards, and shining His glory into this world that so desperately needs it but does not know Him (Matt. 5:13–16).

Finally, Jesus describes the fulfilment of the law being about a *rightness of the kingdom heart*—a right heart. Living eternal life now is about where our heart is aligned, or set, because this will determine the kind of person we become, what course we will set, and what standards we will live by (Matt. 5:17–20). Knowing we couldn't achieve any of this without Him, God gives us Himself: His love, His goodness, graciousness, and faithfulness towards us. Jesus came and fulfilled everything that was necessary to set us right with God and offered a restored relationship with Him forever. When He departed, He gave us the role of being His representatives in the world (Lk. 24:47). God reset, restored, and restarted our lives—if we accept His offer of invitation and respond to it. One author described Christianity as God's marriage proposal to us: He woos, He gives us Himself, He promises to be with us—together forever—and makes His proposal, and then He awaits our response.

What Stops Us from Accepting God's Proposal?

The young man's face fell (much like the look on Baby Huey's face, I suspect); he had wanted to do the right thing. He went away sad, because he had great wealth. The rich young man in our story had a heart's desire for what he determined was good by his worldly misunderstanding. He had a greater love for his worldly possessions, what he could hold in his own hands, even more than he had for the eternal life offered by Jesus. In Mark 4:19, Jesus had already explained that the things which get in the way of people living His call to follow him are often about the worries of life and being deceived by many worldly messages—especially about wealth and possessions. These distractions offer only a false security, and the delusion of being able to possess a good life now. Jesus made the point that the desire for any other thing, other than knowing God and Jesus Himself—first and foremost—will get in the way of us entering into eternal life with Him. As Francis Schaeffer writes, if we go to church to worship and then walk out thinking we can do our own thing, pursuing happiness for the remainder of the week, then all our worship externally means nothing to God[7]—nothing!

Timothy Jennings cautions us about what we worship and cites 2 Corinthians 3:18 as telling us that by worshipping God we become like Him.[8] We become what we worship. Gregory Beale made that statement the title for his 2008 book. And N. T. Wright tells us,

> You become like what you worship. When you gaze in awe,
> admiration, and wonder at something or someone, you begin
> to take on something of the character of the object of your
> worship.[9]

Anyway, like I pointed out some time ago, it has all been said before. Nearly 450 years ago, Richard Sibbes is cited as saying that we become like what we worship and was adamant that our view of God shapes us most deeply.[10] Jesus never stopped loving this young man. I also think Jesus felt kindness towards the genuineness of desire to do the right thing that He saw in the person of this young man. How Jesus must have so longed for the young man to follow Him and to place the desire to live God's standards for life ahead of his desire to put his self-needs first. What do you put first in your life?

Like Baby Huey crying out, 'I found it!', we can think that the standard we hold in our hands has the answer and solution to our life's situation. We often don't realise how far removed we are from God's own standards, particularly of knowing what He sets as the standard for what is good for us, and what His love is really about. While all of us can quote John 3:16, do we go on to read the chapter through to verse 36 (*Whoever believes in the Son has eternal life, but whoever rejects the Son will not see life, for God's wrath remains on them*)? It is Jesus who is both the definition of God's love and standard of goodness—His life reflects the Father's love, and God's goodness and givingness to us. His standards do not change, and following Him means being like Him. This is why Christians ought to be Jesus' disciples—as Dallas

Willard emphasised during his lifetime and made clear in his book *The Great Omission*.

How often can we think that because God loves us, we matter most to Him? Like in the story, God never stops loving us, yet we can forget that His goodness and His holiness are more important than ourselves, because the world, the universe, and all of creation cry out for His goodness. As God Himself tells us, '*It is not for your sake but for the sake of my holy name that I do this*' (Ezekiel 36:21, 22). As Rick Warren tells us right up front in his book *A Purpose Driven Life*, it's not about us. It's actually the other way around: we live for Him, not for ourselves (2 Corinthians 5:15). It is vital for all life, and the created universe(s) to know that God is good to us because we need His goodness. So God is saying, 'Come over to My side. I have the goodness you need. Live by My standards, follow the way of love My Son showed you.' God is good—all the time! He is also faithful and just (1 John 1:9). And He faithfully promises eternal life and goodness when we come to Him (Isaiah 55:2, 3).

Repositioning

Paul, of course, knew all this as he wandered the streets of Athens, among all the idols. I suppose there were several reasons behind Paul's distress, and I am beginning to experience what must be a similar feeling as I see what our culture admires and what we seem to seek after in the pursuit of happiness and the comforts of what we determine is the good life. I think Paul knew that idolatry is more than an offence to God. Worshipping idols means self-destruction. It did when Moses descended the mountain with the Old Covenant, and it remains so under the New Covenant. God's way with us through Jesus is new, but His standard has never altered. God desires goodness for us because that is His love—He wills our good and He wants to give His goodness to us. But we don't trust God to meet our idea of what is good for us. We naturally want to choose for ourselves what we think is good for us, and do not accept God's standard as either reasonable or good enough for us to have the happiness that comes from what the world portrays as the good life. This is why we need God as our centre and not the self.

I find that here we come across a big stumbling block—if not a full blockage—for some people. What do I mean? Am I saying that there are no good people unless they are believers in the Christian God and have been converted, born again, received Christ, and are new creations? Well, maybe I am, in a way, but I don't think so. I am saying that it all depends upon the standard by which one measures goodness—and love, for that matter. Dwight Edwards made this point in his book *Revolution Within* when he said, 'The true standard for goodness and righteousness is given us by God. In fact, the standard is God.'[11] So, if you are comparing different people to one another, then it's OK, but you need to know the standard of measurement you are applying. Edwards says it well when he suggests how easily we 'slip into a street level' view of goodness. Another way of describing human beings' natural way of referring to what we think as good is to say that we view things from under the sun, while God looks at things from His angle, above the sun.

Here now is the opportunity to reset the mark to God's original standard. With the freedom of choice and the responsibility for the consequences, we can rid ourselves of our dilemma in at least the following three ways:

1. Remove any emphasis from God's true holiness, that there is moral truth, and the result is that anything goes, the status quo remains, we keep holding the standard in our own hands and let everything be adrift on the ocean of whateverism.
2. Make all history irrelevant and human beings in history insignificant, and the result is that we are nothing that matters and human life has no meaning.
3. Restore God to His rightful place as the author of creation, our creator, the reference point of moral truth, and the arbitrator of all that is good, and the result is that God is our standard for living, human beings are fully loved, have dignity and significance (meaning) and redemption (restored position).

I'm advocating for number 3. How about you?

The Basis of Measuring Our Position

Back on the survey grounds, we had finally recovered the mark for our primary (first-order) known point, and now it was time to recover the other important two trig stations that were needed to establish the positional control network over the survey area. So altogether there are three stations—all aligned with GDA and integrated in a rigorous triangle that uses the primary station as the crux from which to link the other stations with GDA. The next step is to place navigation positioning systems over the mark of each of these known points. These are high-frequency radio transmitters, which are erected directly over the marks. They transmit radio waves that cover the whole area to be surveyed and provide an accurate measurement from their position to the survey ship's receiver—the distance from them to the ship. Using three of these measurements, intersecting to provide best fit, accurately positions the ship at any time and meets the required quality standards. Importantly, three lines of measurement are necessary.

I will now endeavour to consolidate where we are up to at this stage in the story. My summary of what I have been trying to articulate is that human beings need a reference point other than themselves to be able to understand life and what it means to be fully human. Jesus has been the only fully human person to walk our earth. Human beings need some wisdom other than human knowing to develop a framework for constructing the questions, and to search for the answers to the questions around what it means to be human and exist in this universe. This is their basic human right. So far, I hope I have put the case that God must be our primary reference point, and that our datum—the starting point for this truth—is Scripture. The Bible, in all its versions, has to be our starting point, because it has been established with God-determined accuracy—the only flaws are human interpretations and misunderstandings. While we might seek deeper understanding through the eyes of faith, it is the authenticity and inviolability of God's inspired Word that provides a starting point from which we can seek three essential truths for us to understand our lives—knowing God, knowing ourselves according to God's will for us, and knowing how we are related.

You may be interested in why the original mark was able to be carried in Baby Huey's hands. What we discovered was that the cement used to hold the mark in place was most likely corrupted or diseased—either by contamination of the cement or dilution of the original integrity, or a combination of both. The mixture had also deteriorated over time and not weathered very well because it was thought the shell grit and water used in the mix were wrongly applied, so the result of the decay was that the foundation crumbled, allowing the mark to be removed. We learned the importance of maintaining the integrity of the main substance (cement) and ensuring that the added man-made ingredients followed the correct instructions according to the maker's requirements—not doing their own thing by adding in their own ingredients and diluting the integrity of the mix. Seems a fair analogy of what we do with God's standards? What do you think?

We have restored our primary, first-order station to its original condition and done a reset to keep it firmly in place. Our next step is to seek to describe our three marks further so that we may understand better what we are seeking to measure and have confidence in the accuracy of our measurements according to GDA. The following four chapters will describe the importance of each mark, to the extent that the reader will be able to gain assurance in trusting this way of measuring where we are, whenever we cast our mind over our life's journey—especially through uncharted waters. Again, we emphasise our three marks, which are knowing God, knowing ourselves according to God's will for us, and knowing our relationship with and to God.

Let's go and have a closer look at our three marks.

Notes on Chapter Four

1. Paul E. Little, *Know Why You Believe* (1968), 7.
2. John Owen, *Communion with God* (2007, 2012), 135.
3. Gerald May, *The Dark Night of the Soul* (2004), 66–68.
4. Francis Collins, *The Language of God* (2006), 218.
5. See the following Scripture references for God in Us.
   - **God the Father is in Us** (Jn 14:23, 2 Cor. 6:16, Eph. 4:6, Phil. 2:13, 1 Jn 4:4, 12–13)
   - **Jesus, God's Son is in Us** (Jn 6:56, Jn 15:4, Jn 17:23, 26, Rom 8:9–11, 2 Cor. 13:5, Gal. 2:20, Gal. 4:19, Eph. 3:17, Col. 1:27, Col. 3:11, 1 Jn 3:24)
   - **God's Spirit is in Us** (Jn 4:14 along with Jn 7:38–39, Rom. 8:9–10, 1 Cor. 3:16, 6:19, 2 Cor. 1:22, Eph. 5:18, 2 Tim. 1:14, James 4:5)
6. Brennan Manning, *The Ragamuffin Gospel* (2005), 102.
7. Francis Schaeffer, *Death in the City* (1969), 32.
8. Timothy Jennings, *Could It Be This Simple?* (2012), 22.
9. N. T. Wright, *Simply Christian: Why Christianity Makes Sense* (2008).
10. 10. M. Reeves, *Delighting in the Trinity* (2012), 48.
11. 11. Dwight Edwards, *Revolution Within* (2002).

CHAPTER FIVE

Knowing God

God did this so that men would seek Him and perhaps reach
out for Him and find Him. (Acts 17:27a)

For I desire mercy not sacrifice (Hosea 6:6a)

No one has ever seen God, but the one and only Son, who
is himself God and is in closest relationship with the Father,
has made him known. (John 1:18)

What's God Like?

HERE WE GO *again*, I thought to myself. How do I stay curiously interested in someone as they share their story—especially when it is one that I have heard over and again? I know it is a sacred story and that it is a privilege to be in this trusted place with another person, yet it's difficult to stay focused when it is such a familiar story. It is for me at least. This time, it was a young man whom I will call Ian. Ian was 27 and single when he first came to see me, and I warmed to him quickly and easily. He was refreshingly open and honest, and it was clearly evident that he genuinely wanted to do the right thing in his present circumstances. However, he was anxious that what he thought might be the right thing for him might not be what God wanted for him. And would he trust God anyway if God had other ideas? But in his heart, he wanted to do God's will. You can see why I liked him right off. As Ian shared and I listened, he seemed to gain insight into a way through his problem. He paused, thought for a moment, and then said that what he needed to do was to spend more time reading the Bible and praying because he had been remiss with these practices. I nodded and strived to remain curious. When an opportunity to respond seemed about right, I reflected to Ian that wanting to spend time with God and reading the Bible sounded like a good thing. And I asked him who he prayed to. Looking at me a little bemusedly (because he knew I was a Christian), he replied, 'God.' I responded gently with 'Yes, I understand. What is He like?' Ian hesitated a little, then he began to describe God—then he paused, began again, then went silent. The remainder of our time together was an opportunity to share together what a personal relationship looked like with the person we are intimately relating with, and what we have to say to each other.

What's God like? I am finding more and more in conversations that really matter with Christians that our conversation generally comes around to this question when the rubber begins to hit the road in the story they are telling. The timing is that the question usually appears when the person has finished sharing their immediate concern—or presenting problem, in counselling terminology—and begins opening up their story more widely and deeply. Then, given a little space and having felt listened to, the person usually becomes more reflective and insightful. It is generally very common (for men in particular) to arrive at the insight that as Christians, they ought to be spending more time reading the Bible and attending church more regularly. Now, these are good things—don't misunderstand me here. The point I want to make is that the person believes that they should be doing something— something more. The answer to their problem involves more prayer, reading the Bible more often, and attending church more regularly—as they should. Hence the opportunity to ask, 'What's He like?' Without exception – no, not one – have I yet had anyone respond to the question from a relational perspective. Why? Well, you might think the answer is obvious considering that the person who is struggling might not be feeling very close to God at that moment. But I think that may be simplifying the matter a little. From those whom I have heard respond to the question 'What's God like?', there appears to be something very obviously missing from the way that God is known – and that affects the way we relate with Him.

The Search for the Unknown—A Droggy's Life

What are we actually searching for when we are undertaking a hydrographic survey? During my twenty-eight years as a droggy (Navy jargon for hydrographic surveyor) the advancement in echo sounder, sonar, tide measuring instruments, and positioning technology produced amazing changes. Not only were these technological changes in the systems themselves, but they also drove operational changes in the way we needed to use them and philosophical changes about the way we planned and approached the survey. This in turn produced more particular changes in the accuracy requirements and the standards for the surveys as well. Ships were built bigger, faster, and deeper in draught, and time at sea is costly, so we were always searching for safer and shorter shipping routes. And of course, there were the military requirements as well.

Besides the obvious search for underwater dangers like sunken reefs and shallow shoals, there were also requirements to measure tide heights, currents, water turbidity, marine life, bioluminescence, and bottom sediment types. Suffice to say that the capability of these measuring systems really increased as technological advances occurred. As far as locating objects on the seafloor was concerned, by the time I left the service in 2002, underwater systems could detect a metre cubed object on the sea floor almost anywhere on the continental shelf around Australia. Meeting this requirement to search, locate, identify, and position these unknown objects was more of an art than a science—and very creative too. It was also adventurous, exciting (thrilling at times), and required us to go about our duty with diligence and dedication naturally, but also as though our life depended upon it—as was the case in more than one occasion that I recall.

There was something special about hydrographic surveying for me. The meaningfulness of what we were doing and the wonderful outcome of the navigational chart that was produced for the safety of shipping gave me a sense of purpose and achievement. Being able to see a completed chart with the information gathered during a survey displayed on it gave the greatest satisfaction of a job well done at the end of a survey. But what really stands out in my memory is the loyalty and pride I remember seeing in the character of the people I served alongside in the Hydrographic Branch. It's the relationships and personalities that are most special in my memory. The way they went about their roles and responsibilities, how they undertook the search, the attitude of love they bore towards the profession, and the long hours of hard work in difficult conditions away from our families was truly extraordinary. Our mantra went like this: 'No day too long, no task too arduous, for we are the ships that lead the ships that lead the sea.' Stirring? Sounds a bit like the dutiful servant in Luke 17:7–10, don't you think? Imagine if we could profess something similar to this as Christians: 'No time we have is more precious, nor anything we do more important than for us, His called-out ones, to shine the light that shows the way so that all people may find God' because that is what God asks of us. Aren't we to worship and glorify Him?

I had naively anticipated that writing this chapter would be the easiest of all the chapters and that words would flow freely onto the page because the subject of knowing God is really what all my searching, struggling, hours of reading, and conversations have been about. So many books by notable authors and theologians—the classics and the contemporaries—have wonderfully covered the subject of knowing God. And understandably so, since Jesus defined that this is what eternal life is all about (John 17:3). As I was asking our Father to help me with this chapter, I had a sense that it wasn't to be about how to know God, or a description so much of what God is like—that has been covered very well already by greater minds than I could hope to follow. What I would hope for is to provide the reader with a manner of thinking about God so that they would spend their life in worship and glorifying God while continuing to cast their minds over knowing Him more every day on their lifelong journey of searching and reaching to find Him. And this searching and reaching has to come from you, because grace is not without effort, as Dallas Willard so aptly and earnestly appeals to us. So God looks for our *yes* to His invitation and asks for our participation and perseverance as we seek to know Him increasingly (2 Peter 1:2–8). You may find me repeating myself in this chapter, so allow me to acknowledge this up front and seek your permission to categorise repetition as part of reinforcing how important the subject is.

My way of encouraging you and helping you to cast your mind over knowing God more is to provoke questions and encourage focus so that you will seek answers for yourself. For my part, I hope I present the case that shows you why having this attitude of searching and reaching and desiring to find God is so vital for life, especially life to the full, because it is God who desires to relate with us and wants to be found. More than all our service for Him, He wants to be acknowledged for who He is (Hosea 6:6). In a similar way, I want to encourage and prompt you to reflect on how well and intimately you do know God relationally, what you are doing to seek Him more through broader and deeper exploration, and how well aware are you that this is your deepest desire and higher purpose? If God didn't want us to find Him, there wouldn't be much we could do about that, except change our attitude towards Him and pray something like Paul's prayer at Ephesians 1:17. As we seek God, He in turn will reveal Himself more and more to us through His Spirit. And as we live out and experience our relationship with Him, we will know Him more fully as He truly is.

What Others Say

Before going on, let's look back together at what some of the giants of our faith had to say about knowing God. In the words of Gerald Sitter (2007), we can draw our living water from a deep well. In a sense, this is like looking back either to ascertain we are on the right path in life or to verify that we have maybe taken a wrong turn somewhere, and whether we now might need to make a right turn. Maybe not everyone, but most people I am aware of take a wrong turn at some point in their lives—even those who were fortunate to be born and baptised into a Christian family—and find that they headed down a wrong path. In any case, I am thinking of what people like Augustine, Thomas à Kempis, Calvin, Benner, et al., who say that two vital aspects of our Christian lives become drawn together and cannot be separated throughout the course of our lives—knowing God and knowing oneself.[1]

Importantly, fundamentally, and foundationally, who you believe God to be (and therefore trust that what He promises to be true is indeed true) will affect your attitude and behaviours. And it is these (as is now proven through neuroscience), our attitudes and how we live out our life, which establish and direct our neuropathways. Or, as Bonhoeffer said it, only those who believe obey, and only those who obey believe. Our set ways of believing and thinking, along with our actions, determine our authenticity, integrity, effectiveness, and capacity as Christians. David Benner writes, 'God is the only context in which (our) being makes sense.'[2] Therefore, how we know God is crucial to how we will live our lives. Because if we don't truly know Him, we won't truly love Him, and if we don't know Him and love Him, we certainly won't trust Him. Conversely, if we truly know God, we will know Him as love, *the fountain from whence all other sweetness's flow,*[3] more than anything compared to in this world that we experience as love. But it has to be believed to be from Him, be received from Him, returned to Him, and lived out relationally for us to put our surrendered trust in Him.

Here are some other wisdom encouragements from what earlier Christian spiritual authors wrote.

> Augustine's prayer: 'Grant, Lord, that I may know myself that I may know thee.'

John Calvin, 1536, *Institutes of the Christian Religion*, 'Nearly the whole of sacred doctrine consists in these two parts: knowledge of God and of ourselves.'

John of the Cross. 'When God approaches as who He is, I am liable to feel myself for what I am.'[4]

Thomas Merton (1915–1968), 'There is only one problem on which all my existence, my peace, and my happiness depend: to discover myself in discovering God. If I find Him I will find myself and if I find my true self I will find Him.'

Other recent theologians continue the theme of why it is important how we know God. Oswald Chambers tells us that our knowledge of God affects our behaviours. A. W. Tozer, in his classic book *The Knowledge of the Holy*, wrote, *'It is impossible to keep our moral practices sound and our inward attitudes right while our idea of God is erroneous or inadequate . . . we must begin to think of God more nearly as He is.'* He goes on to say, *'The most important thing about man is how, deep down in his heart, he conceives God to be like.'*[5] Why deep down in our hearts? Because it is in the deep parts of us that we discover our *desires*, our longing to *know* and be known intimately, to *love* and to be loved, and to experience *joy*. Remember, the Bible is an authentic, true love story, and it is important to believe that God loves us and what He promises is true, so that we trust Him relationally.

Neil Anderson wrote, 'The most important belief we possess is true knowledge of who God is.'[6] Gregory Boyd writes, 'Our attitude towards God is completely determined by our mental picture of God.[7] Timothy Jennings asks that we reflect on the question 'Have you considered the possibility that your view of God could be affecting your mental, physical and relational health?'[8] And maybe this one final reference, from Floyd McClung, sums it up: 'Nothing hinders us from receiving the love of God as much as the lies that build up in our minds about who God is or who we are.'[9] I wonder where these lies come from? Of course, there are many other authors, theologians, poets, and songwriters saying the same thing in varying personal and (maybe) better ways—you will have your favourites. But the main thing is that we know and understand this God who is endlessly and eternally, pouring out Himself always towards us—always other-orientated, freely self-giving and outwards-flowing, a perfect and holy love without measure.

Why Is It So Important to Know God?

As I am casting my mind over the reason(s) for it being vitally important to know God, what comes to mind is that it's a bit like the priority and urgency that exists when we are told that we need a heart transplant, otherwise we might die tomorrow. It's really that simple, yet critically essential—we need a new heart. We need a heart that desires God more than anything else and that passionately motivates us to live a new way of life, one that puts us on a new path and ensures we will arrive at our home destination—happily ever after, forevermore. This desire is what God has placed within us all, but this desire gets confused and pushed aside by counterfeit desires. What a great line in the movie from the book *Same Kind of Different as Me* (2008) when Denver Moore said, 'So, in a way, we is all homeless—every one of us—just working our way home.' Some people say it's all about the journey. While I might agree that the journey is important, crucial even, it is the destination that means everything to me.

It is important also because how we live and relate *now* depends on where we are heading, and why we are heading there. Imagine a supply convoy heading out of Sydney, bound for London during the Second World War. The British people and Allies are in dire need of supplies, so the convoy of fully loaded supply ships sets off, escorted by a fleet of warships: a cruiser, aircraft carrier, destroyers, and two battleships for protection. During the voyage, the convoy enjoys great weather, and the crews have a wonderful time entertaining themselves; a really good, happy and safe passage was had by all, and then they finish up by arriving at San Francisco—the wrong destination. I wonder what those waiting in England might think about that?

In some respects, this can be a bit like our Christian journey if we don't keep in mind the destination, why we are heading there, and the purpose for the voyage. Of course, how we manage the journey is important, and so is our experience walking alongside others as we *walk the walk* together. And what joy it will be to arrive at our destination (the right one), having carried out what was commanded of us and having fulfilled our purpose. So we begin to understand the importance of what John Calvin said about knowing God and knowing ourselves, and what Thomas à Kempis meant, and why Augustine prayed as he did. We begin to see why God wants us to search for Him, grope even, and find him. And not for His sake only, but also because He knows that when we find Him, truly then will we find our most true self. It is this journey of discovery that we find ourselves on. It is a spiritual journey about relationships—an interior journey that we can avoid by dancing to our own tune with busy, distracted, full-on lives, or we can pause, tune in to a different rhythm, and begin a new dance along a different path leading to an eternal destination: home, where we belong. I think that's important—what do you think?

Language and Words Are Important

It seems to me that there comes a time and point in a person's life when they actually get in touch with the 'something' desire that longs to be an eternal somebody, forever in an intimate relationship with someone. Now, that is something! So seeking assurance of what we come to believe, Christians look to see whether it is true in God's Word (what we call the Bible), and as we search through the pages with the eyes of faith (not theological certitude), we come to grips with God's self-revelation. God's Word is God revealing Himself to us in human history—it's His larger story being revealed as our smaller story unfolds. But here's a but—language and the interpretation of words are very important. And, we are very dependent on how we understand their meaning, how they are applied, and what set of glasses the people saying them are wearing when they are both speaking and hearing the words. An example of what I am saying is how a person understands the meaning of the following seven words (and there are more): perfection, righteousness, holiness, obedience, love, worship, and glory. There is a separate chapter on love, worship, and glory. So allow me to mention here the other four.

I invite you to reflect on my description of these words and become aware of how they match your understanding of them, and any thoughts and response you might have to what I am saying. Specifically, does understanding them in this way make any difference in how you perceive God to be and in the way you relate with Him?

Holiness. To be set apart from this world and cultures, its worldly ways, and self-centred human nature so as to walk the way of Jesus in the kingdom of God.

Righteousness. While acknowledging that moral and ethical behaviour, along with God's justice and mercy, are part of what righteousness means, in its simplest and basic meaning, it is being in right relationship with God.

Obedience. This is our heart response to God because we want to honour Him and are grateful to Him. In both Hebrew and Greek, it means to listen and take heed of what God is saying and then yield (surrender) and submit ourselves to the God we know, love, and trust because of His love and goodness which are for us.

Perfection. The bringing of something to the completeness that it was always meant to be.

I hope that this helps explain a little of how important language, perception, and interpretation are to knowing God as He truly is. And how implicit to our perceptions, attitudes, and understanding is hearing and reading God's Word in the context of a sacred relationship that we have with Him within the larger story that He is telling? Yes, it is indeed true—our knowledge of God affects our attitudes and our behaviours. And thinking about this through relational lenses, that we too are made in the image of three perfectly holy persons loving each other the way they do, each seeking the interests of the other, giving and receiving to impart joy and goodness to each other ought to affect the way we treat and relate with others. If God is love, is relational, and we are made in his image, then at the centre of our faith is the way we deal with other human beings who share His image. Since God Himself is love, love becomes the acid test of our fellowship and communion with God—all three persons—and with each other. This is our calling—and if it's not, then what is? Our whole understanding (or not) of who we are as persons flows from the Christian doctrine of the three persons who are God—and their relationship with each other and us. To be personal, there must also be *otherness*—I know myself as personal in the context of otherness in relationship with me (or not). If there was no other, then there would be no me. I am aware of myself as an individual and that there is only one like me (my uniqueness) through relationships, which is where I get insight on myself as being wounded and broken and that I sin relationally. Yet it is through relationships and a loving community that I also receive healing.

There's Something About Change

If we keep our eyes on the destination, does this mean that we lose the enjoyment of the journey? Definitely not—it takes the need for control out of the journey so that the journey actually becomes more awesome and exciting: full of thrills, wonder, and amazement at how different we become, how much we change during the course of the journey, and how more like what we most admire to be we become. If I simply put it that we become like Jesus or are transformed into god-likeness, you might not think that it's very attractive or exciting. C. S. Lewis makes the process of transformation sound brilliantly enticing as he described the difference between *Bios* (natural man) and becoming *Zoe* (spiritual man).

> A man who changed from having Bios to having Zoe would have gone through as big a change as a statue which changed from being a carved stone to being a real man. And that is precisely what Christianity is about. This world is a great sculptor's shop. We are the statues and there is a rumour going round the shop that some of us are some day going to come to life.[10]

How wonderfully exciting is that? Of course, this also frightens the life out of me sometimes, as Lewis's sculptor's shop often feels more like being in a stone quarry. Either way, God is shaping us as living stones to build a spiritual house for Him (1 Peter 2:5). But some just turn their music up more loudly, put earphones on, keep themselves busy remaining focused on their idea of a good life, and refuse to consider the inner journey—I get that, and so does God. His goodness is displayed in the dignity and respect He gives us to exercise free will to choose Him or not. And God can see our hearts, so the initiative to reveal Himself to us is all His. He knows the difference between a soul that is earnestly searching for Him and one that is on some journey of self-fulfilment and self-amusement. So never fear if He frightens the life out of you—it is the life you really don't need anyway.

Of course, it's not like we start out thinking we really have to change all that much. I know I'm not perfect. Sure, I mean, nobody is perfect, right? I know that there are things about me that God doesn't like—I don't like them either. But I'm only human, right? Yet despite this familiar mantra within me, I seem to continually arrive at a place of frustration, even desperation that every avenue I go down to try and make my life work just seems to come to a dead end—and I'm exhausted. I know I cannot do my will my way. And I want to do God's will. Maybe I could do God's will my way? What do you think? Maybe there's another way? I know I need God, and I do want to know Him more. Don't you ever wonder why it is that we hardly ever seem to grow or change much when life is going well and we're doing just fine? I'm doing OK, thank you very much—just leave me be. Every time I grow and seem to change for the better, I seem to have to come to this place of, dare I call it brokenness, a place where I realise I just can't do what I want to do to be the man, husband, father, brother, friend I want to be—to the standard of goodness that I desire anyway. And then something changes. Somehow a combination of both my surrendering and my struggle seems to bring it about. Bruce Milne seems to think along the same lines. He wrote, 'Sanctification is both resting in Christ in faith, and wrestling to be conformed to His image.'[11]

Are There Conditions?

Of course, there are conditions that change requires. It would be quite off the mark to think that a loving God would change us without knowing the condition of our heart. And while love does not force itself on a person, inner change—deep in our heart—is something that God does. John of the Cross makes this clear in his writings about two points. First, John says that love is something God does—it is His initiative and activity (Romans 5:5). Secondly, God's love changes a person. We change because our love for God in response to His initiative is our Spirit-given yes.[12] Of course, the challenge to us here is to know God to the extent that our love for Him is unreserved, fully trusting, and openly surrendered so that He has our complete devotion.[13]

I agree with A. W. Tozer that knowing God is both the easiest and most difficult thing in the world, certainly in my life—easiest because it is a free gift, freely given; most difficult because of our natural human resistance, our demand for independence, and our refusal to surrender and trust anyone, especially God. We are so reluctant to accept what anyone else says is good for us, especially someone who says that there are no strings attached, it comes free—just receive. Have you noticed this? Therefore, based on our natural propensity for self-preservation and human nature's antagonism against God, there are necessarily some conditions that need to be met to fully know God intimately. Tozer concluded his classic book *The Knowledge of the Holy* by nominating six conditions he considered vital to our faith journey. Tozer titled this final chapter 'The Open Secret'. The following is my understanding of the six conditions he was openly revealing.

We could describe it in various ways, but basically, it comes down to believing that God exists, that He has our best in mind—He wants for our ultimate good. And He desires that we acknowledge our need for Him as His dependents. In its simplest form, our right condition before God is our yes response to His initiative of the faith, hope, and love He has placed in our hearts. This 'yes' faith response becomes our commitment to be living as it is true to the way God reveals Himself through His Word, the life of Jesus, the Spirit's enlightening within us, and the evidence of His presence in all creation. Our lived-out relational response and willingness to be open to receive God's inflowing of Himself is our surrender in trust to God's grace which we position ourselves to receive by striving, training, abiding (sometimes clinging), and maintaining through discipline and our attentiveness to Him. God provides courage and strength and gives us all the resources we need to persevere in our faith relationship with Him and to recognise and resist worldly attractions that are constantly competing and vying for the desires of our hearts.

What anchors us to our faith and to believing that what is best for us lies in the promises of God is the hope that what He tells us is true and that He is good and His love is always for us. The capacity to stay close to God and in communion with Him requires a committed response with regular pauses in our life's general moving, to spend time in His presence and in His Word as we seek to know Him more. We make every effort without presumption, not taking His love for granted, and with a grateful heart making Him always our 'first love' desire, to journey this life well (2 Peter 1:5–15). Ultimately, our yes response and our humble vulnerability to be open and receive what God pours into our hearts cannot but overflow into the world and those around us. We become God's intimate allies and channels of His grace thereby; as true image bearers, we make visible God's presence to the world. When we live this way, God surely becomes known for who He truly is—and when we know Him as He really is, we cannot do anything but love Him back.[14]

Another condition is our perseverance. Those who are mature in Christ have usually gained much through their seeking to know Him through His Word, Scripture study, and experience gathered along the way as they have walked the walk of their spiritual journey with God. In the end, we have to travel the path ourselves—no one can walk it for us. However, the secret revealed through Christ is that He has already walked our path, so all we need to do is follow in His footsteps—not from a distance. In a sense, even in uncharted waters, hydrographic surveyors understand that there is a lineage of master navigators and surveyors who have been before us and who have handed down their wisdom of certain conditions that either enhance the quality of their search or hamper, hinder, and even threaten their endeavours. HMS *Endeavour* was a wonderful name for James Cook's ship. You can imagine that precise navigation is difficult during storms, poor visibility, or at night. As good a navigator that Cook was, he still ran aground off Cooktown—yet he endeavoured to find a way, because there is always a way.

We are also dependent on the quality of our information. What is the source and who does it come from? Sometimes the accuracy and quality of information being collected is severely impacted. For example, measuring the ocean depth is nigh-on impossible when the ship is being tossed around like a cork in huge seas and large waves. Some days were not conducive to our tide watchers measuring the height of tide because storm surges and strong winds either damaged the tide pole and gauge or destroyed it totally, making it impossible to make tide height corrections. And how difficult is it to see sunken reefs and shoal waters when the sun is ether at too low an angle, causing a silver shine on the water, or obscured altogether by clouds? Sometimes we just need to understand that there are certain conditions that can seriously impede even our best attempts to make a safe passage through life. I am sure you can come up with your own list, but I will name a few, like believing that you can do life on your own and not being part of a community of believers, or seeking to know God through experience alone and believing it is by your own spirit when it does not align with His Word. Even doing good works in the world, if cut off from Christian input and fellowship, can make one vulnerable and weaken the Christian faith through constant negative values, sentiments, and comments from the worldly voices about Christianity. Reinterpreting Jesus seems to be a common practice in our times as we can form a view of Him that fits with worldly values, and before long, He no longer resembles the Son of God or the Christ and Messiah that He truly is. It is always wise to stay close to Jesus and follow the Master and what He has given us in His Word. He came to do the Father's will.

One of those who closely sought after God was author J. I. Packer. In his classic book *Knowing God*, he emphasised three main points. Allow me to paraphrase my understanding of what he was saying. First, it requires that we personally deal with God dealing with us—we must attend to what God is doing in us and take responsibility for it. Second, knowing God requires that we are personally involved in our relationship in all our facets: mind, will, and emotions. And third, we come to know God by receiving and surrendering to His grace—allowing ourselves to be fully known by Him (Gal. 4:9).[15] Love will not force itself on another. Part of that grace that God provides is an enthusiasm, a heightened energy and passion that provides excitement both for our relationship with Him and our journey with others.[16] During the process of progressively being conformed to the image of Christ, we remain in relationship with God and each other. Its relational—it's reflecting God's image as love which gives Him glory. Everything else is an outworking of being loved by God first—our working out what God is working within (Phil. 2:12–13) and a desire to pour out that love into each other, our communities, and the world—a world that does not know this love and is in critical need of it. What is your experience of this love?

Knowing God Through Relationship

When you pray, do you know who you are praying to? It's a serious question, because often when I ask this of a person, they think I am being funny or obtusely clever, yet they themselves admit that they do not think relationally about exactly who they are praying to. Specifically, what I am saying is that when we pray, do we consciously pray to God as one being—the Father, Son, and Spirit in relationship, altogether complete in unity? Or are we specifically praying to one of the persons of the triune God—the Father or Jesus or the Spirit? You can, you know—you can pray to whoever you want. All I am asking is that when you do pray, do you have in mind just who you are praying to and are relating with at that given time? And when you come to prayer in the relationship with the one to whom you are praying, are you conscious of who is praying? Do you have a sense of yourself in relationship with the person to whom you are praying? And then, when you are in the prayer relationship, do you attend to what you are saying during this sacred time of communion?

Prayer is relationship. It is our time of being focused on the otherness of God, conscious of Who He is and who we are, and attending to what we are saying. Or maybe we are listening—I know that I want to do more of that. It is through and in this relationship that God reveals Himself to us and expresses His desire to pour Himself into us to do His work in us—He seeks our yes. God's all-knowingness of us—even before we were formed in our mother's womb (Jeremiah 1:5)—still desires our heart's permission. He knows the depths of our very being because He has searched it, reaching in past our superficial shallowness and blundered attempts of resisting and blocking Him out—not as an intruder but as a divine conspirator revealing Himself to us and revealing who we really are to ourselves. It's all about relationship because it's all about God and what He is doing—because God is a relationship.

In his book *Experiencing the Trinity*, Darrell Johnson writes,

At the centre of the universe is a relationship. That is the most fundamental truth I know. At the centre of the universe is a community. It is out of that relationship that you and I were created and redeemed. And, it is for that relationship that you and I were created and redeemed! It turns out that the community is a Trinity. The centre of reality is the Father, the Son, and the Holy Spirit.[17]

Otherwise, as Bruce Milne writes, how can we know love?

Thus the entire fabric of Christian redemption and its application to human experience depend wholly on the three-in-oneness of God. The Trinity is as important as that. The Threeness of God is also the basis of the fundamental assertion that God is love. God is not a lonely God who needs creation as an object for his love. As Trinity God is fulfilled in himself and does not need to create or redeem. Creation and redemption are acts of sheer grace, expressions of God as free eternal love.[18]

Karl Barth sums it up clearly: *'In short, this God who made the universe . . . with human beings as the crown of his creation, representing him as image bearers, is relational.'*[19]

The Christian God of Scripture, as revealed by Jesus Christ, is a loving and holy relationship of three distinct persons. This makes so much sense. Since God is love (true love), then God has to be more than one person and even more than two. Let me briefly explain with as much sense as the mystery has revealed of itself. True love cannot and does not exist in one and needs more than two. The love that exists as one is narcissistic, self-centred, and turned inwards on itself (Augustine and Martin Luther). And have you ever observed two people in love? The love between two can be a selfish, all-consuming, enmeshed, and unhealthy love that is exclusive of others. God is love, is three persons in a holy, perfectly loving triune relationship—a loving community, in whose image we are made. It is an outwards-flowing, other-centred, self-giving, self-pouring of oneself into another. And it's a fully opening up and inviting into oneself of another. It's a relational community. And love has its way when it is returned. I have come to believe that this is true for all intimate relationships. It is more than just the two—Christ is the third person in all relationships. That's the way God made it to be. Therefore, the most basic community is three, not two, and this includes Christian marriages. It is at its most intimate when the Christ in me meets the Christ in thou.

The truth that God is love and that God is relational is testimony that from eternity past, throughout creation, up to now, the present, and into eternity future means that life *was, is, and will always be* about relationship—*is relationship*. From eternity past, God always existed as a relationship of holy, perfect love between the Father, the Son, and the Holy Spirit. He is one but He is not alone. God exists as fulfilled love in Himself. He doesn't need us to be love. From God's outpouring, perfectly free, self-giving love He created us for relationship with Him and holy, perfect love must be free to choose the object of that love. Made in God's image and perfectly free, humanity turned its desire for love inwards to themselves or outwards towards someone, or something, other than God. As a consequence, it was relationships that were broken, and human beings were disconnected and separated from God, each other, and from all creation. God sent His only eternally begotten son to restore relationship. Through Jesus, we have relationship available again with God, with each other, and with all of creation. For relationships to reflect the image of God, humanity has been given His Spirit as the power of God to live, love, and relate like Jesus. This is how we give glory to God—by making His presence visible in all our circumstances certainly but particularly within our relationships with one another.

For earthly relationships to reflect the same love that exists in God, the love that longingly sits in the deepest parts of us, we need grace, channelled through faith and freely given to us from the Father. And we need to be in communion with Him. To love beyond ourselves requires a power beyond ourselves, the grace for ongoing repentance of relational sin, and mutual forgiveness and reconciliation whenever possible. From the beginning, it was so: love God and love others as yourself. God loves us first. This is first love, true love—real, perfectly holy, and free love. God invites us to join Him in the outwards pouring of this other-centred, self-giving first love into the world and all in it. Surely, the world needs this, yet it does not know this love—*and this is what God is about!* This is where we come in, brothers and sisters in Christ. The same love with which they love within themselves in the reality of the imminent (within themselves) relationship is the love they pour out and give freely to us and work into all creation as the economic (outworking) relationship with us. But it doesn't stop there—not God's vision anyway. There's more! And this very same love, the way the triune God loves within themselves, the way they fully love us is the same love that God told us through Jesus that we are to love one another. I hope that is going on in your Christian community—after all, it is the only commandment that Jesus gave us (John 15:9–12). We must understand this and live it out because at present, this seems to be the missing ingredient from contemporary Christianity.

His Story, Our Story

Imagine what it must have been like for the early disciples whose friend, companion, and leader, with whom they ate, drank, travelled, and slept alongside (and, I like to think, tossed around a goat's bladder and chased it) became Lord, Christ the Messiah, Son of God and equal with the Most High God. Israel to that point adamantly worshipped the one God of Abraham and Isaac and Jacob—these disciples were now worshipping Jesus as the Christ and Son of God. How did that fit with their theology? For them, for those since, and to us now—each one of us has to personally come to grips with who God is, the story about Himself that He is telling us, and just exactly where we fit in. And do we agree that our lives are but a small narrative (story) that sits within a much larger story? Søren Kierkegaard did. He thought of the Bible as a love story.[20]

Larry Crabb agreed with Kierkegaard and was inspired to write his book *66 Love Letters* as letters from God about His love story. The book makes you wonder about God in a different sort of way. Crabb came to believe that God wrote these letters to us to help us understand seven important questions that God asks us in the midst of our smaller story and from the theology we have made of Him.[21] Larry Crabb has since published his book *A Different Kind of Happiness*, in which he gives a chapter to each one of these questions. But the main point here is that the questions themselves are the important matter for each of us to take and use to seek our own answers as God reveals Himself to us through the questions being asked. For convenience, I will repeat the questions below.

Seven Questions

1. Who is God? Core *theology, faith seeking understanding.*

2. What is He up to? Practical *eschatology*, God's plan for us now and later.
3. Who are we? Basic *anthropology*, our nature as image bearers, male and female.
4. What has gone wrong? Essential *hamartiology*, defining sin.
5. What has God done about it? Surprising *soteriology*, undeserved rescue, grace-based salvation.
6. What is the Spirit doing now? Living *pneumatology*, mysterious movement.
7. How can we join in? Purposeful *ecclesiology*, what the church is called to do.

As we seek to answer these seven questions, we can see the story that God is trying to tell us from either (at least) of two main ways: as citizens of this earth and all its realms (the kingdom of us) as finite beings or, as Dallas Willard describes, as '*unceasing spiritual beings*', sojourners and pilgrims here for a while, passing through, so to speak '*with an eternal destiny to be with God*'. And we will arrive in God's good timing at our true home, in God's kingdom, and live there forevermore, where our hearts have always desired to be (Ecclesiastes 3:11).

The Way Is Open

God is inviting us to acknowledge that the deep longings of our hearts, put there by Himself, will be completely fulfilled only when we are home with Him. This has all been made possible through Jesus, and the way is now open. It's where we are meant to be, and this is where the promises of the blessings will be fully realised. Until then, God's desire is that we come to *desire* Him first, *know* Him intimately, *love* Him passionately, and *enjoy* him fully while He undertakes the process of changing us into the image of His Son. Until then, our part is to put Him on display in the way we live, love, and relate. This is why we need to keep searching and groping for Him while in this foreign land—so that we can know God more perfectly, love Him more intimately, and trust Him more sincerely, to the extent that we would surrender ourselves totally into His hands.

God is a loving and holy relationship, and we are made in His image and likeness. That makes us image bearers. In my way of understanding our Western church (us), our theology, and our liturgy, the way in which we represent God has not reflected God's image very well since the seeking to better understand the three-foldness of God went MIA. We seem to have made the spiritual journey of knowing God into an intellectual knowledge about who He is rather than it being more about our coming to recognise more and more who He is through His ever opening-up revelation of Himself to us through relationship. If we are to know this holy and perfectly loving God, we have to be displaying His image in the way we live, love, and relate. This will be evident in how we give glory to God, worship Him, and love Him through an obedient faith—and this in turn will occur when we begin to love each other as the three holy persons of the triune God relate within themselves.

We have the ability to respond to God's self-revelation by reflecting God's glory here on earth. Letham implored that our *prayer and worship are an exploration of the character of the Holy Trinity. It is urgent to ensure that our theology is in line with this most basic Christian experience.*[22] As we conclude this chapter about our primary and first-order mark I will refer to what Larry Crabb says in his book *Finding God*, '*God wants to be found. He delights to be known. He rejoices when we are close to Him. But our search for Him must be on His terms.*'[23] So, plumb-bob yourself over this mark now and ask yourself these questions. How do I know God at this time and place in my life? Is this knowing of God compatible with my searching for Him with the eyes of faith, and is it in accordance with His revelation of Himself through His Word? Is it a knowing as I reach out to Him through the heart of Jesus? Is it a knowing that is completely integrated with His Spirit's quickening inside of me? And does this knowing have the confidence and trust built upon it because of my ongoing relationship with the three-fold persons of God?

How are you going so far? Let's look next at three of His most important terms in the way we respond to Him as we continue on our everyday journey of knowing Him —our love for God, our worship of Him, and giving Him glory. These are the qualities that define our holy, righteous and obedient participation with His desire and plan to bring us to perfection. This is quality assurance for our need to be assured of who God is and set up confidence in the next two marks.

Notes on Chapter Five

1. David Benner, *The Gift of Being* Yourself (2004), 19–22.
2. Ibid., 9.
3. John Owen, *Communion with God* (2007), 50–74.
4. Cited in Iain Matthews, *The Impact of God* (1995), 56.
5. A. W. Tozer, *The Knowledge of the Holy* (1961), 9.
6. Cited in Curtis and Eldredge, *The Sacred Romance* (1997), 82.
7. Gregory Boyd, *Is God to Blame?* (2003), 15.
8. Timothy Jennings, *The God-Shaped Brain* (2013), 20.
9. Floyd McClung, *Follow* (2010), 31.
10. C. S. Lewis, *Mere Christianity* Book II, chapter 1.
11. Bruce Milne, *Know the Truth* (1982, 1998), 245.
12. Matthews, *The Impact of God* (2010), 109, 110.
13. McClung, *Follow* (2010), 29.
14. Milne, *Know the Truth* (1982, 1998), 122–124.
15. Packer, *Knowing God* (1973), 37–41.
16. Ibid., page 24.
17. Darrell Johnson, *Experiencing the Trinity* (2002), 37.
18. Milne, *Knowing the Truth* (1982, 1998), 79.
19. Cited in Letham, *The Holy Trinity* (2004), 21.
20. Larry Crabb, *Real Church* (2009), 99.
21. Ibid., 100.
22. Robert Letham, *The Holy Trinity*, 2004, 415.
23. Crabb, *Finding God*, 1993, 107.

CHAPTER SIX

Quality Assurance

Though He is not far from each one of us. (Acts 17:27b)

I have been seized by the power of a great affection. (Brennan Manning, *The Ragamuffin Gospel* 2005:195)

You become like what you worship. (N. T. Wright, *Simply Christian*)

The glory of God is living man. (Irenaeus, second century)

AT 17 1/2 years of age, I had no sense of calling to join the Navy—I was barely surviving at that point in my life. Signing up to serve on Her Majesty's Australian Ships was a reaction to escape the confusion and lostness of not knowing who I was—or was to be—and to seek relief from the contempt raging in me against anyone who didn't consider my needs first. The world wasn't a good or safe place, people weren't to be trusted, and I had to take care of myself. I needed to escape my life and get out from under the authority of my disappointed and frustrated father who had high expectations of me because up until now, I had done well at school, achieved high grades, was a good all-round sportsman, and excelled at golf. But my people-pleasing days were over. They were replaced with a highly competitive drive to succeed at all costs, a determined wilfulness, and focused self-protection strategies. Yes, I would do whatever was necessary, not just to survive, but to thrive in this world—and to get what I wanted.

It happened this way. In January 1972, Dad took me along with his construction crew to Townsville after cyclone Althea had devastated the area. Late one evening after being up on the roof of the Shamrock Hotel, repairing the damage inflicted by Althea, Dad and I had what was to be our final shouting match. I lay in my bed and filled out a coupon at the back of a popular Australian magazine, headed 'Join the Navy and become a Naval Officer'. Three weeks later, after having been interviewed at two selection boards and sat before a panel of rather impressive-looking gentlemen, I found myself saying goodbye to my grief-shocked mother and on my way to Melbourne, Victoria—excited to be miles from home and on a plane, because I had never flown before or travelled south of the Queensland border. Two years later, having enjoyed the camaraderie and competition of initial boot camp and the sorting-out period, I discovered that I had no heart for playing make-believe naval war games—and I wanted out. My captain at the time was the father of one of my course mates, and he took a personal interest in my well-being. He asked me how I felt about joining the Hydrographic Service. He said that he thought I would like the life and would do well there. I had never heard of the Hydrographic Service. Anyway, I said yes, and within weeks I was posted to a survey ship - and I loved it!

The Navy Hydrographic Service (RANHS) commanded much, expected much, and they trained me well. As long as you gave the Navy your all, it looked after you well. For me, the RANHS provided security, safety, satisfaction, a sense of identity, and a source of community—I believe this saved my life. For 28 years together, we were well matched. The RANHS provided a way of life in which I thrived. It poured a lot of time, effort, and resources into training, equipping, and motivating me to perform at an elite professional level, and it took all that I had to give. I valued all of this highly, and I gave it my all, pouring my heart and soul into performing and achieving well—and I reaped the rewards of prime postings, high achievements, and lots of affirmation and attention. I was fairly popular and well liked, or at least my persona (false self) was—that was the person I presented to the world. I had made it! It was a good life, as far as worldly standards were concerned, and things went to plan—until it all came crashing down.

Henry Wadsworth Longfellow's words ring true for me: '*When lost, alone and in pain, listen in the deep, God is not dead, and neither does He sleep*' (seventh stanza). He is never far from each one of us—and always within arm's reach. When I cried out in my pain and reached out my hand, God came down to me again that day and grasped my hand—just as Psalm 40:2 says: '*He lifted me out of the slimy pit, out of the mud and mire; He set my feet on a rock, and gave me a firm place to stand.*'

This chapter is somewhat about what I have just described, three things mainly: saying yes to what we most desire, giving our everything to what we highly consider to be of most worth, and pouring out all we have within us so as to enjoy the glory of a good life now, and in the future forever. Really, our Christian life journey asks us three questions around this matter. Who do we love most? What, or who, do we worship? And who gets the glory? How we answer these questions will determine the quality of our response to God.

God's Love for Us

There is no doubt in my mind that our moment of conversion is a life-changing event. Receiving Jesus into my heart has been the best decision I have made in life. It's a personal thing, but for some reason the phrases 'born again' or 'been saved' never touched me passionately. I have no particular thing against these sayings, and I certainly value their meaning—they just didn't seem to have a deep sense of relevance for me. When I read Brennan Manning's book *The Ragamuffin Gospel*, the sentence 'I have been seized by the power of a great affection,' went deeply into my soul and seemed to meet me exactly where I was at—in my emptiness and deep longing for something which I didn't yet know. Brennan Manning wrote that he came across this saying when he was doing research down in New Orleans, and said that around that area, the Christians had been using this saying rather than being 'born again' for over a hundred years—it means the same thing, of course. For me, it was the very thing that I had called out to God in prayer not so long ago, when I realised that my search for affection to fill my heart had been the source of such pain and tragedy for so long in my life, and I needed God to replace this longing with His affection for me—and mine for Him.

At the age of 36, I had lost everything that I had valued more than God—my vision for marriage, my wife, my family, my identity, my career, promotion chances, and even friendships. And somehow, what I most valued changed within me, and my life was reshaped and given back in a new way when I said yes to God and received a new heart—His heart. He doesn't leave us standing alone on some isolated rock. In Psalm 40:2, the rock is Christ Jesus. On this foundation, we become a new creation which He reshapes and then He gives us everything that is needed to live a new way—a new purity, a new identity, a new heart, and a new power, that Dwight Edwards so wonderfully describes.[1] And God also provides a new community into which we are to find a place where we can grow. And sometime later, we find ourselves standing at a fork in the road. Do we go along the road signposted 'You can do it', where we remain in control and believe God is saying 'Do this . . . Don't do that . . .', or do we really take the road less travelled that says, 'You cannot—but in Christ you can, with My grace.' And then God says, 'I will give you . . .' (Ezekiel 11:19–20; Ezekiel 36:24–27; Jeremiah 31:33–34; Hebrews 8:10–12) everything you need, says Peter (2 Peter 1:3). And He simply, lovingly, asks us to receive. And this is exactly what He does—God gives and pours out Himself. Do we receive?

If you have experienced something similar, then you will know what this turning around of life is like. If you haven't already (maybe you won't), God touches us differently and relates personally and uniquely with each of us. But, if you would like to, you could try praying this prayer of Nicholas of Flue:

> My Lord and my God, take everything from me that keeps me from You.

> My Lord and my God, give me everything that brings me closer to You.

> My Lord and my God, detach me of myself so I may give my everything to You.

If you want to pray Nicholas's prayer but are a little apprehensive about what God might do, might take from you, be reassured by what Teresa of Avila tells you;

> Let nothing trouble you, let nothing frighten you, everything passes: God never changes. Patience obtains all things. Whoever has God wants for nothing; God alone is enough.

What do you think? The greatest respect that I could offer anyone reading this section is to allow you to take responsibility for finding out for yourself the love God has for you and to choose for yourself how you will respond. As I briefly set the scene for this chapter, I will mention God's love for us, but again, great books have been written on this, and it is far more exciting when you search the answer for yourself. As a way of being encouraging, maybe it will be helpful to understand some more about God within the context of this book. There is a desire in me and, I believe, also in you that longs to experience real love unconditionally, and no matter how great our human experiences are or have been of receiving this true love, the experience never seems to reach the quality or the quantity we desire and never seems to last— and the desire remains. What can fill it?

Letham writes, 'The one being of God is never to be considered by itself, for God is the Father, the Son, and the Spirit in relationship.'[2] That is the crux of what I want to say, but this is so crucial that it needs to be emphasised and reinforced because as Richard Rohr so eloquently put it, the Trinity seems to have been missing in action for seventeen centuries. Let me offer you this quote: 'Could it help explain the simple ineffectiveness and lack of transformation we witness in so much of the Christian world? When you are off at the centre, the whole edifice is quite shaky and unsure of itself.'[3] If you, like me, want to be integrated at the centre, firm and certain on where we stand, then let's plumb over the mark. I invite you to stay with me now as we look at just what is the only thing that is able to love us as we long to be loved, give us all that we desire to be given, and pour into us every good thing necessary to meet all our needs.

The starting point from which to know God must be God Himself because we cannot know God from our human sense. Human beings look for God where He reveals Himself, and we seek Him through the eyes of faith. God is Spirit. He is supernatural—God is above the natural (creation). God is everlasting from eternity past to eternity future and has placed eternity in our hearts (Ecclesiastes 11:3). This is the eternal life Jesus offers to us—not only are we saved from death to live forever, but eternal life is offered to us now through an ongoing relationship that is full to the brim of life. This is why Jesus defined eternal life as knowing the only true God and Jesus Himself (John 17:3). The only true God, the God described as being love (1 John 4:8), whom Jesus explains, and as quoted by Letham above, is the relationship going on between his Father, Himself, and the Spirit (John 16:12–15). Love is what exists because of this eternal relationship.

The early theologians came up with the Greek word *perichoresis* to describe this holy, perfectly loving relationship of the three persons of God as they mutually indwell as one being, as love – literally, from the root words, it means 'like a *circle dance*'. This is a dynamic and living relationship in which the three Persons mutually indwell and inter-penetrate one another in 'ceaseless movement' stirring up love. There is no 'they' in the relationship, only 'us'. Each person is fully open to the other(s) and directed towards them in love, and holds onto nothing of themselves but is given fully to the other who fully opens up and invites to receive.[4] This onto-relational (relationship of persons as beings within community), spiritual, and intensely personal way of relating is what Jesus is saying to us (John 15:9–12) and prayed for us (John 17:21). It is also the reason why human beings long for connectedness, relationships and love—because we are made in the image of a holy, perfectly loving community. I urge you to read that last sentence again and again.

This continuous, never-ending, everlasting relationship is one that gives, pours out, and invites to receive. The outflowing givingness of love is pro-creation. It is for life, and it gives life—no wonder we are seized by the power of this great affection. This is what we long for in the depths of our souls. Our Christian life is an ongoing love relationship with our Christian God, seeking to know Him fully and allowing Him to know us fully according to His will for us (1 Cor. 8:3). Christian life is not about getting life right and certainly not about having to be right. It is all about allowing ourselves to be loved the way in which we most deeply desire—opening up to receive it and responding in the only way possible when we fully realise who our God truly is. Allow me to paraphrase what John of the Cross described God as saying to him, 'I AM yours, and I AM for you, and I AM pleased to be as I AM that I may be yours and give Myself to you.'⁵ This is why Jesus came—to make it possible for this to happen.

So it is understandable that being made dependents of this *love*, human beings would have in us a DNA that longed to be a part of our origin. Our desire will be for God, whether we realise this or not, and whether or not we spend all of our lives trying to fill this desire with someone or some other thing—but it will never be satisfied until we are finally with God, which is exactly what Augustine was saying back in the fourth century: *'Our heart is unquiet until it rests in You.'* This is our story, and every story has an author—God is our author. The history of human beings can only be found within His story. Without having a part in the larger story that God is telling us about Himself, what He is up to, and where our place is in it, where would we be? Is there an alternate story? For hundreds of years, human beings have been trying to renounce God's authorship and plagiarise it to write their own story—or at the very least, make out their stories to be larger one. But despite all historical evidence of humankind's hopeless vanity and self-deprecating pride, the best narrated story humankind can author without God begins from nothingness with a random eruption, a chance occurrence then fills it with futility and meaninglessness until it offers a future without hope, finishing with a return to nothingness. Do we really believe this? I know we don't desire it. Perhaps someone can write another one—perhaps you can author your own.

Our Love for God

We human beings are made by God and are created in His image—like God but not God—and are made to be dependent on God. We are dependent on God for our very lives—we breathe in for the first time, and we are alive. As natural beings, we breathe out for the last time, and our body dies. We were created by love, with love, for love, to love—this is life, and when we live this, we have life. What then is our response to God's initiative—His givingness, His outpouring of Himself, and His invitation to receive from us? Those who believe God and turn to Him to receive His love have their need for love fulfilled. Those who do not believe in God—and all of us when we turn from Him to seek love elsewhere—are never satisfied, and our need for love is not met. Unmet needs become demands, and a human being will do whatever it takes to have their needs fulfilled—that is the natural self-determined vow we make to look after ourselves and have our needs met. And when God doesn't come through for us as we believe we are entitled, we might even shake our fist at Him to let Him know of our severe displeasure. Those who don't usually take it out on themselves and others.

What do you think is in us that desires to give of ourselves to another person? I mean fully giving everything of ourselves, holding nothing back. Emptying ourselves sounds so unhealthy in the assertiveness of human rights in our present day, if not totally scary, yet that's what love does—it gives. This is why 'Love the Lord your God with *all* you heart, with *all* your soul, with *all* of your strength and *all* your mind' means giving all of ourselves to God. It is our response to Him loving us and us recognising what this means. Curt Thompson informs us that our relationship with God will directly reflect the depth of our relationships here on earth—even our most significant ones.[6] Could it be this basic? When we love someone, it is a giving love—not loving so as to receive. The reason why relationships are in so much of a shambles is that we have love around the wrong way. First, we turn love inward—we love ourselves first—and then we look to receive it from others. When we are loved this way, we feel good, so now the other becomes responsible for making me feel good—for the rest of their life at least. And when I don't feel good, then you are not loving me enough, so I don't love you anymore. Dallas Willard defined love as willing the good of another, not willing the good of self through another—not making someone else responsible to make me feel good, and not loving someone else so I will feel good. So what has changed in human nature since back then in the Garden, when Adam and Eve chose this selfish way of love—when they decided to seek their own good first? Nothing!

God came down—this is where Christianity differs from all other religions. God came down to reset, remake, restore, and restart His vision for us which went askew in the garden when selfishness set in. Jesus came to give everyone an opportunity to eliminate the selfishness that is destroying God's creation and allow everyone to take up His invitation to relationship as it was, and was always meant to be. That's why love is other—it overcomes selfishness. If we know this to be true and we know that God's vision is for His creation to reflect His goodness so that we will desire Him as our first desire because we know that this is our greatest good, what is our response? Is it total and utter gratefulness? Will you receive His love? If your answer is yes, then you really ought to understand how large and deep and wide and high His love is, because your yes to Him will realise His promise to do whatever it takes to bring you to Himself—where Jesus is, where your complete goodness is to be found. And you must allow God to love you to the point where He will capture your complete devotion.[7] When you, too, are seized by the power of this great affection you will want to worship Him forever. But if you do choose to worship God as your greatest treasure know that you are also choosing to pick a fight. Nothing hinders us from receiving the love of God as much as the lies that build up in our minds about who God is and who we are and how we are in relationship together,[8] and this is a battle. It is a battle for our hearts, minds, and souls as the deceiver continues to persist, even in defeat, to take as many souls with him as he can by being the instigator of lies.

Our Worship of God

To worship God alone, to acknowledge His love for us, to gaze on His splendour and majesty and proclaim His holiness (you may recognise the worship song those inspired words come from)[9] very much affirms that Christians set apart God from everything else so as to hold Him up to be of most worth in their lives. I have been reflecting on the theme of worship for some months now—reading what various authors write, Googling it, and discussing it during conversations about God that really matter. A friend asked me to share a message at his church on the subject and so I gathered my thoughts together and spent much time seeking what God might reveal during prayer. By the time I had done all of this, I felt I had a pretty good handle on what our worship of God is, so writing this section seems timely.

Yesterday, I took an early morning drive to Cape Byron—the most easterly point of the Australian mainland—with my friend Don. I wanted to reconnoitre the trig station which was somewhere near the lighthouse because I thought it might make a good cover shot for this book, and if I could get to the place before sunrise, that might make for a special backdrop. The evening before, I had resurrected the ol' digital camera—no longer in use because of my mobile phone camera capability—and then set off at 5:40 a.m. the next day to pick up Don and catch the sunrise. The carpark at the top of the cape was still locked when we arrived with seven minutes to spare prior to the predicted time of sunrise. People were everywhere (tourists mainly), and there was no place to park. So Don offered to drive the car away as I made my way up the hill, hurrying to walk the 300 metres to the lighthouse and locate the trig point before the sun rose. Regulating my breathing and pulling my wind jacket around me to protect me from the bitterly cold early morning air, I saw the trig point in very close proximity to the lighthouse. So I made my way through the gathering crowd who were congregating around the lookout on Australia's most eastern point to see the sunrise over the Pacific Ocean on a beautiful Monday morning in July. I managed several shots with the digital camera, with only a father and son spoiling an otherwise great shot. Then they moved, and I was able to get a couple more shots before the sun rose too high—great. I then took one shot with the smartphone just to send a picture to Susan and then walked down the hill to rendezvous with Don. As we drove off to find a cafe and enjoy breakfast together, I reviewed the shots I had taken, but there weren't any, because the memory of my digital camera was full—no, not one.

Arriving home later that morning, I told Susan about my misadventure and disappointment and then spent some time in the reading for the day—which was on Psalm 131 and about being calm and quiet in the midst of disappointment, discomfort, or pain. 'What might You be saying to me?' I asked God. I believe He asked me to reflect on the morning's activity. Well, it was dark leaving home; there was Don waiting by the side of the road, eager to escape the cold wind, and gratefully, he accepted the hot flat white coffee I had prepared. The forty-five-minute drive to Cape Byron seemed to pass quickly as we engaged in conversation, but already my mind was on the task ahead. Will we arrive in time? How will I find the trig point? Will I get a good shot? And then we were thwarted in getting a park. People everywhere—why couldn't they just move aside out of the way, just a little? *I need this to be a good photo. I wish I could get a better angle, and I'm a bit too close.* Could I stand outside of the safety rail? And after all that effort and concern, I had no photos to show for it. What was that about, God? And I think I heard God respond gently, 'John, did you at any time give glory to Me? Did you thank Me for the time you and Don had sharing together and the safe and timely arrival at this most beautiful place? What did you think of the glorious sunrise I provided today? This is the day that I have made! Was I in your picture?' It's that moment when, like Job, you just need to put your hand over your mouth and humble yourself—know who you are in God's presence. I hadn't invited God into the picture this wonderful morning—and the picture was really His, and for Him, I had thought. I could have enjoyed a sacred time (God and me; God, Don, and me; us all together), and what a privilege it would be to remember that time whenever I looked at the front cover of our book. The next section I was up to in the book is about worship. I'm sorry, Lord—I was off the mark yesterday. Forgive me for not thanking You for inviting me into Your picture or taking that opportunity to show You how much You mean to me. Can we do it together next time?

There is a good example of how not to worship. That morning, I didn't even acknowledge God—not even for a moment, let alone give him my everything. Floyd McClung writes, 'Our choices and attitudes in every aspect of life can be a form of worship to God, or we can divorce God from our everyday lives and limit our understanding of worship to singing a few songs on the "holy day".'[10] Our worship of God is making evident that He is our first love—we love Him more than anyone or anything else and hold Him up as what we value as being of most worth in our lives. Jesus was putting this message across in His interaction with His disciples when He told the parable of the treasure in the field (Matthew 13:44–46). Jesus' emphasis on true worship was the cause of sadness that the rich young man felt when Jesus opened his insight to the fact that he cherished his wealth (or other things) more importantly than following Jesus. This story appears in all three synoptic Gospels (Matt. 19:16–22, Mark 10:17–23, Luke 18:18–25), so it must be very significant. Even though the young man was pious, religious, and he gave God all the worship that was required by Jewish religious law, it neither made him good nor gave him direct entry into the kingdom of God. And when Jesus engaged the Samaritan woman in John 4:19–26, He took her direct question in verse 20 about whether Samaritan worship or Jewish worship was correct and turned it into an opportunity to tell the woman about the Gospel and what true worship really is.

Let's think together briefly on OT meanings of worship and what Jesus was saying to the Samaritan woman. Jesus tells the woman that an important thing is about to happen (verse 23), *'But an hour is coming, and now is when the true worshipers will worship the Father in spirit and truth.'* Jesus, by His coming, was reshaping worship just as He reshaped love, by pointing out the change from the old covenant to the new. Under the old covenant way of worship (where: the Temple; how: by rituals and practices, and at certain times), all were important. But in the new covenant, the new way of worship, Jesus is the new temple (John 2:19–21), and by worshipping Him with our all, we too are being built into a holy temple in the Lord (Ephesians 2:21; 1 Peter 2:5). Thus, *where* we gather to worship is secondary. How and whom we worship is primary. Interestingly, prayer—our sacred time with God—as contemplation literally means that we come *with a temple.*

People can mistakenly think that if they go through the proper externals of worship, maybe even feeling the rapture of a beautiful worship song, then things are OK between them and God. As long as they attend a church service, sing heartfully, and commit to church programmes, they figure that everything is fine. These are all good things, but if they haven't dealt with God on the heart level and if they haven't repented of their sins in thought, word, and deed, are they in right relationship with God? We can't properly worship God on Sundays if we're not worshiping Him throughout the week. So Jesus tells the Samaritan woman that it's not the externals that matter as much as the internals. What's going on in the heart? We must make it our priority to become true worshipers of God in spirit and truth. As Jonathan Edwards argued, God created the world for His own glory.[11] That God, Who is love, wants to be reflected in His creation, for the good of *all* creation, and that includes us, the jewel in the crown. So God is seeking worshipers who will bring Him glory, not just for an hour on Sunday, but every day through all their activities (1 Cor. 10:31). Why do you think this is so? I think it is because the world, and all of us in it, drastically and essentially need God's goodness displayed, and that's the role God gives to His people—that's us. God desires true worshippers, and it's a priority. What do you think?

In verse 24, Jesus says that these true worshipers *'must worship in spirit and truth'* (italics mine). It's a necessity. It isn't optional; it's essential. If you worship God, you are indicating that you hold Him up to be 'first thing' desire—He is of most worth to you in your entire life. Therefore, we must live this out or it means nothing, says Francis Schaeffer. Timothy Jennings, in his book *Could It Be This Simple*, cautions us about what we worship and cites

2 Corinthians 3:18 as telling us that by worshipping God, we become like Him.[12] We become what we worship. Gregory Beale made that last sentence the title for his book, saying, 'What you revere you resemble, either for ruin or for restoration.'[13] N. T. Wright tells us, 'You become like what you worship. When you gaze in awe, admiration, and wonder at something or someone, you begin to take on something of the character of the object of your worship.'[14] Anyway, like I pointed out some time ago, it has all been said before. Nearly 450 years ago, Richard Sibbes is cited as saying that we become like what we worship and was adamant that our view of God shapes us most deeply.[15] Jesus never stopped loving the young man in the story He told. I also think Jesus felt kindness towards the genuineness of desire He saw in this person to do the right thing. How Jesus must have so longed for this young man to follow Him and to place the desire to live God's standards for life ahead of his self-needs. What and/or who do *you* worship?

God seeks true worshippers who will worship Him in spirit and truth. Jesus repeats this twice so that we don't miss it (John 4:23–24): '*But an hour is coming, and now is, when the true worshipers will worship the Father in spirit and truth; for such people the Father seeks to be His worshipers. God is spirit, and those who worship Him must worship in spirit and truth.*' In Spirit—to worship in spirit is to worship from our innermost being. It does not mean ritual and religious ceremonial activities by those whose hearts are not right with God (Matthew 15:8). Thus, the most important factor in becoming a worshiper is to guard and cultivate your heart for God. I am not saying that song and external expression is not part of worship—worship in spirit is, in part, emotional or felt—but it must spring from our spiritual centre. Worshipping in truth, as God revealed Himself to us in His Word of truth and supremely in His Son, who is the truth (John 1:18; 14:6; 17:17), means that we offer worship to God as Jesus did—as His Word says. Worship is your response to the truth that God has revealed in His Word about Himself and us, what He has done, and how we are related, because this is what you believe and hold to be of most worth. Prayer is relationship and helps you remain in communion with God. Without spending consistent time alone with the Lord, your soul will shrivel up—and you won't worship in spirit and truth.

As we've seen, personal worship is not restricted to a few moments on Sunday mornings or before we take part in some Christian event. In the context of 1 Corinthians 10:31, our worship of God is in everything we do. The point is, you can't live a self-centred, worldly life all week long and then come to church on Sunday and worship. Why do you come to church? If your focus is to get something out of the church service, then I suggest you check your life's instrument controls, because I think you might be flying upside down. Your focus should be to give praise and honour and thanks with all the saints to the God who gave His Son for you. The real audience is God, and the entire presentation is offered to Him, for His pleasure and glory. So the issue when you come to church is not 'Did I get anything out of it?' but 'Did I give God the heartfelt praise and thanks and glory that He deserves?'

John Piper wrote, '*Missions is not the ultimate goal of the church. Worship is. Missions exists because worship doesn't. Worship is ultimate, not missions, because God is ultimate, not man.*'[16] According to John MacArthur, '*Worship is our innermost being responding with praise for all that God is, through our attitudes, actions, thoughts, and words, based on the truth of God as He has revealed Himself.*'[17] And later, he made his thoughts simpler by writing, '*Worship is all that we are, reacting rightly to all that He is.*'[18] I think Steve Cole, senior pastor Flagstaff Christian Fellowship, quoted as saying, '*Worship is an inner attitude and feeling of awe, reverence, gratitude, and love toward God resulting from a realization of who He is and who we are,*'[19] sums it up for us—what do you think? We don't worship God to gain eternal life; we worship God because He has loved us first and has given us eternal life with our yes response to His love. Worship is our 'everything' response to God's 'everything' to us. The world is constantly competing for our worship. We cannot love, worship, and give glory to God unless He has our all—we all belong to God, and He is worthy of our all (1 Corinthians 6:18–20).

Three Relational Communities

The military, or the Australian Defence Force (ADF) as we know it in Australia, consists of three large communities—Navy, Army, and Air Force. Each of these three arms of the ADF holds different codes and philosophies of how they view their role within Australia's strategic defence strategies. The Royal Australian Navy, of which I was a member for more than thirty years, is also made up of numerous communities, which are normally referred to as branches of the Navy. Some of these include the Seaman Branch (including subspecialisations), the Submarine Branch, the Mine Warfare and Countermeasures Branch, the Supply Branch, the Engineering and Electrical Branch, Musicians, Naval Air, Naval Police, and, last but not least, the Hydrographic Branch—in which I specialised and served for twenty-eight years—which sits within the Seaman Branch. All of these branches play out their roles in different ways but are still part of a core purpose. In a similar way, Christians can be seen as being one body like the Defence Force, with large communities of different denominations within which there exist smaller branches. Different churches form under worldwide, national, state, and local bodies—the smallest community of which is usually a home group at the local church level. It is this local church level that I will be addressing as the third community. But first, let's briefly relook at the other two communities that have already been discussed.

The first, foremost, and core community is God—the Father, Son, and Spirit in relationship. This community has been described under the heading 'God's Love for Us' in this chapter. It has also been described in the previous chapter and is a major part of this entire book. The first and core community is *who* we are getting to know as our most intimate friend. We have looked at how the Three Holy Persons indwell and relate within that triune community—fully giving of themselves to the other, fully pouring out all they are towards the other, and the other totally opening to receive. Since this 'circle dance' is continuously ongoing and everlasting, it gives and pours out into the second community and invites back. The second community is human beings existing within creation, including the wider universe(s) and all living things. God gives Himself fully to us and pours out His very life into us. God invites us to receive Him fully and give of ourselves in the same way back to Himself as our first love offering. Our love for God is our 'yes' to His initiating action and invitation. Our worship is our giving of our 'everything' to Him first because we hold Him to be of most worth. When this is happening, we are in communion with God. We now come to our third community and a third way of relating in our local communities—our local church, home group, and/or relationships with one another, wherever there are two or more of us who have come together in His name.

The Third Way of Relating

If we read Philippians 2: 1–8, we might be encouraged to relate as Jesus did with the same love as He, and we might agree that immediate felt self-interest is not to be our dominant and controlling interest when we relate—if we are to relate as Jesus did. I invite you now to look at the mindset of Jesus as you reflect on His prayer to our Father in John 17: 1–26. As Christians, being real to what God has put in you at conversion, would be to have the same mindset, the same attitude as Jesus—an attitude towards relating that was the same as the three persons of the triune God relate with one another. This is the same attitude that Jesus related towards His people and as He commanded us to relate with one another, always a pouring out of self towards another, outward focused and other orientated.

Jesus glorified the Father in all He did. When He did this, He was revealing the Father's heart towards people. Jesus revealed divine love. To love as Jesus did is to love in the truth of who God is—and is to live, love, and relate as Jesus did. Jesus's nature as God—as love—is within a loving community. Jesus wants us to realise the joy, which we desire, is actually available to us. *To enjoy* God is what we most desire to enjoy: the joy of loving with a better love. Jesus wants us to realise the joy, that what we desire, is actually available to us. Jesus tells us that the cost of this relating is great; and in this life, we will not experience this joy as much as we would wish and hope to because we are left here in this world, groaning and longing for what is to come. We are partakers of Christ's mission, resisting 'self-centred' relating and settling for nothing less than being witnesses to Jesus's way. As Jesus did willingly sacrificing 'self'. Jesus glorified the Father as the only glory that was worthy of praise, and this cannot and will not be shared. ('My glory I will give to no other.') No one is to love well in order to be noticed. God gives us nothing for our own glory or works other than what gives God the glory. We are to receive from the Father through Jesus by the Spirit all that is required and worship God by putting Him on display by the way we live, love, and relate. Jesus came so that we would have the truth so that we would know God as love—to know Him and to make Him known by being like Him. This is the third way of love, brothers and sisters in Christ. It is not your way or my way—it is the way of Jesus.

Giving Glory to God: The Third Community

While reflecting over some thoughts I'd written in my diary, I noted on one day I had written, *'I have the ability to respond through the power and glory of God given to me to put Him on display by the way I live, love and relate—not naturally but supernaturally—and I don't do it! Saying, "I am only human," just doesn't cut it for me anymore. My sin is not about my failure to be like Jesus but rather that I excuse my failures as being merely human and deny my relational guilt, and so fail to repent.'*

Christian couples often come to counselling seeking a better marriage. This is a good intention, you might agree. As good as that intention is, I am really curious to find out how they are loving each other. You may have noticed some debate over marriage in recent years. What really interests, and concerns me, is what marriage means to Christians in this time of political correctness. I am interested to know how the way we love and relate to each other as a Christian community is seen as so special that it would set marriage apart from secular relationships. So my question is, *how are we loving each other and living out our relationships so that it puts God's glory on display?*

It is man's—as in both man and woman, mankind's—responsibility to glorify God. This is in the Westminister Charter, which is good, and more importantly in God's Word to us. 1 Chronicles 16: 29 tells us, *'Ascribe to the LORD the glory due his name; bring an offering and come before him. Worship the LORD in the splendor of his holiness.'* Psalm 29: 2 says, *'Give unto the LORD the glory due unto his name; worship the LORD in the beauty of holiness.'* And Romans 11: 36 says, *'For from Him and through Him and for Him are all things. To Him be the glory forever!'* Amen we say. How do we give glory to God? I think the answer is to be found in how we put our hearts into action (1 Corinthians 6: 20) and in whatever we do (1 Corinthians 10: 31). In all things, as we are appealed to in 1 Peter 4: 11.

If I attempted to describe God's glory, it would probably be the revelation of Himself in His holiness and in His divine nature as 'love', as was revealed to Moses and also in the Gospels. It was fully revealed to us in Christ. Three times, the Father spoke to the Son with love (Matthew 3: 16–17; 17: 4–6; John 12: 27–29). On all these occasions, Jesus glorified the Father as love through the way He loved His Father and us—through His life, His attitude to His Father, and what He did in His Father's name. But for me, nothing is more powerful than the description of God's glory in Jesus: *'For God, who said, "Let light shine out of darkness, made his light shine in our hearts to give us the light of the knowledge of God's glory displayed in **the face of Christ**"'* (2 Cor. 4: 6). Consider what would be revealed to you if you gazed into the face of Christ? How do you see Jesus's face? Why did God give His glory onto Jesus? God's glory was given to the Son to reveal it to us. Jesus revealed His Father's glory (in truth) in the way He lived, spoke, and related here in His life on earth. That is, Jesus, through His obedience to God His Father, put God's glory on display by the way He lived, loved, and related (John 7: 18). Always showing us what and who love is. Always for His Father's glory, not His own. *'And I will do whatever you ask in my name, so that the Father may be glorified in the Son'* (John 14: 13). And for me, the greatest work of faith has always been to change a heart so that it would love God more than anyone and anything else. That we would worship Him first and then obey (yield, surrender, trust, and submit) to Him by loving others and thereby be His visible presence on earth and reflect His image. This would truly reflect His love for us.

The Father giving glory to the Son and the Son giving glory to the Father—this gives us some understanding of *who* they are as they give, always to the 'other'. But wait, there's more! It doesn't end with the Father and the Son! Jesus in prayer with His Father reveals that we now have been given this glory (John 17: 22–23). The Message Bible reads, *'The same glory you gave me, I gave to them. So they'll be unified and together as we are—I in them and you in me. Then they'll be mature in this oneness, And give the godless world evidence that you've sent me and loved them in the same way you've loved me.'* Jesus was given the ability to put God's glory on display; and He did that through the way he lived, loved, and related. He has given that glory to us! Irenaeus (AD 130–202) is accredited as saying *'The glory of God is living man'* and *'The life of a man is the vision of God'*. This is indeed man fully alive! Jesus came so that we could have life and have it abundantly (John 10: 10). The act of bridging the immense gulf between God and the physical cosmos, drawing human beings into a life like His, was no haphazard afterthought; it had been the plan and intention of divine love from the outset. Us, we are to be His image bearers! We are to represent Jesus to the world. That is our purpose for our time and place. And the fruit of our lives as disciples—faith, hope, and love in the world—gives glory to God. *'This is to my Father's glory, that you bear much fruit, showing yourselves to be my disciples'* (John 15: 8), being like Christ, Christlike in how we live, love, and relate.

We have been given God's glory and the power to live it. It is possible you know, and it can be done practically. It is very relevant for today, and it is also very necessary. We must not ignore God's gift to us! How different from the world's way of being—from our culture and self-focused society—never seeking our own glory but putting God's glory on display in the way we live out our lives, loving and relating to others. The writings of John the disciple of Jesus, the beloved disciple and one of the recognised apostles, in the fourth Gospel and his three letters refer to the Christian community. This is the third community, and the way of love has always been that of a third way—not your way and not my way, even if one or both of us are close. No, the third way is always the way of Jesus, and that is the way He commanded us to love. Just as they love one another within the Holy Community of three persons, as God loves us, so we are to love one another. When we do this, we give glory to God, and we are truly worshipping in spirit and in truth, and our love for God is evident (John 15: 8–17).

As we come to the end of this chapter, I am feeling like I've done a worthwhile, hard day's effort on the survey grounds. The writing of it took a lot of effort. How was it for you? I think it was important to set the quality of our first mark with God determined accuracy GDA before moving ahead. If we are to adhere to the principle of continuous improvement we will need continual awareness, verification and validation of our attitude and our approach to the purpose of the survey. This will provide our quality assurance. Now it's time to return to our survey area. Come with me as we cast our mind over our second known mark.

Chapter 6 Notes

1. Dwight Edwards, *Revolution Within*, 2002, page 55.
2. Robert Letham, *The Holy Trinity*, 2004, page 283.
3. Richard Rohr, *The Divine Dance*, 2016, page 26.
4. Letham, 2004, pages 208, 327, 351, 382.
5. Cited in Matthew, *The Impact of God*, 1995, page 26.
6. Curt Thompson, *Anatomy of the Soul*, 2010, page 24.
7. Floyd McClung, *Follow*, 2010, page 29.
8. Ibid. page 31.
9. Song of Praise, 'Let Our Praise to You Be as Incense' by Brent Chambers.
10. McClung, 2010, page 54.
11. See John Piper, *God's Passion for His Glory*.
12. Timothy Jennings, *Could It Be This Simple?*, 2012, page 22.
13. Gregory Beale, *We Become What We Worship*, 2008, page 11
14. Article by Tony Reinke, 'We Become What We Worship', 22 August 2012, *Desiring God*, www.desiringgod.org/articles/we-become-what-we-worship, accessed 30 October 2018.
15. Michael Reeves, *Delighting in the Trinity*, 2012, page 48.
16. John Piper, *Let the Nations Be Glad*, 2004, page 17.
17. John MacArthur, *The Ultimate Priority*, 1983, page 127.
18. Ibid. page 147.
19. Source unknown.

CHAPTER SEVEN

Knowing Yourself

For in Him we live and move and have our being.
—Acts 17: 28a

*And I see your true colors shining through. I see your
true colors, and that's why I love you.
So don't be afraid to let them show, your true colors.*
—Cyndi Lauper

*A humble self-knowledge is a surer way to God
than a search after deep learning.*
—Thomas à Kempis, *The Imitation of Christ* (1993: 20)

I WOULD LIKE TO place a different emphasis on this chapter than in chapter 5, which was about knowing God. Hopefully, the way I present the need to know yourself will raise questions of how well we do or don't know who we really are as human beings, as a person, and as a man or woman. Other important considerations in this chapter touch on some things that get in the way of knowing who we really are. The main one would be the effect that culture has on how men and women are perceived and how gender identity is approached and presented. Anyway, see what you think. It is better that you decide these things for yourself. What I would like to achieve is to provoke your thinking as you continue to cast your mind over the matters we are looking into so as to navigate the uncharted waters of life.

There has been enough said already about our Western society and culture in the earlier chapters, and I do not wish to go over old ground. But I do want to make this important point to keep in the forefront of your mind: culture is man-made. It is about the way of life that a people choose to live so that their life works well for them. It is about a worldly way of life, not a life within the kingdom of God. And it is not the place where God's effective will is carried out. There is sufficient evidence of this in Scripture; and the view I put forward is the basic assumption that, as a Christian, you cannot have a foot in both camps—it's fully in one or in the other. To think that you can have this worldly life, and God as an insurance policy on the side, is as dangerous as trying to straddle a high razor wire fence, particularly for us men.

Asking the Question

What does it mean to be human and to exist? Although I don't go along with the reasoning existentialism philosophy has advanced since the nineteenth century, this basic question seems to have been around for thousands of years. The writer of Psalm 8 seemed to wonder out loud to God while Job seemed to ask God the question more directly (Job 7: 17). Providing we use our reference point, our Christian faith clearly asserts that we are God's created dependents (Psalm 104: 27–30; Proverbs 3: 5–6; John 15: 15), His offspring, His children, His sons and daughters, His friends, and His intimate allies in this created world. And despite where existentialism has ended up, its genesis originated from those who believed in God: Søren Kierkegaard (1813–1855) is generally regarded as the 'father' of existentialism; and Dostoevsky (1821–1881), a Russian philosopher who also believed in God, warned us that 'if there is no God, everything is permitted'. Yet despite all the knowledge gained and handed on throughout human history, the questions of who we are and why we exist seem to cause each and every individual to seek an answer for themselves. It seems like every one of us has to go on an individual journey in search of our answers, and it doesn't seem to be any easier if a person is born into a family that believes in God and knows of God and the Bible—or not. Then at some point, at least by my understanding, most people seem to lose sight of whatever reference point they were given or once held in childhood and choose one for themselves in their search once more 'to find themselves'. This search typically begins in the teenage years, and as Erikson's life stages depict, the teenage years are mainly about understanding identity.

If knowing God, knowing yourself, and knowing how we are related to God isn't a difficult enough quest from the outset, what about the difficulties caused by hurdles we come across on the way? You might wish to pause here and consider how your own journey has been to this point. How did you go? My childhood was complicated, confusing, and traumatic. So very early on, I learned to be an 'imposter'—it wasn't safe to be my real self. I soon developed a persona that disguised my fears and gave me successful strategies and ways of coping so that I would be well liked, accepted, affirmed, admired, and loved. Still, my best efforts were occasionally, and inevitably, challenged by someone along the way. I had to face my fears on more than one occasion, which wasn't a pretty sight in the way that showed up. Remember back when these used to be fighting words: (Challenger) 'Who are you?' (Responder) 'Yeah, and who are you?' And then it was on. I never knew who I was back then, anyway. Then, when I was a teenager, my dad would often ask me, 'Who do you think you are?' I didn't know. Why is he asking me? Doesn't he know?

Somewhat early into my naval career, I had an unfortunate disagreement with a very senior officer, who, after our confrontation, was heard to exclaim, 'Who does Paterson think he is!' I knew that it wasn't a question. This incident didn't help my career much. I learned from that incident, though. In the Navy, as in life, it didn't matter what I thought of myself—it was what others thought of me that mattered. And it has taken me a long time to unlearn that lesson, to let go of the vow I had determinedly made to protect myself at all costs and to accept my true identity in Christ. I know that it is God's opinion of me that matters above anything else. It just took a long time to live out my true identity. Now I play to an audience of One—or at least I try to.

A Self-Made Person

It was 1989, and I had been given my third command in succession—and my most valued. I had served in every officer position on the survey ship HMAS *Flinders*—treatment of oily birds officer (competes with laundry officer as the lowest job in the ship), third officer, supply officer, survey boat officer, navigating officer, senior surveyor, and twice as executive officer. Now I was in command and in charge of surveys. I was at the top of my profession. I knew who I was, at least I thought I did. I had worked hard, performed to impress, and competed well to arrive at this position. Life was all about me, of course. To all those who had used me for their own purposes and to those who thought I wouldn't amount to anything, I had proved them wrong. I was a self-made man. I could look after myself now, and I didn't need anyone.

Well, you know what happened next. I had walked away from my true self to arrive at this place of success, and my then wife decided that I didn't need her or the girls. That's the sort of man I was projecting. Almost twenty years of building up an identity so as to leave the lost and confused 17-year-old boy at home, I found myself lost once again. I was confused and without any sense of who I really was, except that I had squandered away what had mattered most to me—being a husband and a dad.

Have you ever paid attention to how our worldly language honours someone who appears as being successful? Often in admiration of their success, we will say something like, 'He or she is a self-made person.' What is actually being honoured and admired in the statement are qualities such as independence, a strong self-will, resourcefulness, as well as a determination and ability to get what they want. And the fact that the person did it all by himself or herself makes it all the more wonderful. It's as if they didn't need anyone else. It's not true, of course. We all need someone 'other'—even if it is to use them to get what we want. There's enough of that going around. But there is no such thing as a completely self-made person. There cannot be because we are who we are in the context of relationships. *'I am a part of all that I have met,'* says Ulysses in the poem by Henry Wadsworth Longfellow.

Beneath the qualities that characterise us—the good and the bad, those great ones and those lesser ones, the positive and the negative—there lies a determination or decision to be like, or not to be like, certain people who have or had a significant impact and/or influence on us. Add to our determinations and decisions the subtle voices and messages constantly infiltrating our unconscious awareness, from a host of projections, and supplement all these with the conditions of the environment we live in, then answer the question 'Where on earth did I get the idea that I can do life all by myself?' How did you go? How can we admire independence as a character quality when we are made to be dependent on our Creator, God, and interdependent on close others as we live together in community?

We are indeed biochemical, psychosocial, relational beings. A virtual 'pea soup' of determinations, decisions, influences, ideas, and conditional factors that epigenetically—by both nature and nurture—integrate and instruct our DNA to control and express our genes as they were activated, or 'switched on'. Just put it all in a sausage maker, and it comes out with skin on. But we are much more than that. At the core of the 'self'—in the spiritual centre of our very being—that is where we know our 'self' as personal. And it's in this place of our deepest being that we either receive or accept our true identity from God, or yes, we can choose any other identity from the shelf of worldly false selves and portray ourselves as whoever we wish to make ourselves out to be. That 'self' would indeed be self-made; and it would also be an illusion, a false self, a persona. That's the person we hide behind and display to the world for a whole lot of reasons, but usually based on some deep fear(s). The search for an answer to the question of who you are is to be found in how you understand yourself and experience yourself as being loved by God. *'Neither knowing God nor knowing self can progress very far unless it begins with a knowledge of how deeply we are loved by God,'* writes Benner.[1]

Knowing the Self as Loved by God

Knowing yourself is the second mark from which we measure where we are at any point on our life journey. Remember, the first and most important mark is knowing God. But how do we know ourselves? It has been said of human beings that we are the only species or 'thing' that doesn't seem to know who we are. Now this may seem a little weird, but I understand what Benner is getting at when he says that dogs, rocks, trees, stars, amoebas, electrons, and all other things *'all give glory to God by being exactly what they are'*[2]—all except for us human beings. While at times I have wondered about cats, when it comes down to it, they know they are a cat whenever they are stood on or chased by a dog or purr to manipulate their way out of you. Why is it that human beings seem to be the only creatures that need to 'find themselves' and appear to be so busy, sometimes frantically, searching for who they really are in all the wrong places? And in the process, we seem utterly determined to make ourselves out to be whoever we and others think we should be. Is it because we don't like ourselves as we are? What do you think?

We live in a time of information overload. Billions upon billions of ideas and information clutter the airways and seek to occupy the human mind, amassed with possibilities that entice us through fantasy and fiction to construct a view of 'self' that most pleases us and informs us that we can be, and should be, whoever we want to be. So we play Russian roulette with the Internet, seeking due to inquisitiveness, the need to know, or some quest for the 'Holy Grail' that which will define us as we want to be known. But, we still don't know who we really are. All the while we are unknowingly unaware and in conscious or unconscious denial of the truth that only in God can our desire to discover who we truly are be satisfied. Determined to self-destruct, human beings demand their right for independence to self-construct whoever and whatever they want to be. Seemingly, deaf to what Paul is saying, *'For in Him we live and move and have our being'* (Acts 17: 28a). And apparently, blindly, stubbornly, and arrogantly refusing to agree with Thomas Merton that *'if we find our true self we find God, and if we find God, we find our most authentic self'.*[3]

Once again, in the midst of all the noise and busyness within society that seeks to entertain and distract us and positioned on the unstable foundation that an independent self is constructed and tossed around by the shifting sands of Western cultures, we need our datum. It is God's Word to us that tells us we are loved by God. The reason why this starting point is so fundamental to understanding who we are is that if we are going to experience being loved by God, then we have to believe it so as to trust it before we will live it. If we don't take on the 'mindset' of Christ (Philippians 2: 5–8) and live the way that Jesus has modelled, we create a gap in the reality of our lives. This sets up a cognitive dissonance, which means we do not really believe what we say we do. Old patterns and old neural pathways seem to be stronger and more credible than our new way of thinking. The 'old ways' have become our reality because that's how we experience our self. Then we live out of the identity that we have socially constructed, built up, and come to accept as who we are; but we are never known as we truly are and as we deeply desire to be known. It takes a long time repeating and reinforcing new beliefs so that the new neural pathways become the dominant motivators. The last seminar I attended around sexual identity informed us that there are now (last count, anyway) seventy-one genders that people have constructed for human beings; as an aside, heterosexuality was not a specific one but fell in the category of cisgender. Isn't that amazing? How's that for evolving—we have already added another sixty-nine on to the two that God made!

Do you feel like you're in some dark hole? Hurding tells us that *'the only way out is to lose the self, to let it go and once more willingly become an object again—not an object naively fused with the flaws of life . . . nor an object to be controlled by others, but an object in the love and service of* God*'.*[4] So we need to start from some reference point that is not the 'self', but which one? Other than the 'self', the only one I can recommend is our datum—known to GDA as Scripture, which God has given to us for this very purpose. Because knowing ourselves must begin by knowing the 'self', which is known by the One who created it, there is no other 'self' that exists.[5] And this is what John Owen was saying 350 years ago when he urged us to know ourselves *'in reference to the will of God concerning us'.*[6] Are you willing?

Self-Acceptance and Self-Awareness

So far, I have written about the focus on the 'self' with a negative connotation. It may appear confusing to now shift the perspective to a more positive one. But the reality is that you are a person who has a 'self'—this cannot and must not be denied but rather embraced. What's more, you are an individual and unique 'self', just like everyone else in the world. Imagine how awful it would be if we were to think of ourselves as just a drop of water falling into an ocean that consumes the small drop totally. A person would not only lose a sense of their uniqueness and individuality but would also cease to exist—simply be a part of the ocean. The ocean is such an immense body of water and so deep in places. Sometimes to break the monotony of our survey routine, we would heave to (stop the ship) and go swimming over the side. 'Hands to swimming stations!' would be broadcast throughout the ship; and within minutes, there would be people jumping, diving, bombing from all parts of the upper deck. I would always get a sense of how vulnerable and small I was and how big the fish were whenever I dived into such deep blue and seemingly bottomless water. I still experience myself as fragile, vulnerable, and very small sometimes. But now I try to keep my hand outstretched and live with the assurance that whenever I sink, God will reach out to me with His left hand—because that's His mercy hand—and take my hand in His; and I will rise from the deep into the loving arms of my Father.

Some spiritual people actually believe that when we 'die', it's like we become part of an all-consuming ocean. That somehow 'love' is something we become rather than it being the relationship that exists between persons—I do not. It goes against my understanding of what a truly personal relationship is like. We are not lost in the 'other' to the extent that we become so joined that we lose a sense of where we end and the other person begins. That is enmeshment rather than healthy self-differentiation. Don't call it love. No, the 'self' that we are to lay down, put to death, and lose is not our true self—it is the false self that we are to lose, the self we have constructed to both protect us and to project into the world so that it actually hides and denies our true self. This is extremely important—when you receive God fully, you become fully who you are and who you were always meant to be. You gain your life, your soul, and your true identity when you surrender your self-made one.

Whenever all four Gospels give an account of what Jesus said, you can be assured of the importance of what He was expressing. Take, for example, the following passages: Matthew 10: 39, 16: 25; Mark 8: 35; Luke 9: 24; John

12: 25. However way you choose to say it—whether it's denying self, losing self, or crucifying self—it means the same thing. We are not to put self-interest or anything that hinders our faith-lived life ahead of following Jesus and our desire for God, first and foremost. So we lose the 'false self', the worldly one, to gain the true self that is found in God. I don't know if you noticed, but I didn't use the term 'dying to self'. I do so intentionally because, for me, it is not a category in which to be thinking; and there seems to be some sort of human arrogance and resistant pride involved about 'dying to self'. I think we need to put the 'I' aside because we really are to die to God, not to self (Romans 14: 7–9). Practically, it's more helpful to think this way because I don't feel as resentful towards God when I freely give Him something rather than when I think He is demanding and/or taking something (good) from me.

Someone once said that change begins to happen when we begin to accept ourselves and receive acceptance from others. If we go to God first, we will find this acceptance. His words are real and true. He tells us that He loves us with an everlasting love. He says it's beyond measure—the length, breadth, height, and depth of it. It is beyond our wildest dreams, this self-poured-out love. And all we have to do is receive it and accept it as it is true. If we believe and accept this to be true and trust in it to live it out, we will begin to experience it as true. We have to accept being found by our Father in heaven to be restored to who we were always meant to be, becoming who we already are through what Christ Jesus has done. This is what the parable of the lost son or loving father (Luke 15) is about. It is not (just) about changing our thinking and our decision to return—it's also about becoming self-aware and understanding our need to be home where our well-being lies. It's about returning to the Father because of who He is—because He is loving, merciful, and kind—and accept being found by Him as we truly are.[7] When we go to God and receive from Him all that restores us to who we really are, we are better able to give our true selves to others. And that is really good, so good that it brings real happiness.

Trusting and receiving acceptance from God will bring down the walls we hide behind from shame and fear of rejection and better enable us to receive acceptance from others. God is the only one who loves us unconditionally. Even the greatest of human love cannot begin to match the love our hearts desire. We have to allow God's love to penetrate the very depths of us because He knows us and sees us as we truly are—I AM sees our true colours shining through Christ Jesus, and He loves us. So don't be afraid to let them show, your true colours. Don't you know that's why these words that Cyndi Lauper sings sound so wonderful? There is a person who loves you just as you long to be loved, and all you need to do is say 'yes' and receive Him into your soul—then you will know yourself as loved by God. And we live this as true when we trust in His promises and the assurance of His faithfulness to us, not ours to Him.

From False Equation to True Equation

Allow me to seek your agreement to turn my primary focus towards men, Australian Christian men (ACM) in particular, as I write the following sections on identity, culture, and masculinity. I hope everyone can glean from what I am saying, but I speak mainly from my experience as a man. Imagine what we set up for ourselves in life when we live by the following equation:

My self-worth = my opinion of myself + what others think

As I have shared already, this is the equation I lived by for forty years. It was never going to work. I suppose you could tell straight away. I was kept totally exhausted trying to make myself look good so that I would be accepted and liked by others. And since everyone's different, I too had to be different to please everyone else. I'm feeling exhausted just thinking about it again. No wonder I never knew who I really was. Even when I became a Christian, this strategy didn't change for some time. In fact, I think it got worse before it got better. I really wanted to be a 'good' Christian, and I really wanted to fit in and be accepted by my chosen community, so I think my performance rate picked up. I was obedient (military trained), loyal, performance orientated, a self-starter, and a high achiever. So I was fully primed for serving. I'd do whatever was asked of me and still look for more—the roadie in music ministry, serving in children's ministry, volunteering for men's camps. I'd arrive early to set up and was always ready to help clean and pack up at the end. By the way, I'm not saying that there is anything wrong with that. I am saying that my self-worth and neediness were the wrong motivations.

As I reflect on the early years following my 'yes' to God and the years since listening to other stories, I can see the way churches across a whole range of denominations were places where performance was overtly encouraged and plainly admired. Most churches I know place a major focus on knowing God in their different styles and ways, but there is also a significant emphasis on service, and that can overly encourage a performance-orientated focus. What I find missing is what David Benner writes about in his book *The Gift of Being Yourself*, where he observes the contemporary church ignoring the second part of the Christian journey—that of knowing ourselves. That might seem a bit out of place in some Christian circles and a bit too much like 'me, me, me and I' at times. But it is crucial to our journey to know God because if we do not truly understand who we are according to His will for us, then we will not understand our need for Him—and that is essential.

I invite you to pause here and consider how you think relationships in our communities, our families, our marriages, and our society generally are going. Be really honest. Do you see any shipwrecks? When I ask the question 'Who do you think you are?' it is in the context of significant relationships. We are who we are in our relationships, and something just doesn't seem to be like it should be because our relationships are in serious trouble. Most people who come to counselling are in pain or are lost and confused; otherwise, they wouldn't be there. They sure don't seek out counselling just to meet me. Some come to make things better, but most come because their life is pretty much a mess, and they can't fix it. So what do you think needs to happen for people to change their thinking so that they might accept the following equation as being true?

True equation: *my self-worth = God's opinion of me*

A Man-Made Culture: The Total Way of Life of a People

STORY: *Two Australians appeared at the pearly gates of heaven, catching the gatekeeper—bouncer or doorman—completely off guard because he certainly wasn't expecting to see any Australians in heaven. So he asked them to please wait at the gates while he went to verify their credentials with St Peter. When Peter was informed about the two applicants from down under, he too was surprised and taken aback, and he decided to accompany the doorman back to the pearly gates to see these two unexpected visitors. But when they arrived at the entrance, crikey, the Australians were gone! And so were the pearly gates.*

What are your thoughts? Did you have a laugh or maybe smile a little? Does this reveal something about us as Aussie blokes? When we laugh and are cynical about ourselves, is this a good thing, or does it concern you? Anyway, I visualised our two larrikins returning and saying it was just a lark—that they really did want to come in!

Most Australian Christian men I have had a conversation with really want to be good brothers, sons, husbands, fathers, mates—and they try hard. But what I have observed is that they are trying to bring together two diametrically opposing forces. They are trying to live out a contemporary Christianity from however their church is presenting it; and they are trying to get their masculinity, their identity of what it means to be a man, from the myriad of messages coming out of the various voices of a secular humanistic society and hedonistic culture. But this inevitably sets up a duplicity and causes what Benner (2004) describes as a 'chasm' and Willard (2006) calls the 'gap' in what we say we believe and how we live. And this is inherently weak because there are flaws within our cultural identity and what our Western society deems a man should be like. There have to be. All cultures are man-made, and Jesus was countercultural. Natural man is 'hostile' towards God (Romans 8: 7; Colossians 1: 21), and Jesus did the Father's will to glorify God above all else. The disturbing thing for me about the above story is that when I first heard about it, it wasn't told by an Australian. I was even more surprised when I heard a response by an overseas psychologist to a comment about Australians being cynical and negative. 'I'd heard that,' they said. I wondered where from. Does it make you wonder?

Let's hear a little of what two well-known Australian authors say. The first is Steve Biddulph, a psychologist and family therapist for more than twenty-five years. His book *Manhood* (2010) attracted my interest. Steve is interested in rehabilitating men and in reconciling men and women after generations of wounded relationships. Here's what he wrote: *'The problem can be put very simply: most men don't have a life. What we call our life is mostly just a big act, a mask that we clamp onto our faces each morning and don't take off until night. Most men are flat out every day living a lie . . .'* On love, he writes that we are like *'refugees from loneliness'. 'Their happiness totally depends on the other,'* and *'deeply insecure, they watch intently for any sign of diminished love.'* On spiritual matters, Biddulph says, *'Reality is real, but it's just not the way we perceive it. Our perceptions are short-cuts, "handles" on the world we occupy.'* Biddulph concludes, *'There is a truth and most (Australian men) are living a lie!'* What do you think is the 'truth' that we are not living?

Hugh Mackay—another Australian man who is also a psychologist, a social researcher, and author—identifies in his book *What Makes Us Tick? The Ten Desires That Drive Us* (2010) ten key 'social desires' linked to personality, identity, relationships, and that influence our approaches to love and friendship, family, work, and community. The chapter titles reveal subjects that immediately resonate, like the desire to belong, the desire to connect, the desire for love, and the desire for control. He speaks of a threefold need of connection: with our inner selves, with others, and with the natural world—each of which may suffer when we allow the *virtual* to replace the *physical*. Or maybe to replace what we are created for by something '*not real*'. He emphasised the need to connect with 'who you are'. He is at pains to illuminate the danger of focusing on happiness above wholeness. Mackay thinks that when people talk about wanting to be happy, they are thinking of a narrower and vacuous (empty/void) feeling related to the desire for control of 'something' that is obviously out of control or maybe from a sense of powerlessness.[8]

A Reference Point for Masculinity

As Christian men, we must consider *masculinity* as referring to what it means to be a man as God intended. What did God have in mind when He created gender? We must avoid descriptions and perspectives of *masculinity* that are merely culturally determined and continually discern God's perspective of what He had in mind when He created men and women. Specifically, how does God want to manifest His character and activity in each male? There are plenty of good Christian authors who write on this topic: Payne, Dalbey, Crabb, Eldredge, and others. And I commend them to you. So why is it that we don't readily adopt God's standard for masculinity? I offer you four possible reasons—there are more, of course.

1. Man's own ideas and desires are very often selfish and self-serving— they serve us better (we think) than God's intentions for our good.
2. Culture is man-made and has historically followed man's search for the 'good life', including our enticement towards depravity—our attraction to the 'forbidden fruit'.
3. Role models today basically consist of very flawed, if not immoral, heroes of our sporting culture, movie stars, and rock stars.
4. The higher educational systems of the day, in academia and media, are, for the most part, based on secular humanistic standards and principles. God is not in the picture.[9]

Well, I don't know about you, but I have spent more than half of my life trying to be someone who I am not just to please others—and also to make my life go well. I became so confused and tired from the energy it took to keep faking it that I made two decisions: first, to accept my God-given identity; and second, to live my life showing others the real me. The road is steep and rocky and has made my Christian journey both a humbling and healing path, which is why Thomas à Kempis's words at the beginning of this chapter are so meaningful. And believe me when I say I needed to take the path towards humility. We need to know God, and we need to know how much we need Him. But here's the surprising thing. I found the path not only to be about being made low—there had to be times of that necessary experience. But more than that, the journey towards humility is much more about coming to know who I really am as I stand before a holy God who wants to be fully known and who wants me to know who I am as loved by Him. I am not saying it has been easy. Sometimes (mostly) I have felt lonely and persecuted (by secular organisations, courses, university, professional peers as well as rejected by friends), afraid, and hurt. But the overriding sense has been that of peace, clarity, fullness of meaning, and deep inner joy. That does not mean that at times I don't still feel like I'm flapping around like an Australian plains turkey (bustard) instead of soaring like an eagle or that I don't have anxious moments of fear and doubt. But more and more, I feel like I am becoming who I already am in Christ and as I am known by God—as I am loved by Him.

As Australian Christian men, we can choose to find our masculine identity either from society and culture or from our Maker. So how is that identity appropriated today? What's required of us? What do I do? You will not find your manhood either in the mythical heroes of culture, the false idols and values of a lost society or through the embracing of women—not in girls, gold, or glory. Here's what Leanne Payne (1995) says: *'The power to honour the truth—to speak it and be it—is at the heart of true masculinity.'*[10] So it's okay if you want to be a rebel and an outlaw. Just ensure that it is a rebellion against this world and its culture of distorted myths and lies[11]—and not God, just as Jesus did!

Where is our 'moral compass'? What's true north, just a Christian rock band? No, of course Jesus is! Otherwise, we are 'off course' and mainly because we haven't made the necessary adjustments for society and culture's variation and deviation away from God's standards and intentions for men. To follow Micah 6: 8, *'to act justly, admire mercy and walk humbly with your God'* requires us to be certain of who God really is and to know who we are. To know your 'true' way, you need to know where you are heading and where you are—that's navigation theory 101. Our Christian morality cannot be reduced to a set of rules or punishments. John Paul II wrote that the two central tenets of what constitutes the moral Christian life remain[12]

1. the willingness to pursue to be the imitation of Christ and
2. the practice of brotherly love—as opposed to self-centred love.

The manner of our response lies in the depth of our heart, *'whom do we love, whom do we prefer and choose to follow?'*[13] It's a heart response, an interior law—not written on stone, but on the human heart. This is our new covenant with Jesus as foretold by Jeremiah (Jeremiah 31: 33) and confirmed by Paul (2 Corinthians 3: 3). C. S. Lewis tells us that it comes from within. *'Every time you make a choice you are turning that central part of you into something different than it was before. . . . Either into being in harmony with God, or in a state of conflict and hatred with God.'*[14] It's that conflict of choice again. Note I didn't say that it's a conflict of not knowing what to do. We know what is good and true—what we will choose is the real question. Lewis reminds us that the universe is at war, and it's a civil war, a rebellion. And we are in enemy-occupied territory—*'that is what the world is.'* So whose side are you on? Still got a foot in each camp? You are free to choose—God's way or the world's way. Or perhaps you have a better one.

Taking everything that has been said so far, here are the qualities that I believe define an Australian Christian man.

- Knowing ourselves in relationship with a loving Father God through our brother and Lord Jesus with the fellowship of the Spirit
- Having an open and willing heart that we bring in surrender and submission (trust and obedience) to His love
- Sacrificially loving our wives and families
- Loving and blessing our children
- Living in brotherly love with others
- Serving our communities
- Standing for what is good and true
- Moving into the world with the purposes of God

Identity

It's a little strange to get one's head around the truth that our Christian identity is really a journey of coming to know and accept ourselves as who we already are. *'But now in the Lord you are light'* (Ephesians 5: 8). Paul tells us we are light now—Christians have the very life of Christ alive in them. The light shines in through our cracks, and then we seem to block it from shining out again. And it makes sense that that light will show up the 'darkness' within. Henri Nouwen acknowledged this point and chose to move towards the light, asking for grace to continue to allow it so. It is God's light shining on us for us to reflect. We are not generators of light but reflectors of light! We are already as God sees us! So what has to happen for us to arrive at the same view as God? The more I am getting to know God and allow Him to love me, the more I am beginning to trust and accept His view of me. As I reflected down the years of my life journey and of how I knew God during different periods and across certain ages, I gained some insight into how my knowing God affected my response to Him, how I related to Him, and therefore how I lived out my life. Let me explain.

1. Ages 3–11. My childhood God was the God of my father. How I viewed God was as my earthly father modelled Christianity and as I knew my earthly father.

2. Ages 12–18. The God of the rebellious. I rebelled against my earthly father's abuse and understood God as an authority figure who punished wrongdoers, of which I was foremost.

3. Ages 19–35. The God of the irrelevant. As I was making my way through life seemingly in control of making myself relevant, competing and performing out of fear of being irrelevant, God had no place in my life. To a large extent, He was irrelevant, although I never said that to His face.

4. Ages 36–38. God the earthquake. All of my life structures crumbled, and the foundations I had built on shattered. I needed a new foundation and new building blocks—I needed God.

5. Ages 39–48. The God of love. God showed me His 'father's heart' and brought me under His wings into a loving community. It was a time of reforming.

6. Ages 49–60. The God of living waters. God had become the fountain for my thirst and the table for my hunger. I was kept longing for more—hungry, thirsty.

7. Age 61–continued. The God of eternal life. I want to know You more. I want to know Jesus. And I want to love others with a better love.

As you can see, there is still more to come. If you are still alive, then you still have more to learn *from* God—emphasis mine because I am not saying that the person reading this has to learn more *about* God. What I am saying is that our faith and search to know God is His work in us, and He will continue to perfect our faith and reveal Himself until He calls us home to Himself (John 6: 29; Hebrews 12: 2). While we still breathe and have blood running through our veins, God's Spirit is at work. Our whole life is about knowing God—that's His purpose. I wonder about how we use the time He allocates us for that purpose and how much we waste on other matters not nearly as important. How about you? Are you searching for God? Are you reaching, fumbling, groping for Him? Do you really want to find Him? He will change you—you know that, don't you? Maybe that's why we resist Him and block His light within us.

Our human capacity for denial, self-deception, and blindness around personal faults seems to sit equally alongside our self-centredness as incredible human traits. What really fascinates me as an ex-military man is how good human beings are at defence strategies. People with no military knowledge can develop such amazing self-defences. And people with no legal training can be so fluent in their ability to act as their own consummate defence attorney. This should be no surprise because these are natural, innate human capacities—they are our powerful default weapons of self-protection. These strategic capabilities are not necessarily a conscious matter or something we have to choose to employ. They occur automatically, and they are very useful. They are effective at keeping us (in denial) from seeing the need to make changes to our character and/or behaviour(s). They enable others to be the cause of our problems and to be to blame for how our lives turn out. David Benner makes an honest character assessment of himself when he wrote, *'I seem to be programmed for selfishness and egocentricity, not love . . . my motivation is never as pure or noble as I wish it to appear.'*[15] How honest is that? I think he speaks for all of us. What do you think?

Well, there should be no surprises here really. This all began back in Eden when our first representatives felt that they were too exposed, and they discovered the ability to blame the other for their fear and shame and through their pridefulness decided to assume the responsibility to look after themselves first rather than rely on God. This is why if we are to find and know our true self, we must come back to God—turn and return. Benner offers us three things that are crucial to a complete knowing of our true self in relation to God: First, we must know ourselves as deeply loved. Then we must know that in this life, we are being redeemed and restored, which means we are undergoing a regeneration process to take us out of our natural state and awakened to a new reality of who we are (already) and who we are becoming as fully human—like Christ. And finally, we must recognise and accept ourselves according to God's will for us.

Knowing Our Father

Dalbey's view is that the struggle for identity is linked with a man's (a son's) struggle to bond with his father.[16] Often, it's a matter of lacking the ability to communicate genuine feelings for each other. And so I often hear men say, *'I know my dad loved me—he just wouldn't say it and never showed it, not in the way I needed it anyway.'* Even so, still, there was either an imperfect or no experience of love—remembering our hearts long for unconditional love. And it never does seem to take the hunger (to be loved by the father) away from deep within. It is not always the case, but it is worse still for those men who live their lives under the spoken words of an angry and condemning father. 'You'll never be any good! You idiot! You're a complete failure! You loser!' And again, for those who were violently punished and abused by a disapproving and angry father. Where are most of us in our quest to discover real manhood if the following saying holds true? *'A man is never a man until his father tells him he is a man.'*[17] Did your father ever tell you that you are a man?

Are you able to picture this scenario? *'So knowing that he is a loser, the man/boy was forever protected from having to try, and from ever experiencing defeat.'*[18] This is a self-defeatist defence strategy and a way of coping with awful pain and suffering. Its purpose is to protect us from the experience of having to remember or of feeling that sort of pain again. So the person develops a self-protection mechanism, a mantra in their thinking, that might go something like *'I'll never be able to please him as a son, so why try?'* You might agree that this is not a useful life principle for a Christian man. Our knowledge of God determines our behaviour. If we view God as a frail old deaf and insignificant grandfather figure sitting in a rocking chair mumbling, 'That's nice. It's all very nice. Isn't it wonderful?' or as a punishing, authoritarian father, then no wonder we see Him as irrelevant today—and little wonder we have no problems rebelling against His will for us. If God is an authoritarian, angry, and disapproving father, we could never please him anyway. So why bother?

The 'truth' is that God exists whether we believe it or not. And He is who He is and will be from eternity past to eternity future. It is man who is irrelevant in this sense. And God is who He has revealed Himself to be through His Word. We have already addressed this point in chapter 5. But the full and final revelation of God, and especially as Father, is revealed by Jesus. Gregory Boyd makes a crystal clear statement about this in his book *Is God to Blame?* when he stated that if our impression of God is anything other than as revealed by Jesus, then that impression is most surely mistaken. The question is, since He exists, what do we choose to do—tremble and trust?

If we experience God as an absent, distant, uninvolved, and uncaring father, then this too will affect the way we relate with and trust God as Father. *'The resounding truth is that God is always there, never turning his face against those who are his. To believe he did so with Christ is unthinkable.'*[18] Henri Nouwen's *The Return of the Prodigal Son* (1994) is a story of homecoming. Nouwen exhorts us, *'Do not ignore or neglect God's First and Everlasting Love for you. Do not deny His great love for you.'*[19] Our Father God longs for us and is waiting for us to return to Him and receive our true inheritance as sons (and daughters). Since God has now made His home in us, He is wanting men and women to return to their true eternal home. There, they will find Him and find their true selves according to His will for them.

What does psychology say? Well, I think that the Bible is the greatest book on psychology ever written—and the one most plagiarised! For Alfred Adler, ultimately, healing was directly linked to the person's willingness and courage to face the road ahead.[20] I find psychology very useful insofar as it reveals scientific facts about the human psyche and helps us understand ourselves a little better in our time. However, at its centre is the human self. In the words of Paul Vitz, humanistic psychology is *'the cult of self worship'*. Ultimately, you cannot find your 'self' and identity in secular humanistic psychology. And you will never find your true self in the 'images' presented by a world, society, and culture steeped in the deception of false idols and distorted truths. As men, the experience is like *'walking beside ourselves'*[21]— separated from the power to see ourselves as a man. The reason there is the anger of confusion, the fog of unknowing, the anxiety of uncertainty, and the fear of aloneness is that nothing can fill the void of nothingness—nothing except God.

You can only discover your true identity in your Father God, and you can only discover your masculinity through God as Father. If true freedom is freedom to do the good and if real hope is hope in the good and if true love is really good, then it is no surprise to me that *'masculinity is the power to do good'*.[22] It is a distorted and perverted masculinity that would turn this power towards a selfish and/or self-serving cause, and that includes self-protection or, even worse, such as the rampant nature of male violence in our societies now. Let's pause for a moment here. Do you think that a man who knew who he was as a son of a loving Father, sent into the world to be a power for good, if he knew that, would he be violent? The crisis in masculinity is always a crisis in the truth of knowing who God is and knowing who we are as men according to God's will for us, accompanied by a sense of powerlessness to do the good and right thing. Payne warns us, *'When a nation or an entire Western culture backslides, it is the masculine which is the first to decline.'*[23]

Knowing Ourselves

Previously in this chapter, we looked at how important it is to know ourselves as loved by God. I want to address three matters that John Owen[24] pointed out to be the primary things that are necessary for the knowledge of who we are in reference to God's will: 'sin, righteousness, and judgement' (John 16: 8). I will use my own words to describe these three things. You may see it differently, but the important point about them is that it is the Spirit who convinces us and our honest appraisal of what is going on in this world and that these three things are true.

John 16: 9 is saying that the reason why we (sin), 'miss the mark', is because we don't know God. John Bevere describes this more powerfully to the point, I think, as 'missing the true end and scope of our lives, which is God'.[25] But whatever distinction is used, every one means the same thing— sin is an obstacle to knowing God.[26] Because if we knew God, we would believe in Him; and we would love Him, trust Him, and obey Him. The proof that we miss the mark or, worse, that there is no mark is self-evident when we declare, 'I haven't done anything wrong.' When this is the case, it is as C. S. Lewis declared in *Mere Christianity* that Christianity has nothing to say to those who have done nothing wrong and don't need forgiveness. The human condition defaults to the 'self'—it is our natural position. So it is not so much what we do but rather what is naturally present within us—a desire for anyone or anything other than God as our first desire. Again, I am not saying that everything else is bad. Rather, it is not first-order good when we place it ahead of giving glory to God (1 Corinthians 10: 22–24), and 'sin' is the offspring of putting these other desires first (James 1: 14).

Conversely, when we are off the mark at the centre, even a little bit, the farther we move away from that mark, the more the error increases, and the harder it becomes to orientate ourselves to what is true. And it becomes more difficult to find God. We become weaker relationally, emotionally, physically, and mentally. We begin to double our efforts for some control over our lives and do all we can not to admit our powerlessness and need for God. Before we realise it, we are back on the way of the 'old' covenant—looking good on the outside, doing this and not doing that, following the rules, faking it to make it, and forgetting that our sacrifices are insufficient. Our worship turns into religion, and we know we are not being real. Shame first turns to hiding, then into contempt for our protection. It's all too hard we cry, 'I can't do this.' And already in our hearts, we have walked away from God. I know—I've been there too.

In regard to righteousness (John 16: 10). When we are off the mark, God becomes a God too far away. He is too distant and no longer there for me, and He demands the impossible of me. After all, I am not perfect—I'm only human. Trying to find this God through distant theological binoculars or telescopes only serves to keep Him at a distant safe enough to not have Him in my heart. If we invite Him into our mess, He might clean it up, and we might have to change. If we love Him first and every other good and important thing second, it will mean His will and His way, and not my way. Yes, God is good, but He is not safe—not safe enough and not good enough for me anyway, to the extent that I would surrender all and allow what Christ has done to be all and sufficient for me. We will have to let go of everything we are holding on to that is not from Himself and in our wretchedness, shame, and mess accept His grace as sufficient (2 Corinthians 12: 9). We are His, and all of our outstanding debts have been paid.

In regard to judgement (John 16: 11). I understand that we cannot have a foot in each camp. We cannot say we believe in God and then interpret God (the Father, the Son, and the Spirit) to fit into our life's purposes. We can say this in various ways, such as not serving two masters (Matthew 6: 24). Either we are of the world or of the kingdom of God. C. S. Lewis was quoted as saying that his greatest fear was to ever hear God say to him, 'All right, Clyde, your will be done.' It's either God's will and God's way or our way and the highway—and I am not meaning the highway in Isaiah 35: 8 because the only way we can be holy is when we are set apart from everything else for God first and primary. The problem to believing that this is true is to be living it as it is true. God tells us that it is done—it is finished. He has made the way open now; the invitation is extended, and He has given us the power to live in the kingdom now. God doesn't have to judge us. We judge ourselves as we choose. What will you do?

We Know Who We Are in Community

How do we know we are a person? What does it mean to be personal? When we look to answer the question 'Who do you think you are?' we know that we need to begin at the point where you know yourself as you are loved by the triune God who is for you, with you, and in you. This must be our beginning point because every human being is more than matter and matters much more than they are able to imagine to a holy and perfectly loving community who longs for them to receive their love. God is love in action in community (i.e. Father, Son, and Holy Spirit find their identity and intimacy in communion). Made in this image, our identity and sense of who we are are to be found in community and needs to be lived out in community. We take our identity from God and live this out in the context of who we truly are at the core of our being, within our most intimate relationships. There, we find our true self in the 'we' and 'us' and in the 'you' and 'me' and, even more intimately, in the deeper meeting of the 'I' and 'thou'. Even so, this will be like a morsel compared to the real thing. Every human being is a spiritual being, made in the image of God, whose very soul is their person and within which God has placed a deep desire to be loved and to love. And it is this desire that only God can satisfy—we are destined to live within a holy and perfectly loving community forever.

Where to Next?

I was seeking to understand more about myself recently at some training for spiritual direction, and I came across this quote from Noel Davis in *Together at the Edge*: 'The Love that sees our beauty enfolds us, holds us, opens our hearts, reveals us to ourselves.*[27]* God knows our heart. It was God our Maker who put the only perfect desire we have in our hearts—the desire for love, to be loved and to love. Why don't we accept this and trust God to receive what He longs to pour of Himself in us? He wants us to know His heart so that we will believe how truly good He is, and He wants to give us His goodness, only asking that we would receive it and then pour it back into the world.

The intimacy that is involved within this relationship is so deep that we can almost not bear the ache to savour it. But we can, and we must because it's only a taste that we get for now. Yet the taste will be so good that it will keep you wanting more. It will never be fully satisfied, not until we are with Him completely forever. Then it will be a full-on banquet!

When we truly know God, we will truly know love. But to experience the love that we most desire, we must go to God and receive it in a totally surrendered, vulnerable, unprotected, and openly invitational state—just like the three persons of the triune God intimately receive from one another, just like that. We come into God's intimate presence just as we are—holding on to nothing and bringing nothing but our true selves and our 'yes'. His embrace will be higher, wider, and deeper than the deepest oceans.

In 1990, we passed over the Mariana Trench—its deepest part is the Challenger Deep at almost eleven kilometres deep. I remember experiencing an unsettled vulnerability at having that much water beneath us, an insecurity that only goes away when standing on solid ground. Catherine of Siena in her *Dialogue* gives a similar sense of God: *'Thou, O Eternal Trinity, art a bottomless sea into which the more I plunge the more I find, and the more I find the more I seek Thee still.'* I imagine the vulnerability of exposing myself to God's love to be similar, in a way—a challenge to us all, I guess. But we know His response. He will wrap us in the best robe of righteousness—forgiven, pure, whole, and clean. He will put His ring on our finger, the inheritance of eternal life and His promises identifying us as His son or daughter. And He will give us footwear to assure us of our freedom just before throwing the biggest and best party we will have never experienced the likes of (Luke 15: 22–23). And then we will truly be happy—but first, we have to come home.

We have now cast our minds over our second mark—knowing yourself. This will be used to measure where we are. We have established its importance by looking at how it is related to our primary mark—knowing God. We have also seen how necessary it is to know our self in accordance with God's will for us and not a false self if we want to maintain integrity with our positional accuracy. These are two vital marks from which to measure where we are, but there is still the third and final mark to establish. Come with me now as we find our third and final necessary mark—our relationship with God.

Chapter 7 Notes:

1. David Benner, *The Gift of Being Yourself*, 2004, page 49.
2. Ibid. page14.
3. Cited in Benner, 2004, page 15.
4. Hurding, 1986, page 231.
5. Benner, 2004, page 47.
6. John Owen, *Communion with God*, 2012, page 135.
7. Kenneth Bailey writes insightfully on this theme from his extensive studies of Middle Eastern culture in his book *Jacob & the Prodigal*, 2003, InterVarsity Press, Downers Grove.
8. Comments by Simon Smart, ABC Radio Religion and Ethics, 27 October 2010.
9. Francis Schaeffer, *Death in the City*, 1969. Schaeffer identifies this to be so for nearly 100 years now. Imagine the impact.
10. Leanne Payne, *Crisis in Masculinity*, 1995, page 41.
11. Gordon Dalbey, *Healing the Masculine Soul*, 2003, page 194.
12. John Paul II, *Veritatis Splendor and the Renewal of Moral Theology*, 1999, page 20.
13. Ibid. page 33.
14. See C. S. Lewis's *Mere Christianity*.
15. Benner, 2004, page 64.
16. Dalbey, 2003, page 130.
17. Payne, 1995, page 77.
18. Dalbey, 2003, page 3.
19. Wayne Jacobsen, *He Loves Me!*, 2007, page 127.
20. S. L. Jones and R. E. Butman, 1991, page 237.
21. Payne, 1995, page 17.
22. Ibid. page 81.
23. Ibid. page 83.
24. John Owen, 2012, pages 153–169.
25. John Bevere, *Killing Kryptonite*, 2017, page 134.
26. Larry Crabb, *Finding God*, 1993, page 83.
27. Noel Davis, *Together at the Edge*, 2011, page 17.

CHAPTER EIGHT

Knowing Your Relationship with God

We are His offspring.
—Acts 17: 28b

Yet to all who received Him, to those who believed in His name,
He gave the right to become children of God.
—John 1: 12

Do two walk together unless they have agreed to do so?
—Amos 3: 3

WELL DONE SO far if you are reading this. We have come a considerable way in establishing the 'infrastructure' required in our survey network that enables us to position ourselves for the search to make the unknown known. But this is only part of the picture. It was always a great reality check to discover that when we were on the survey grounds responding to the challenges, undertaking the necessary everyday things to keep the ship and the crew functioning, and finding a way through unknown waters, our experiences seldom fitted neatly into the theoretical framework of the manual of surveying. Despite all our knowledge and experience, things didn't often go as planned, nor did they turn out exactly as we might expect. What we relied upon to keep us moving forward and able to carry out our searching was our training, discipline, preparation, and ability to respond well. This was not so much a matter of being in control, but rather an equipping with the confidence required to adapt and overcome the diverse scenarios we encountered. In a sense, it was more about 'knowing' what we were about rather than the knowledge we possessed.

The three marks that we are setting up so as to prepare us for the ongoing search—casting our eyes and minds over the survey grounds of life—cannot be fully known through knowing about things, possessing all the necessary information, or having all the facts and good ideas. Nothing wrong with any of those things per se; but knowing God, knowing yourself according to His will for you, and knowing how you are related are the 'knowings' that can only come from actually knowing your relationship to each mark—and this is vital. It is your ability to respond and the willingness of your 'yes' to keep moving forward from the secure starting point—the datum you have chosen, which provides the confidence, assurance, and certainty that what you know is good and true. But always keep in mind that the datum is your starting point—your reference point, the place to which you refer whenever there is any doubt that you might have moved off the mark.

Our need for knowledge about the world, people, and all manner of things comes out of a sense of insecurity. 'Knowledge itself is power,' writes Francis Bacon.[1] We are comforted by the illusion that a sense of security brings us and by a sense of being in control. But a relationship is not something we can control. On more occasions than I can remember, I have heard personal stories of controlling behaviours that are so damaging within relationships. I have sat with couples and observed their well-learned and creatively inventive strategies that they use to control and avoid being controlled by each other—for a whole range of good and not-so-good reasons. The reasons are usually very understandable and can make sense, but they never work in the long run, and they can be very destructive. That's the problem with relationships—it's God's problem, and it's our human problem. You just cannot force and control someone to make them love you. It's never worked, and yet we seem to keep trying to make it happen.

Love Is a Gift

So how do we proceed? I invite you to stay with me now as we grapple together with this great mystery of God's love in action as evidenced in the human experience of relationships. Please keep in mind that love cannot force its way on another. Love is always freely given for the good of another and has to be freely received. It's a gift. And love has its way when it is returned. 'Love is life,' says Leo Tolstoy, and it is the very core nature of who God is—the giver of life. But as we have already understood, His love is not of this world. God's love is a poured-out, self-giving, other-centred love. God *gave* His only Son so that we might live. God *creates* life, is *for* life, and *gives* life. Timothy Jennings writes of this giving love of God and describes it as a 'circle of love'—out of God, always giving, giving back; being received and returned. This is a 'never-ending circle of giving'. If we stop, look, and gaze upon God's creation, we can see this circle of life all around us; and the theory of relativity begins to make sense at last.[2] This is God's vision for us. He created life to be relational and to give lovingly for the good of another *is* life.[3]

Why is it that a sense of being *in love* is so vital for us? It seems too simple, yet true, to say that this is the very nature of our personhood. To reach our full potential actually means to be transformed through a process of coming to be in love, says Rohr.[4] As the myth of hedonism—that our life fulfilment will be found in the pursuit of happiness for ourselves—is debunked, a malaise has set in with endemic depression and anxiety around the fear of being alone. Yet disconnection and insecurity abound in our Western societies. This is understandable because our sense of significance and security is to be found only in coming to know who God is, who we are as His offspring loved by Him, and through an ongoing, eternal relationship as His sons and daughters. Being an independent person is an oxymoron. The whole concept of being a person has always been something shared with others.[5] All the energy in the universe is to be found in relationships. Check it out. 'Everything is in relationship with everything else,' says Rohr.[6] And as the bishop said in our recent famous royal wedding, *'There's power in love!'*[7]

A Second Chance

Most people would know of a story about being given a second chance. Certainly, Christians would have one. Let me tell you a little about my captain back in 1973. He was the CO of HMAS *Vampire* (a Daring-class destroyer). Four of us midshipmen were posted to *Vampire* for the sea training required prior to being selected (or not) for commissioned service. Our CO lived across the harbour from the naval base; and it was part of our midshipman training, as the duty boat's driver, to pick him up each morning and return him to the ferry wharf at Mossman in the evening. Sometimes the CO would be met by his wife, who would be standing on the wharf to greet him as he disembarked from the boat. This particular captain was the epitome of a naval officer. He always wore his uniform and was very impressive in his character, appearance, and presentation—a real gentlemen. However, he also had this unnerving trait of standing on the bow of the small and highly manoeuvrable boat without holding on to anything. Then as the boat made a close-enough approach, he would step gallantly onto the wharf without missing a beat, all in one seemingly graceful movement—on most occasions.

You may sense already what is about to happen. On one fateful day, when I was the duty boat driver, the weather was not conducive for enjoying a boat outing on Sydney Harbour. The wind was affecting the boat's normally good stability and had chopped up the sea into sharp little waves, causing some handling difficulties. In such conditions, it is best to keep more speed on to ensure that the boat isn't tossed about uncontrollably. So as we approached the wharf, I was very aware of two things: we were approaching the wharf more quickly than normal; and my captain was maintaining his usual stately, handsome, and commanding appearance on the bow—but he was still not holding on to anything. As I found reverse gear, more purposefully than usual, I was surprised by the immediate reaction of the boat and felt a sickening feeling in my stomach as I watched the CO being propelled forward. Fortunately, he managed to wrap his arms around a pylon on the wharf, which prevented him from falling into the harbour. His wife seemed very amused and gave me a smile and a wave before assisting her husband to gain composure once more. I steeled myself for what seemed inevitable following such an embarrassing situation for him, especially since he was dressed in his naval uniform. So I was bemused when, without missing a beat, my captain greeted his wife and, with amazing dignity, walked away arm in arm together along the wharf without even giving me so much as a glance.

I had a restless sleep that night, and the next day, I heard my name being requested to attend the executive officer's (XO) cabin. He was in charge of the ship's seamanship department. The XO was delighted to inform me that the CO had selected me to be his personal boat's driver for a week. That's seven days in a row, although he had no understanding why. I saluted, greeted, and spoke with the CO all that week as he embarked and disembarked twice each day for seven days; and he never once mentioned the incident—not ever. During that week, I learned much about small boat handling and became a much better boat's driver (coxswain). I also felt encouraged, motivated, and more confident within myself.

Sometime later, before posting out, when I was dancing with the CO's wife at a party in the officer's mess, I said to her, 'You know, he has never mentioned the incident—not once.' She responded, 'You know that he really likes you, John, don't you?' That went deep. My faith in both the good character and excellent professionalism of my captain increased, along with the belief in myself that I could become a competent seaman officer. You could say that I had been given a gift by my captain. This was the same CO who I approached later to say that I didn't think I was suited to being a naval officer and that I wished to resign. And it was he who suggested to me that I might really like the Hydrographic Branch. He subsequently arranged for me to be posted to a survey ship. Do you see? He believed in me and had given me a second chance—it was a powerful gift for which I was very grateful.

The way I understand belief to work is that a person's thinking becomes a conviction when they see proof of the belief being acted out, and this continues to deepen the conviction until it arrives at the place deep within us we call 'our heart'. Something deep within us tells us whether we can trust a certain person, fact, or thing to be good for us—or not. My captain in 1973 gave me a gift of goodwill—he liked me and desired my good. His attitude towards me and his personal investment in me, even at the cost of embarrassing himself, were gifts of faith, belief, hope, and confidence to me because I had an opportunity to take on board what he had given to me within myself and respond to his initiative. And there was more—I wanted to be like him. Years later, when I became a CO, I had opportunities to act in a similar way.

One of the more difficult challenges for me to endure as a CO was to remain in my cabin at night whenever new officers were on watch by themselves for the first time. They were required to gain experience and confidence as the officer of the watch before being awarded their bridge watch-keeping qualification. Some situations were especially hard, like when they would phone down to inform of the nearness of approaching ships or if they were about to change course particularly when navigating in coastal and confined waters. Of course, when prudence called for it, I would go to the bridge and sometimes stay with them so as to provide a sense of reassurance. Whichever was the case, either remaining in my cabin or when I came to the bridge, the purpose was to impart a sense of trust, confidence, and faith to the officer by allowing them opportunities to seek and respond to their own inner strengths and sense of judgement. It's a 'self' gift, poured out for the good of another, that when received begins to grow within the other—like a seed of faith sown, which is now ready for watering.

Well, if ordinary people can instil a sense of faith, belief, trust, and confidence in another person, how much more able and powerful is a father figure? I use 'father figure' purposefully for a number of reasons, but specifically because it is the name 'father' that in itself has such a powerful impact on all of us. As was mentioned previously, a boy does not become a man until his father tells him he is a man. If that is even partially true, then we can glean a sense of what is so horribly wrong within us blokes. After some 450 years since God was recorded to have spoken to His people in the book of Malachi, we see God speak again in the Gospel of Luke (3: 21–22). Here, we have Jesus emerging from the waters of the Jordan River after being baptised, and the heavens opened, and a voice was heard to say these three things (in my words): *'You are My Son. I love you. I am pleased with you.'* Imagine how different our world would be if every father spoke these three sentences into the lives of their sons.

Could it be that this is something like what God does for us? I happen to believe so. Look how far we have come since chapter 1—being aware of something inside of us, something already there, and understanding that our deepest desire to be loved is actually a desire for good, and it is there for a reason. We know that the goodness we long for comes from God, is God, and that He loves us and desires only good for us. Knowing this, we get the sense of how much we are worth to Him—that we are the *'apple of His eye'* and that He really likes us. We've been given a sense of knowing ourselves as loved by Him. He speaks life to us through His Word; and He empowers, encourages, comforts, and accompanies us in Spirit. When we believe this to be true and seal this conviction in our hearts with a surrendered trust, we live our lives in ever-growing faith—the assurance and certainty of our hope in the eternal future of His promises.

Psalm 62 assures us of these two seemingly opposed principles when it comes to human experience—that God is both strong and loving. Matthew Henry comments that *'a smiling world is the most likely to draw our heart from God, on whom alone it should be set'*.[8] How easily we are attracted and enticed towards the promises of men and the delights of the world only to be let down, left disappointed, or, worse, have our trust damaged or destroyed. Yet the leading of our heart away from God was enticed by our commitment to make life go well for ourselves—only to find that it was towards weak promises and second-rate fulfilment that is the best the world can offer. When we look into the face of Jesus, we see fully the love of someone who is for our greatest good and who is able to be trusted. His love is strong. Only God can hold these two principles together in loving integrity. He is strong in His capacity never to be hurt, rejected, manipulated, or threatened by us to the extent that He would stop being loving towards us. Therefore, only He can be trusted fully and completely.

The greatest gift we have been given is love. Love is the greatest gift because love gave fully of itself for the world and all humanity. McClung writes in *The Father Heart of God* that there are two things we must do to become children of God: we must believe in His name. Jesus Christ, and we must receive Him.[9] I know this to be true because I recently completed a sentence beginning with 'God is' with 'everything good that I desire and need forever'. We have the capacity to receive His love—to will it and to desire it. When we open ourselves to fully receive and believe this gift of love, it brings forth many other gifts—the gift of eternal life, a relationship with the triune God now and forever into eternity, and salvation is implicit to this gift. All—everything—that has been received is a gift from our good, good Father. And every gift from Him is perfect and good for us (James 1: 17). How might our particular theological stance be different if in humility and gratitude we acknowledged and received all gifts that come from God rather than debate over 'which' is the gift (as is argued over in verses such as in Ephesians 2: 8–9)? Might we trust the giver more? If we did, would more people receive the gift? What prevents us from trusting and receiving from another?

The Need To Be Right

Once again, I mistakenly thought this chapter would flow easily—just think 'union' and 'communion'. As I began to cast my mind over this chapter, I stumbled into that enormous chasm that exists between how people understand God's sovereignty and human responsibility—what is up to God and what things we need to take responsibility for ourselves. We all know it's not really one or the other, don't we? Everyone knows that relationships involve mutual responsive giving and receiving and that the most important thing is to be loving rather than fulfil our need to be right. The answer is that it is 'both and . . .' God is sovereign, and people have responsibility. Anyway, I fell into a hole that seemed to get deeper and deeper, and I was finding it difficult to see a way out. Have you ever looked at the debate between those who follow Calvinism and those who follow Arminianism perspectives on the Internet? I came away just crying out to God, 'What on earth are we doing?' Either be relieved or otherwise forgive me because I am just not going to go there. The proponents of both sides are so knowledgeable about their understanding of Scripture and how it is viewed through their theological set of glasses that what they argue seems so right—both sides—and they argue and present their information so very well.

But when both sides have a need to be right, any subject becomes nondebatable because neither side is listening to the other. And where has love gone? It reminded me of all those people I know who are in relational crises. We are seeing this more and more in relationships—the need to be right being expressed in the most unloving ways, and it shatters the essential trust needed for love to be believed and received and for the couple to be able to willingly move forward with their relationship. Richard Rohr candidly describes the preoccupation with being right as having an impact on people's personalities; and they become 'judgmental, preoccupied with themselves, and very often not in love with God, in love with life, or in love with their fellow human beings'.[10] Relationally, people end up cut off or shut off, and the relationship is called off—that's really off, I think. But it is not how it is meant to be. We end up back where we started—I mean right back where it all started. God told Adam not to eat that fruit. But you know the story—they did. And ever since then, human beings have determined that it is more important to be right than to be loving. What has been the impact relationally? It is both traumatic and complex. Let me explain.

There is much evidence from research across various models of counselling, from family of origin work, attachment theory, couple work, and the neuroscience into complex trauma that shows us that human beings carry within them the capacity to build or to tear down, to love or to hate, to accept or to reject, or to encourage or to destroy any relationship with any 'other' human being. Attachment theory looks at whether we experienced both safety and security from our primary carer/nurturer and within our significant relationships in the first two years of our lives. Complex trauma is the outcome of multiple and repeated exposure to interpersonal traumatic relational incidents over time. It doesn't have to be overtly abusive even to adversely affect us. When our experience is that those who are supposed to love us just don't love us as we have deemed to need to be loved, we can be very hurt. It all happens within relationships; it hardwires our brains for further relationships, and it disrupts every part of our lives. And this is especially so for our relationship with God the Father because we learn about the unseen through the seen. The person's attachment style—the way they experience or not deep levels of intimacy—will align with their spiritual way of relating. Some authors say it more simply; our relationship with God mirrors the way we conduct and experience our earthly relationships.

In the strongest way, I would exhort us all to get rid of the need to be right from our relationships. Just stop it! It destroys trust and prevents us from receiving love. Here's how. When one person has a need to be right, that need is a self-centred need. A self-centred need requires others to agree with me and affirm me, and if they don't, then I will demand that they admit they are wrong—or else. We will never trust another person who we believe is more about having their own needs met over and above what is for our good. We know that is not love. But there is always a third way to look at things, and it is the way of Jesus. His way is clearly signposted and asks you to be directed by your considered responses under three main headings: First, seek the Spirit's vision of what is God's will—goodwill—for the other in the circumstances. Then before considering the detail, seek to understand how the matter fits into God's larger story that He is telling about Himself and how we fit in. Third, ask yourself if you are looking at the situation through relational glasses and if you are seeking to love this person with a better love for their good. I urge you to try this way and see if it's different from other ways you may have tried so far.

I wonder how it might have turned out differently for me had my captain responded in a different way. Imagine the scenario once more. Rewind to the CO hanging precariously onto the wharf pylon dressed in full naval uniform. He turns around to me, utterly livid. His face a bright red flush and full of indignant humiliation, he blusters out in the well-known language of the old seafarers exactly what he thinks of me and my boat-handling ability. He gives me a full broadside loaded with shrapnel to cut through my sails, and he and I become the centre of public attention. How would that represent the Navy? Where do he and I proceed from that point? What might have been my plight? How might it have affected my confidence, my belief about authority, the Navy, and myself? And how would I have thought of him? This is all conjecture. But I know, and probably you do too, of how similar circumstances have impacted us all and taken our lives down certain directions, usually motivated by the determinations we make within ourselves never to allow such a thing to cause us such hurt, pain, humiliation, or shame—ever again. People are not safe, and I will never trust anyone.

When our heart makes such a determined vow, little do we know that our relationship with God is also not based on complete trust. Allow me to propose four ways in which we can explore our relationship with the One who holds the ownership rights to our world and everything in it—because He is our Creator (Psalm 24: 1–2). The first is how we are all related to God.

The second is how we are united with Him because of Christ. The third and fourth ways are closely linked as being our communion with and our walk with God.

We Are All Related to God

What does it mean when the Bible tells us that we are God's offspring? We know that we are made in God's image and likeness (Genesis 1: 26)—not God, but like God. We know that He formed us, gave us breath, and made us a living being—every human person (Genesis 2: 7). We know it to be true that God is Spirit (John 4: 24) because Jesus said it. So somehow in our spiritual nature, we have a likeness to God and bear His image. We are image bearers of the living God. We are akin to God, not a kin of God, which means we are of similar characteristics. We are related to God by the very nature of being a creation of His outpoured love that gives light and life to the world. In Him, we live and move and have our being, and He holds everything in the universe together. Imagine coming up with the coefficient for gravity? And we know that He loves *all* of us because anything made by love He sees as very good. We are His offspring, and He loves us. Gerard May sees this as confirming that union with God already exists when we are born.[11]

Our spiritual life journey through the course of our life becomes a 'deepening realisation' of what already exists.[12] This is also how John of the Cross describes our spiritual journey. Richard Rohr agrees that we are all united to God in this way and adds, 'But only some of us know it.'[13] Or might we say only some of us show it, meaning that to say we believe in something is to be living as it is true. We are up against a human ego that is determined to be self-made, and we naturally reject the possibility that there is an 'other' who would desire our good above and beyond our own capacity to even grasp the concept of this being true. This is why trust or, more accurately, the determination not to trust is so vital to our spiritual relationship and hence our spiritual well-being—with God. Allow me to grope for an explanation.

Nearly every professed Christian I know can quote John 3: 16. I think it vital to understand what Jesus is saying in verses 16–18. First, let's look at the word 'believe'. We probably all are aware that it is not just a cognitive head thing—even the demons believed who Jesus is. Rarely do I presume to know Greek, but the word used in verses 15, 16, and 18, which is *pisteuo* from *pistis*, according to *Strong's Concordance*, actually means to '*believe in*' as having faith in. Expanding this faith further, it means to entrust, commit to trust, put trust in the truth itself. In this case, in the truth of the incarnation (that the man, Jesus, is the Son of God) and in the OT prophesises of the Messiah that He is the Christ and in His revelation of the truth of who God is, especially as the Father, and in His promises of eternal life. This entrusting is so vital for Christian 'faith living'. It is also a tautology because it is declaring our acceptance of this truth and announcing our response—our 'yes'—to entrusting our eternal spiritual well-being into a committed ongoing relationship of living a new life with our spiritual Father as a new person, with a new identity, having been born again, from above—anew. This is our moment of self-judgement—this decision to believe in God or not. God's love has given Jesus to the world and to all people within it so that whoever receives this gift and fully embraces it and allows God to fully pour Himself into their soul becomes as one with God. And that person will be in a spiritual relationship with God from that time forward to eternity.

Whether or not anyone agrees that it is God's will for all people to accept His love and saving grace is a matter of personal choice. As many spiritual giants and theologians who believe it is God's will for everyone to receive Him, there seems to be equal numbers who disagree. To go any further would be like trying to understand the mysteries of God found in His threefoldness, the incarnation, the sacrament of communion, God's foreknowledge, His initiative into the souls of individuals, and the ways of His love towards us. Human minds do not have the capacity to grope with these mysteries, let alone be able to put language around them. At least mine doesn't. So I am not worthy or qualified to say—except that if we do not believe that we are both the pursued, the sought after, and the loved, as well as the searchers, the seekers, and the lovers of God, then we really have a problem. And if God, who knows already what we will choose, does not give us His mercy and grace, we simply will not reach our most desired destination that He Himself has put in our hearts.

God has poured out His goodness onto all of creation. That's what love does—pours out itself towards another and invites the other to receive it and return it. There's power in this love. The power is evident in God's kindness, patience, and faithfulness that He has made known to the world so that there is no one who cannot see it (Romans 1: 20). He does so because this is who God is, and He desires that we accept His poured-out love and turn to Him (Romans 2: 4). He wants all people to be saved and to come to the knowledge of the truth (1 Timothy 2: 3–4). I would simply put it to you that God loves all His offspring and that it is His will that they would receive His love, believe in His goodness, trust Him, and love Him back. God cannot be impartial because there is no partiality in God (Deuteronomy 10: 17; Job 34: 19; Acts 10: 34–35; Romans 2: 11; 10: 12; Ephesians 6: 9; Colossians 3: 25).

There seems to be enough agreement around to understand that we are living in the 'last days' where God has had the last word by speaking through His Son, who has now sat down until He calls full time (Hebrews 1: 1–3). It's a time when God has also poured out His Spirit into the whole world and on all people as He said He would (Joel 2: 28) and confirmed in Peter (Acts 2: 17). I believe that His Spirit searches the hearts and souls of all human beings and finds those who would choose Him—those who respond with their 'yes' become the ones God is asking to shine His glory into the world (Acts 15: 8–9). That is not to say that He won't initiate and work His love in and through any other He so chooses—for His good purpose (Philippians 2: 13). God's ways will always remain above the ways of men, absolutely sovereign, and known only as He chooses to reveal Himself. But this we know—God is love, and love by its nature seeks union. G. K. Chesterton spoke of 'the furious love of God' that pursues us, which Brennan Manning went on to describe as *'the enormous vitality and strength of the God of Jesus seeking union with us'*.[14]

The crucial point I am stumbling to make is that I believe God chooses that all people would come to Him, but not all people choose God. God is for us, and for us He gives—but not all will receive. The purpose of His loving kindness is that we will turn/return our hearts to Him, recognise who He is and who we are, realise that all of our goodness lies in Him, and receive Him into ourselves (Romans 2: 4). Love loves—that's what love does. Love seeks union and communion (more on communion later). But neither union nor communion occurs without the unforced, uncoerced, heartfelt 'yes' response of the other. And love has its way when it is returned—because the circle of life is a circle of giving and receiving. If we remain open to receiving God's grace in true humility, knowing who we are as we stand in naked humility before God and entrusting and honouring our spiritual well-being through a living relationship in the intimacy of prayer, I believe we could all be God's favourites—if we so chose to receive His gift (John 1: 12). But we have to be open to receive all of Himself that He chooses to pour into us. Faith requires our full trust and total obedient response to His undeserved gift of gracious love, not having a bet each way.

Union with God through Christ

It seems to be a common human experience that no matter how close you are to someone and how well you think you know the person, there comes a moment when you realise that you never knew certain things about their lives. This is the case for me at least, and as I reflect on this matter, the moment holds a hint of sadness for me that perhaps I could have spent more time and got to know the person deeper. And I begin to wonder how well I really knew them at all. If this is true for us human beings, then how infinitely more so does it apply to God? How well do we really know Him? Do we know Him at all? How do we fathom the depths of God's mysterious ways? This is precisely the reason why we need to rely implicitly on His self-revelation. The previous section was mostly an exploration into the mystery of our union with God using, as best we can, His revelation of His ways and attitude towards us as being both strong and loving and His nature as gracious, merciful, patient, and full of kindness and faithfulness. Now we will cast our minds over God's perfect revelation of Himself through the life and ways of His only Son. More specifically, how we are united to God and one another through Christ, by His Spirit, when we willingly open ourselves to receive Him and to invite Him in—this mystery of Christ in us.

Few of us would not be able to recall the moment, the time and place, the way, manner, means, and/or process of our experiencing what we might call our conversion—of being born again from above, of being saved, or (maybe) of being seized by the power of a great affection. Whatever we choose to call it, the occasion marks our 'yes' to accepting our need to receive Jesus as Christ in our lives, our commitment to follow Him by God's grace, and our resolve to trust Him with our lives and spiritual well-being. It is also the moment of our rebirth as a new spiritual being with a new spiritual Father in heaven and the beginning of regeneration, a transformation into the image of Jesus becoming fully who we were always meant to be. I would be curious to know your thoughts upon reflection on the following question: *how are you different now that you have the Gospel in you?* Allow me to bring to mind some things concerning Jesus. He was, is, and is to come. He came down to us. He calls us to follow Him. He showed us the way. He told us to love each other. He died and rose again and lives to show us the way. He prepares a place for us and will come and take us to Himself. He is now with the Father and yet also with us. He is seated because His work is finished, and He waits for us. And that's the Gospel truth.

Even as I am writing this and stumbling over the words to use in my desire to be clear and concise, I know that this subject is the matter for books and chapters of books and can in no way be contained in one section of this chapter. So here's my offer. I will continue to fumble my way through this chapter in an endeavour to provide sufficient matter that will establish a starting point for further exploration; and you, the reader, will continue to conduct your own search as you progress the survey of your life. But as Rankin Wilbourne so aptly put it, here is our starting point: *union with Christ means that you are in Christ and Christ is in you*.[15]

Part of a Team

There are two occasions in my life that come to mind, outside of being married and being a father, where I felt extremely privileged and honoured—two words that are bandied about too superficially to give justice to their meanings these days. Nevertheless, these two very different occasions were, first, when I was given command of three Navy ships—one at a time of course—and, second, when I was asked to lead a start-up community of people that God had raised up to live a way of life covenanted to Him and to one another.

The CO of a Navy ship has overall responsibility to the admiral of the fleet for the operation of that particular ship and to uphold the values and standards of the Navy. He represents the ship and is the representative of all the men and women who serve in her—we always refer to a naval ship in the feminine. So wherever you go and whenever you turn up to some naval occasion, operational situation, or briefing, the COs of the various ships would be addressed by the names of their individual ships. For example, I was called Brunei or Ipswich or Flinders, and each of the other COs was addressed accordingly. The admiral might ask, 'What does Flinders' think?' or 'What part will Cook play in this?' Sometimes it went slightly differently, like 'Nice of Hobart to join us' if a CO turned up late, for example. Of course, this is not an uncommon thing. Often, sporting organisations and teams operate similarly—members are addressed by the team they represent.

The point that I want to make is that the ship's crew or the team members or the people being represented by a particular church group are *'in'* the name of the particular unit they represent—like Christians are *'in'* Christ. Remember, this is the starting place for us to understand union with Christ. You are in Christ, and Christ is in you. To be united to Christ is to have His

Spirit within you.[16] I remember an occasion, not long after having taken over command of *Ipswich*, a Fremantle-class patrol boat. *Ipswich* was the then holder of the Golden Star, which was awarded to the ship that was recognised as the most efficient ship in the Navy for that year. About a dozen of her crew and I were walking back to the ship after having been beaten in a volleyball competition, and it was *Ipswich*'s first loss in some time. Someone commented to me that it was my fault that we had lost, and I curiously asked how so. The crew informed me that the previous CO had always yelled at them and directed their every move, and I hadn't. Hence, it was my fault for not yelling at them to play better and win. I was really impressed at the 'spirit' in which they seemed to have pride in their ship, and I reassured them that it was them, the crew, who were awarded the Golden Star. They were *Ipswich*, not the previous CO. We had a really good twelve months enjoying the team spirit *Ipswich* showcased to the Navy in our time together.

This is how it is meant to be within the body of Christ, and it is Christ in us who is working to make us more human, not less human.[17] And that is why I don't like to hear men in particular say, 'But I'm only human.' While I sort of have an understanding of where they are coming from, often, it seems to be more of an excuse and a cop-out for not taking responsibility for their (in)action than an opportunity to access the power given to us to claim Christ in us and to strive to be who we already are in Him. Imagine what happens when the same attitude is expressed within a marriage union. Paul is telling us that somehow in this mystery of our union in Christ, it is the same way we husbands are to love and treat our wives (Ephesians 5: 25–33). Declaring that I am only human does not cut it—or at least it never has for me. But it should prompt us to seek His grace and strive to receive the courage and strength necessary to love our wives with a better love, with the love of Jesus. This is what is possible through the life of Christ poured out for us. As Hubert van Zeller put it, 'Christ's at-one-ment reconciled man and woman with God by grace,'[18] which makes us all part of a team together—husband in Christ and wife in Christ with Christ.

We have now arrived at the point of looking at our relationship with one another in the whole body of Christ—the worldwide church. This is probably a good place in which to find ourselves, following on from the previous paragraph. Let's look briefly at Galatians 3: 27–28 because this verse, along with those quoted at the beginning of this chapter, defines our relationship with God and one another. We are God's offspring. We are those who believe in the name He gave us all to represent Himself in the world. We are His children—His sons and daughters.

> You are all sons (and daughters) *of God through faith in Christ*
> *Jesus, for all of you who were baptised into Christ have clothed*
> *yourself with Christ.*
> *There is neither Jew nor Greek, slave nor free, male nor female,*
> *for you are all one in Christ Jesus.*

That's who we are as soon as we say 'yes' and receive and believe. I know I have mentioned this before, but you might agree that it seems to need repeating and reinforcing for today—to believe means to be living what you claim as your faith as though it is true. That's what it means to be a Christian 'believer', one who believes in Jesus as the Christ and who stands on the words of Jesus as being truth and then in His name lives out His words. That is why Christ's Spirit is in us so that through our responsive 'yes', He can do His work in us and out into the world (John 6: 29). Brennan Manning is quoted as having said, *'The greatest single cause of atheism in the world today is Christians: who acknowledge Jesus with their lips, walk out the door, and deny Him by their lifestyle. That is what an unbelieving world simply finds unbelievable.'*[19]

I believe this to be sadly and simply true. That many, most even, of those who represent Christ and carry His Spirit within them seem to live and serve another cause. And it's a self-centred one—we have addressed its destructive powers already. It destroys all Jesus came to reconcile and reestablish—our relationship with our spiritual Father, with one another, and with His creation. We do this by simply not following His one and only commandment: love one another as I have loved you. In this way, the world will see God's glory on display. We are in Christ. This is the ship we serve in all together as God's children—His sons and daughters. And it is not a warship, brothers and sisters—it is His worship. Can you sense something inside of you that says 'Yes, I want to be part of this team'?

Our Communion with God

Through Christ and like Christ, we now have access to the Father by the one and same Spirit (Ephesians 2: 18). Union with God becomes *'the doorway to communion with God'*.[20] Before we go further, allow me to make an assumption, which is in the manner that I will be referring to *communion* as separate from our *union* with God. Our communion is us being as one with God in our relationship through our fellowship. In a sense, it is like *immediacy*, one of counselling's core conditions, that is used to check in with the relationship between two people in the present moment. How are we going—you and I, I and thou? So while a person may have union with God, that does not mean that they are in communion with Him at any particular moment; it depends on the state of the relationship at the time. There's a sense in which it's almost like we have been building up to this point—maybe we have. What do you think?

There is a meaningful passage of Scripture that, for me, provides a way of defining our communion with God and each of the three persons. It also corresponds to any relationship we may have where we say we are in communion with someone or somebody of people. My experience of 1 Corinthians 10: 14–22 is that it is both mysteriously beautiful and agonisingly heart-rending in the message it brings to me. Would you take a moment to read it now? How was it for you? Did you gain a sense of the deep communion in humble gratefulness with God that it offers? And was there a sense of immense responsibility that verges on being an ominous forewarning? Does this impact you in any way? Because we are not able to have it both ways in our life—we either worship idols in our life, or we worship God. It is one or the other. You have come to realise this, haven't you? We cannot hold up even those most important people or things in our life ahead of God. God's rightful place must be as our 'first thing' love—if we are to have communion with Him.

You might say that the moment of communion, defined by our priority of attitude with God as our first love, defines true righteousness. It is the moment and time in our lives when we are right with God—when we are in right relationship with Him, as it was always meant to be. You will know these times, of course, whether in your conscious awareness or in your unconscious 'gut' experience. Some would call this your intuition. You will either have a sense of deep joy and inner peacefulness based on the assurance and conviction of your faith walk, or you will feel 'differently'—agitated, irritated, annoyed, unfulfilled, dissatisfied, maybe angry and depressed or harassed by the 'shoulds' that pester your mind. There may be a sense of guilt because you haven't spent the time at prayer that you 'should', or you haven't been reading your Bible as you 'should', and you 'should' really be spending more time with your Christian relationships in your community. Usually, the outcome is that both fellowships suffer—the vertical one with God and the horizontal one with our important others. That's why the Christian symbol of the cross is so perfectly apt; getting both relationships in right order seems so much like a cross to bear sometimes.

But for me, there is an even more substantial message that comes from Paul about our communion with God. It also means that we are partners with Jesus who participate and share in His life work to pour out His life, love, and goodness into our world—a world that is so void of this grace and so very needy. We are either partnering God through participating with Jesus by sharing in His Spirit, or we are participating with idol worship whether we are aware of it or not. And our response shows up what we hold to be of most value—what our hearts most desire.

Imagine the two lovers in the passage at Song of Songs 1: 7–8 meeting at the beginning of that very descriptive of love stories. The scene is like an enticing meeting of two new loves where a tantalising dance of intimacy begins through an underlying and coded invitational message that might read something like *'I desire you, but I'm going to check you out first. I'm not going to give myself fully to you only, not yet. I want to, but not until I have sussed you out some more.'* It seems to me that the lovers take a little while to adjust to the rhythm of the dance before they understand the necessary steps required for some reassurance that they won't get their feet stood on or worse, and trust begins to build towards the other. God woos us to Himself as a lover who promises to give Himself fully—His best for our good—and not hold anything back. He pursues us, inviting us to trust in His goodness, fully inspired by His desire for communion with us. The Gospel is His marriage proposal to us. Our 'yes' is our acceptance and betrothal—united in the wedding feast at conversion and consummated in what Augustine calls the 'marriage bed of the Cross',[21] where we reach communion through perfect completeness of our union in every way. Then our Christian faith life is the marriage itself, where we are schooled in love—at the higher education level, I think—until we graduate at our full and final union with God.

Given that our minds are hostile to God in our natural state (Romans 8: 7), both our union and communion with God have to be by His supernatural grace. Our relationship is initiated, sustained, and accomplished by God; but since it is an intimate love relationship, it must be voluntary, of our own free will, and by our unrestrained consent. Love does not force itself on another; yet that does not discount what Rohr describes as the divine dance or what Willard would say is a divine conspiracy, where God as our lover pursues and woos us, His beloved, inspired by His desire for us. If only we could somehow grasp the depth of this desire both to be with us and for our perfect good and understand that His greatest heart burden—His deep grief and sadness—is when we don't believe the boundlessness of His love.[22] And if we do stop running and/or hiding from Him, He comes gently alongside us, stands lovingly before us, and knocks tenderly on the door of our heart. His kindness gets our attention and causes us to rethink our attitude towards Him. His assuredness of His faithful love invites us to trust Him and receive from Him. His words tell us that while it is still today, don't harden your hearts—surrender, yield, open to Me, and trust in My promises. Allow me to paraphrase John Owen:[23]

> *Our communion with God consists in His communication of Himself to us, with our return to Him of that which He requires and accepts, flowing from our union with Him based in Jesus Christ. It is both perfect and complete; and initial and incomplete.*

God desires our 'yes' response to Him to the gift of His Son and all that comes with this. Our response is completely voluntary, but necessary. With it come fellowship, intimacy, and all the rights of being His child—right now in this present time and continually—while we are walking with Him and being transformed to the likeness of His Son.

Walking with God

Have you ever wondered how the world, and we, would be different if Adam and Eve had continued to walk with God instead of slipping away from the path to raid the tree and then hide? If only they had been able to stand naked before God with repentant hearts, yet confident in His goodness and love. And what would it be like to have the kind of relationship that Enoch had so that he got to walk with God. I imagine it to be similar to our hearts burning within us just like the two who got to walk with Jesus on the road to Emmaus (Luke 24: 32). To me, walking with God brings together my sense of being in communion with God. It brings a sense of companionship, fellowship, joining in, and being bonded as we share the same path and head towards a common place. This is our spiritual journey, of course; we don't have to be out walking in a garden. It can happen anytime, anywhere, anyhow. This is the manner of our faith walk with God; and it brings together, I think, the joy, hope, and companionship that set our relationship with God into a sure foundation that is accurately aligned to our reference point.

Walking with God is a life lived in faith through a relationship with Him, which is expressed as presence, pleasure, participation, and partnering (Genesis 5: 24; Hebrews 11: 5). Within the mutually agreed communication of this relationship, there exists a giving and receiving of a way of love that holds us in a common union. It is initiated by God the Father through the real presence of His Son and by the power of His Spirit. It is then received by us, yielded to, responded to, and returned to God through the same way by us—and then love has its way. We know this love by the stirring in our hearts when we recognise it as being from Him because our hearts burn as we hear His Word and realise our need for Him and His kindness. And when the 'eyes of our hearts' see this love we have been searching for and longing for, revealed on the face of Jesus, it becomes a fire. It is this fire that becomes an all-consuming love that we receive fully, abandon ourselves to, and then return to God in the fullness of our union. John Owen wrote, *'When the soul sees God, in His release of love, to be infinitely lovely and loving, and rests upon and delights in Him as such, then it has communion with Him in love.'*[24]

Allow me now to paraphrase Owen when he wrote of six things that were required for our walking with God. First, we are bonded by our agreement to walk together. Quoting Amos 3: 3, *'Two cannot walk together unless they are agreed.'* Also, we are free to walk whatever way we choose, although it is wise to listen to His voice as we stand at these crossroads and choose the good way (Jeremiah 6: 16). Second, we need to make acquaintance with one another. We need to introduce ourselves and get to know one another—more importantly, sharing about who is in our family. During our becoming acquainted, we find out who each other is; and this sets the tone of our continued walk because He is God, and we are not. The third thing, then, becomes the way of both the manner in which we walk and where we are heading. For most (all) of us, this constitutes a *'new and living way'*, as we continue to *'draw near'* to one another (Hebrews 10: 20–22). Fourth, we soon discover that His way is far too difficult for our natural capability, and we hear Him saying to us, *'Apart from me you can do nothing'* (John 15: 5). We realise that we need His strength and are assured by His words that we *'can do all things through Christ'* who strengthens us (Philippians 4: 13). Soon, it is as though our relationship has reached a depth level whereby our trust and confidence increase as we continue walking together. The fifth thing necessary for us to walk together is when we are real with one another in our boldness to discuss openly and honestly the things that really matter in life—even shameful things that would otherwise damage and adversely impact an authentic and intimate relationship. Finally, we come to realise how alike we really are and that our hearts burn with the same love, that we have the same end in mind, and that we can hardly wait to get there and celebrate together—forever.[25]

A Moment of Returning to Communion

There are times when I see God as some obtuse authority figure. I know the Father is for me, that Jesus is with me, and the Spirit is in me. I just don't experience that as constant. It's almost like I am waiting for the hammer of the great judge to come down on me sometimes. But here's the thing. As His children—His sons and daughters—we can boldly stride up to His throne of grace. Whether at that moment God seems more like a thunderstorm than a loving Father or whether He seems like an ineffective pithy breeze, you can walk right up and stand before Him and boldly say your piece even though your knees may be trembling. Or you might just rather wearily climb onto His lap and let His loving arms enfold you. Either way, or anywhere in between, is okay—just turn up!

Very recently, as I was sitting in my prayer chair, trying to be present with God and to understand why I was in a pit of despair, God took the moment to reveal the source of my despair as crippling fears that are so disabling for my relationships with others—those who are intimate with me and those who I hardly know. These fears exhaust me physically, mentally, and emotionally; and they cause me to hide behind walls that I build for self-protection but that block the openness and honesty needed for the real intimacy that my heart cries out for. In-to-me-see—I long for it, and I fear it. Fear of hurting others and of being hurt by them. Fear of offending others and of being offended. Fear of rejection, of inadequacy, of not being good enough, of saying and doing the wrong thing, of not being able to please others. Fear of fear itself— so much fear. In this pitiful state, I cried out to God to take away my fears. And He did, but not before I fell into and was enfolded within the embrace of His strong and loving arms. It was a priceless moment of deep communion with our Father.

Whether I am feeling confident and assured and experiencing God's abundant joy or whether I am feeling wary, suspicious, and neglected, I can be certain through faith in Jesus Christ of the love the Father has for me and how

He simply beams with delight any way I turn up in His presence. Sometimes simple prompts are helpful to guide me into His centre of being. Like the PAPA prayer described by Larry Crabb and the prayer of the Trinity by Richard Rohr or breathing the seven-syllable prayer that Brennan Manning offered: *'Abba, I belong to you.'* There are many more forms of such prayers, and I encourage you to search and find those that are meaningful and helpful as a way of bringing you into this communion. And when you are tired and weary of praying or you simply run out of words to say or maybe you feel your spirit has just dried up, listen quietly, remain open, surrendered, and welcoming to whatever gift or not, blessing or not, word, song, or silence or not that God reveals or not in this time with Him. This is contemplation because you have come with your total self—body, soul, and spirit—*'with a temple'*, offering your everything and your nothing up to everything that He is to you.

So we *'walk the walk'* on a narrow path that follows the *'good way'* in the footsteps of Christ. That's 'true north'! We always need to know where true north is so that we can know when we are heading in any other direction. It's also important for us on the journey to understand 'why' we have chosen this path and be able to describe it to others, if we are going to be any safe sort of guide, and express it with any sort of energy and passion. Often, along the way, as we live out our lives, we find we are changed and shaped by our experiences and relationships. Scripture uses terms like 'change', 'growth', 'becoming mature in Christ', and 'transformation' to mean the process of sanctification where we are being (slowly) transformed into the image of Christ—becoming Christlike. This is our spiritual journey on earth, and it is the journey of a *'long obedience in the same direction'* (Eugene Peterson) following Jesus—that's the walking path. We could break into the old worship song 'Trust and Obey'. Obedience is yielding to the love of the Father. His love forms His will for our utmost good. Every loving father understands this.

Confirming Our Third Mark

As we cast our minds back over this chapter, I hope I have given you some means by which you are able to measure where you are, at this present time, in your relationship with God. I have tried to describe a measure of continuity where your relationship could be anywhere from a place—where at one end, you are united to a Creator that is beyond knowledge and our imagining or at the other end, where you have a deep and loving communion with the three persons of the triune God of Jesus Christ. Or you could be anywhere in between. Or elsewhere? The encouragement I would like to provide you with is to keep searching for God and reaching out to Him, sometimes groping for Him, and remaining open to how this God, who has somehow put something immensely desirable in you, will continue to reveal Himself to you. I also hope that I have helped to instil some enticement into you to seek out a personal and intimate depth relationship with God so that He will be your joyful partner in celebration of the good times in your life and the assurance, comfort, and anchor when storms and bad weather wear you down. Whatever is your present situation, I hope that when you attend to how you are related with God at any point in your life and you have set a plumb bob over that place, it will serve as the third mark from which to measure where you are.

Let us now take stock of our survey preparations to ensure we have the means to determine our position anywhere across the uncharted waters of our survey grounds. We have established three marks that can be known with confidence to be of God-determined accuracy because they are based on our starting point—the datum that we have chosen—God's Word as revealed in Holy Scripture, the Bible. Using this known reference point, we have established three critical marks from which we can measure where we are. The first of these is the primary mark of knowing God. Second, from this known place, we can establish the important mark of knowing ourselves in accordance with His will for us. Our third and final mark, which is accurately determined from the other two, is knowing our relationship with God at any time in our life. When we use all of these three marks together, we are able to know accurately where we are at any given time in our lives. So come with me now and let us look at how best to measure our position this way.

Chapter 8 Notes:

1. Bacon's *Meditationes Sacrae*, 1597.
2. Although Einstein deduced that there is no fixed point of reference in the universe, everything is in relationship. Everything is moving relatively to everything else, hence his theory of relativity.
3. Timothy Jennings, *The God-Shaped Brain*, 2013, pages 22–30.
4. Richard Rohr, *The Divine Dance*, 2016, page 77.
5. Ibid. page 85.
6. Ibid. pages 56–69.
7. The wedding of Prince Harry to Meghan Markle speech given by Bishop Michael Curry.
8. Matthew Henry commentary on Psalm 62: 8–12.
9. Floyd McClung, *The Father Heart of God*, 2002, page 65.
10. Rohr, 2016, page 68.
11. Gerald May, *The Dark Night of the Soul*, 2004, page 43.
12. Ibid. page 48.
13. Rohr, 2016, page 109.
14. Brennan Manning, *The Furious Longing of God*, 2009, page 29.
15. Rankin Wilbourne, *Union with Christ*, 2016, page 43.
16. Ibid. page 51.
17. Ibid. page 52.
18. Hubert van Zeller, *Spirituality Recharted*, 1985, page 52.
19. Brennan Manning quote, https://www.goodreads.com/quotes, accessed 24 November 2018.
20. Wilbourne, 2016, page 85.
21. Sermon Suppositus, 120: 3.
22. John Owen, *Communion with God*, 2007, page 49.
23. Ibid. page 31.
24. Ibid. page 53.
25. Ibid. pages 171–177.

CHAPTER NINE

Where Are You?

*Therefore . . . we should not think that the divine being is like gold
or silver or stone—an image made by man's design and skill.*
—Acts 17: 29b

But the Lord God called to the man, 'Where are you?'
—Gen. 3: 9

*The Lord looks down from heaven on the sons of men to see
if there are any who understand, any who seek God.*
—Ps. 14: 2

'WHERE ARE YOU?' An interesting question, don't you think?
Especially out there on the survey grounds. It is always so
crucial to be able to determine where you are at all times while carrying out
hydrographic surveys, mostly because we are usually operating in uncharted
waters. But the main reason for being there is to make known what is unknown.
When we find something as a result of our searching and investigating, we
have to be able to establish its position on either the existing chart or on the
new chart about to be produced. So we have to know where we are and very
accurately because ships are getting bigger, faster, and deeper; and they rely
on electronic navigating systems to give them an accurate position. But there
are other important reasons, beyond being geographically embarrassed, as
to why we need to know where we are at any moment, as I will venture to
tell you in this final chapter. But first is this short story of being asked *the*
question by my CO.

'Lazy, lazy, lazy, lazy, lazy!' was all my captain could manage to yell at me
up on the bridge of Her Majesty's Australian Ship *Moresby*. It was a wonder

he could speak at all given the extremely agitated and stressed state he was in; apparently, he hadn't had much sleep the previous night. I found myself quite lost for words also because I had never before found myself standing in front of a CO who was this upset with me. Just when I thought the CO was about to blow a boiler, he paused for a deep breath, and I took the opportunity to tell him the reason why he hadn't been able to locate where I was. As best as I can recall it, it went something like this.

The *Moresby* was the Australian Navy's survey mother ship, some 310 feet long and slender in width. She carried three thirty-four-feet survey motorboats (SMBs) and a helicopter. The three SMBs were used to do shallow-water surveys in coastal and confined waters so that the ship wasn't put in danger. During this particular survey in 1976, the survey boats were deployed to survey out of the southern Western Australian coastal seaside town of Mandurah and as far out to sea from the coast to the deep water contour line. Meanwhile, *Moresby* was surveying in deep waters some 200 miles farther south. So we were a detached survey party living in a local pub and very much running our own show—and loving it.

Anyone who knows the local weather in and around SW Western Australia would know about the afternoon sea breeze called the Fremantle Doctor or, in local lingo, the Freo Doctor or just Doctor. This is a breeze that comes in from the sea in the summer months sweeping in across coastal areas as the land heats up, usually from around midday or early in the afternoon. When playing the game of cricket, the bowling side just loves it when the Doctor comes in because it usually causes the ball to swing and move around considerably. But the batting side doesn't like it at all. Golfers don't appreciate it either. And neither do hydrographic surveyors who are out in small boats trying to carry out quality survey work when the Doctor blows in. Usually, the strong wind dies down around midnight, and sea conditions settle for the remainder of the night and into the forenoon of the following day.

Now as you can imagine, surveying in rough weather is no fun. Whether you are the person steering and trying to keep on a survey line or you are sitting in front of the echo sounder watching the sea-bottom trace while the smell of the stylus burning the carbon paper fills the breathable close-cabin air or whether you are the engineer trying to check on the equipment while bouncing around, rough sea conditions can be really testing. Besides taking a toll on both the boat and the crew, the quality of the data is also adversely impacted. Therefore, as officer in charge of the survey boat, I came up with a routine to solve the Doctor problem. If it was too rough to survey, we would come to a mooring in sheltered waters and tidy up the boat and get some shut-eye before heading out again around midnight. So as to ensure we slept well, we also shut down the engines and turned either the radio off or the volume down. This routine was working well—until one fateful day.

We were all fatigued and catching as much sleep as we could when at about 9 p.m., a search and rescue (SAR) boat came alongside us and asked whether we were the Navy survey boat SMB *Fantome*. We confirmed we were, and the skipper of the SAR said, 'Great', and told us that we were thought to have been lost at sea. Apparently, a flare had been sighted out to sea, and a call had gone out to all boats in the area to verify if they knew of anyone missing. My CO in *Moresby* had also received a call and was asked if any of his boats were in the area. He said, 'Yes, SMB *Fantome* was out there somewhere in the vicinity.' The CO wasn't aware of our well-thought-out routine, and he had tried to call us on the radio for a few hours, but he hadn't received any response.

After being unsuccessful in making contact with us, the CO had ordered for all three generators to be put in the loop to work up maximum speed in *Moresby*, and she set off at full steam towards our survey area. The CO also sent off a signal to the admiral at fleet headquarters to inform him that one of his boats was lost at sea. As the SAR boat departed back out to sea to continue their search for whoever did send up a flare, the skipper suggested that we might like to contact our CO. It was a rather unfortunate compounding of events, really. It was fortunate that we were not lost but rather had simply not heard the CO calling out to us over the emergency channel 16, '*Fantome*, where are you?' Unfortunately, everyone, including the admiral by this time, thought that we were indeed lost. As quickly as I could, I called up *Moresby* on the radio to let the CO know that we were all okay. The flare that had been reported hadn't been ours, so there was no need to worry. A familiar voice of the officer on watch in *Moresby* informed me that the ship would be off Mandurah at 0800 tomorrow, and we were to come alongside immediately after she came to anchor. Since we were not lost, I couldn't understand why *Moresby* would come 200 miles off her survey area when we were all okay, although something told me things were not well with the world.

As we brought *Fantome* alongside *Moresby*, pretty much right on 8 a.m., I saw the executive officer leaning over the guardrail; and after a long draw on his cigarette, he said, with what I thought was more of a smirk than a smile, 'The CO is waiting for you on the bridge, John.' On reflection, I think the smile said it all. That's probably the only time in my life when I wished that

I had actually been lost at sea. Anyway, I was eventually able to convince my CO, when he stopped to get his breath, that we were genuinely working well and that the routine was productive. I apologised for not informing him, and yes, the radio remained on 24/7 after that incident so that the CO knew at all times where we were and what we were doing.

I think these are important lessons for our Christian journey also. In a similar way, knowing where we are requires that we remain tuned in to our faith, attending to what our minds are actually paying attention to and being in regular communication with God about it all. At least life seems to go better for me when I do. Still, it was some time before my fellow officers stopped saying 'Lazy, lazy, lazy, lazy, lazy' to me whenever they saw me. It must have really impacted me because some forty years later, that's exactly what I say to my 14-year-old red kelpie dog as she lies around all day and hardly moves—except for her eyes that don't leave me whenever I walk outside.

Back in the Garden

Unlike my CO in *Moresby*, God does know where we are at all times. Whether we are hiding from Him because of fear or shame, whether we are seriously lost, or whether we have purposely walked away from Him and are far off the path, the one that He would have us walk, He still watches over us. So why did He call out in the garden back then, 'Where are you?' And why did God only call to the man, Adam? Since it was a rhetorical question, what point do you think God was making to Adam? Might God have been trying to get across that it is utterly useless trying to hide from Him? 'Adam, I know where you are. I know what you've done, and I know what's going on. I could destroy your hiding place (Jer. 23: 24; 49: 10). I've seen you naked, Adam. I know everything about you. I'll keep pursuing you until you give me your response. What's it to be? Where is your heart right now, Adam? Are you still for me?'

What on earth was Adam thinking? How did he understand God after all the time spent together in the garden? Didn't he know Him by now? I am assuming they must have walked together a lot—I could be wrong because Scripture doesn't specifically say. And why hide, as if God would blush about seeing him naked? God had formed him and had given him life and breath and everything—he was God's offspring. Look at the fallout since—shame and fear abound as well as broken relationships, the will to independence, self-preservation, and self-determination of our own good, the need to be right, destroyed trust, and more. The cycle of love is broken, and now we do not receive anything from another unless we have decided that it is what we want and that it is good for us. It was Adam that God had told not to eat the fruit off the tree of knowledge—does it make you wonder? Was there a specific responsibility that God had in mind when He created men to be masculine? Back in chapter 7, I quoted Leanne Payne writing, *'The power to honour the truth—to speak it and be it—is at the heart of true masculinity.'* Adam did neither, and as Larry Crabb writes, he didn't remember and move.[1]

God would not have needed to ask Adam that question if Adam had been walking with God. If only he had remembered what God had said to him and moved into the situation with the purposes of God and had spoken up when he was there with Eve. Or if Adam hadn't hid in fear and shame and had rather accepted being found by God and then stood before Him fully naked, trusting in God's loving kindness. If only Adam had a contrite spirit and a repentant heart and had not blamed God or Eve. If only Adam had been courageous and willing to take responsibility for his silence and for momentarily seeking his goodness elsewhere rather than in God's ultimate goodwill for him. If only Adam had recognised and realised that his heart desired God more than any other person or thing (including Eve) and that being with God was where he and Eve were always meant to be. But he didn't. And instead, with a shameful, arrogant heart; a dark, lost heart; a weak, traitorous heart; and a pitiful, selfish heart, Adam brought about a disease that would infect the heart of human beings for the course of the natural world. If only . . .

The following two scenarios would have made the world of difference, I think, to the dilemma we find ourselves in today if either one of them had occurred. Preferred scenario: Eve has just been handed the piece of fruit, which looks really appealing. Adam, standing right there beside her, remembers what God said to him; so he moves into the situation and speaks up. 'Honey, even though the fruit looks really good to eat, I remember God saying not to eat of it, so it would be great if we listened to Him because He loves us and knows what's best for us.' And Eve replies with, 'Sure, huns, the fruit looked so good that I forgot about everything else except wanting to eat it. Thank you for speaking up and reminding me. I really love the way your heart yearns to please God and how you were moved to speak up.' Second preferred scenario: Adam forgets and joins with Eve in tasting the fruit that the stranger assured them was great for them and that God had been holding out on them. Realising their mistake and now enlightened by the knowledge that they were naked and felt ashamed, still, they stood and waited as God approached and, with repentant hearts, believing in His goodness and mercy, said that they were sorry and asked for His forgiveness because they knew that their hearts wanted more than any other thing to be with God and with each other in relationship forever. The first scenario was how it was meant to go, I reckon. But either of these scenarios would have turned out a whole lot better for humankind than the one that we were left with. What do you think?

Two Questions in One

Back on the survey grounds, we now find we are able to know where we are with confidence. Once an electronic positioning system has been established over the first survey mark and transmits to the ship's receiver, the distance between the station and the ship can be measured. Now we have our first line of positioning. This is the master station and will set the timing and transmitting instructions to the other stations. So we can now passage across the survey area knowing where we are according to the distance to our first station, but that does not give a very secure feeling because we could be at that distance away from that station along any bearing within 360 degrees. By establishing our second positioning station, we now have a better knowledge of our position because the two lines of measurement—the distances from station 1 and from station 2—intersect. We now know the ship's position is at the intersection where the measurements cross each other. This is good, although not accurate enough for hydrographic survey standards because errors in the positioning system's hardware and software can cause too many errors with only two lines of measurement, and what if we lost one in the dead of night approaching a reef? We need to remember that ships' navigation systems rely on very resolute positioning these days. Therefore, the way to maintain confidence in the accuracy of our position is to have three lines of position intersecting one another and calculating our position within the small triangle caused by three lines crossing over one another. We know where we are when we are within the triangle.

So it is as we cast our minds over life's survey grounds, by which I mean are our circumstances, situations, environment, phases and/or stages of life, and our relationships. As Christians, we can use the same principle to know where we are at any time. This is not new because I have been guided by all those navigators and surveyors of our Christian heritage who have gone before us, with particular credit to John Owen, who helped me locate our third measuring parameter. Framing an answer to the question 'Where are you?' within the metaphor of hydrographic surveying is simply using the stories of my life in the survey navy to articulate what I believe God is saying to us to help us understand our search for Him. He wants us to know Him and to seek Him with 'all our heart, soul, mind, and strength'.

As exciting as life in the survey navy was and as exciting as the sea and ocean can be at different times, these things nowhere near hold the awe and wonder for me that God invites us to look upon in His kingdom. Hopefully, I have imparted to the reader that I have not ventured to offer a 'how-to' in this book, but rather an 'appeal to'—to search for and to keep seeking and reaching to find God. We have to because He is too immense to grasp and take in, in one go. It takes our whole life to know God as we attend to how we are living out what He is working on inside of us. It's about knowing God in a deep and meaningful way, knowing yourself as you are loved by Him, being confident in knowing how you are in relationship with Him at any particular time on your Christian journey, and to be continually seeking to understand where your faith lies when you measure where you are, in the way Jesus encouraged, by asking, seeking, and knocking (Matthew 7: 7–8) so as you can be guided as to where to place your next step. It's a question that every Christian can give an answer to, and maybe it is a better question for us to be asking each other when we meet so that it can stimulate real authentic conversations rather than the superficial 'How are you?' and 'Yeah, fine. Busy. Going great', which tends to occur in the majority of cases. Instead, ask, 'Where are you?'

Four times (so far) I have changed my mind, endeavouring to settle on the title for this book. Originally, I had thought to call it Unknown God? But I didn't want to appear arrogant by suggesting this was yet another book that had the answers you need to hear. Then I came up with Missing the Mark before quickly getting lost in what I was trying to say. I think I got close with my third attempt in Where Are You? The Need for a Reference Point because I thought that this might pose two questions for the reader to think about. There's a rhetorical question, to make the point about how far our Western societies and their particular cultures, and the world in general, seem to have moved off the mark and no longer know that they've moved because there is no reference point other than the individual 'self'. Everyone is moving together. And there's the question of 'Where are you?' I have settled for a title that, I hope, hands the onus over to the reader to do their own searching with eyes wide open. I hope I have also provided you with some ways that you can measure whether or not you have moved off the mark and some encouragement to attend to what you might do next.

In this final chapter, I would like to spend a little more time around the second question of 'Where are you?' I think the real point behind the question *'Where are you?'* speaks personally to each and every one of us at any time in life. Whether we are lost, confused, in some dark place, hiding out of fear or shame, or simply don't know in what direction to take the next step, God wants us to know that we are never alone. He assures us that He is for us and with us and is the power within us so that we can know at all times where we are as we take our next step into the uncharted waters of our life's journey.

Off-Centre

What happens when we are off-centre? Our search for the unknown God will always be off-centre when we have not plumb bobbed directly over the pivotal dot that is the centre of each mark. I am of course referring to Jesus Christ as revealed with GDA in our datum. And the farther we move away from the known marks that God Himself has revealed to us, the greater the error will become. This is what is evident throughout Western secular societies with man-made cultures whose highest goals and deepest desires reflect the drive to pursue happiness and self-determination of their greatest good for themselves—without any fixed or known reference point other than their 'self'. We are moving farther away from the heart of the Father and, therefore, farther away from knowing what actually *is* our greatest good.

This movement away from the heart of the Father is a searching in itself. Within the parameters of what we determine to be the 'good life' and the self-centred grasping for what we believe we are entitled to, we are trying to find this 'unknown', missing thing, person, or wisdom that will reveal the treasure that will satisfy all our heart's desire. Have you found what you are looking for yet? Let me confirm what you might be thinking. Yes, this is worshipping idols; and in our self-entitled, independent, and wilful responses, we even reinterpret God as Father, Jesus, and the Spirit and skilfully reconstruct them into images of our own making so that they conform to our will for them (Acts 17: 29). Does that work? Has it opened up a better life and a better way to live? Does it fill your heart with deep joy and comfort. If it does, then I wish you all the best in your ongoing journey.

Be very wary of seeking the 'good life' apart from God to the extent that you are comfortable and satisfied with this life. That is idol worship. Rather, be thankful that God may bring us to a place where we admit our need for Him and fall in awe at His feet at what He has done because of His love for us. Then 'regeneration' can begin. We were made to be dependent on God and interdependent with our brothers and sisters in Christ. Yet human nature, by its very essence, will demand independence, the right to meet its own needs, to control, manipulate, and do whatever is necessary to get what it wants. And we will continue to do that until we arrive at a place where our lives and dreams are shattered. Until we lose our way. Until life becomes a mess, and we realise we can't fix it. And it is *we* who then cry out, 'My God, where are You?' Then we have an opportunity to seek Him more dearly and cry out from our hearts, knowing that He promises to hear us. And then His agenda kicks in, His plan to be with us and provide through His body, the community of God's people, the means to ensure that no one should have to face their struggles in this life alone. The words of that old song came back to this 'fair-weather sailor' son today: *'With Jesus in the boat I can smile at the storm. Smile at the storm. Smile at the storm. With Jesus in the boat I can smile at the storm as I go sailing home.'*

When It All Goes Dark

These days, I find myself more and more reminding God the Father that I am His 'fair-weather sailor' son. I like the sea—and life—when things are going well, when I can see and anticipate trouble, overcome challenges, and enjoy the passage. I would hazard a guess that we've all had moments when things go from bright and bubbly to dark and scary, but allow me to tell you what it's like out on the survey grounds in unchartered waters and the 'lights go out'—when things don't go as planned and we cannot tell where we are.

During the cyclone season on the east coast of Australia, some cyclones can turn out to be pure ornery and unpredictable. They can move slowly or pick up speed, track into the coast or away from the coast, change direction at a whim—north, south, or any direction in between. During one particular survey, we were searching for a new route through the Great Barrier Reef so that the huge coal ships coming into Hay Point near Mackay could save time and money by using this quicker route. Some of the experienced sailors and fishermen who knew the area well would tell of a passage through this particular labyrinth of reefs. It was up to us to find it and survey it thoroughly. Well, we had just reached the stage of the survey where we are up to in this book so far. The three electronic positioning stations had been erected over known marks, and we were able to position ourselves anywhere in the survey area when a cyclone began honing in on our position.

Our primary station had been erected on the peak of a high island at the northern end of the Whitsunday Island group, and it was very exposed to the weather. The gas generators, gas bottles, batteries, and all the electronic equipment would have to be protected; so we made passage to High Island and sent the team up to secure the heavy stuff and rescue the expensive bits. No sooner had we weighed anchor to head for shelter ourselves than the cyclone warning was cancelled because the cyclone changed direction and was now heading away from us. We remained off the island overnight, and when it was safe to do so, we sent the team back ashore and reestablished the equipment. But here's the point: as we kept our eye on the cyclone for the next three weeks, we repeated that procedure three more times. It's just so vital—when in uncharted waters and things go 'dark', you still have to be able to know where you are if you want to be able to search for a passage through the turbulent waters of life. HMAS *Flinders* did complete that survey and did find a passage through the reef for the large coal ships—it was named Hydrographer's Passage.

The purpose of that small story was to describe how 'in the dark' we can be when we lose our means of measuring where we are. There are many more stories of things going dark on the survey grounds, particularly in bad weather or due to natural causes like fires destroying a number of camps. Once, there was a water buffalo who took a particular dislike to the camp and personnel being in its territory. That was exciting—and terrifying for the two camp attendants. But when the lights went out, when we lost our bearings and were not able to see the way ahead of us—when it was dark—we had to come to anchor wherever we were and wait patiently until we were able to proceed into uncharted waters. This wasn't about a lack of faith; rather, it was the knowing gained from prudent practice.

I imagine you have had times in your life when things went dark, and you couldn't see a passage through the circumstances at the time. In my life, when darkness closes in and I think I might be lost (again), I find myself asking the question, 'Where am I?' Do you? And I know that I wouldn't need to ask that question if I was walking with God at the time. There you have it, and I call myself a Christian. Yet occasionally, I still find myself going out for a walk, looking for something or someone, to make my life at least have some appearance of being good. And before I realise it, I am either looking for a hiding place or feeling like I have taken a wrong turn, and I find myself

WHERE ARE YOU?

heading down some wrong path. So what do I do, especially when I am in uncharted waters? When I am trying to make passage through life, either I have to be able to determine where I am by measuring my position from the known marks described in this book, or I have to come to a stop and find the anchor for my soul until hope lights the way again. And for that hope, I look to Jesus—the pioneer and perfecter of our faith (Heb. 12: 1–3).

Measuring from the Centre of Our Known Marks

In the very centre of each brass plaque that forms the core of our known marks is a small triangle with a dot in the centre. This dot is what surveyors plumb bob over to accurately position themselves in the centre of the known station—our mark—all referenced to GDA, of course. This is also how the Christian searcher measures himself or herself, by plumb bobbing over the very core centre of our mark of faith—Christ Jesus. Jesus is the 'fixed point' that Pascal was referring to in his *Pensées*.[2] How often have you and I cried out to God because we feel lost, confused, and in some dark place? A lot of men I know—and I include myself, insofar as I know myself—see themselves more like the first 'Adam' than the last 'Adam' (1 Corinthians 15: 45). Yet we seem to be the ones who see ourselves this way. God sees us as His children, and Jesus sees us as His brothers and sisters and calls us His friends (Hebrews 2: 5–18). And since Jesus is our brother and God's only Son, into whose likeness we are becoming, it just makes sense that we look to Him who is at the very core of how we know God, know who we are according to His will for us, and know how we are related.

Jesus is the 'one and only' who has been at His Father's side and knows Him fully (John 11: 18). And Jesus is the only one whom the Father has sent to reveal the truth about who the Father is to those to whom Jesus chooses to reveal Him (Matthew 11: 27). To close the loop with this thought, Jesus will only reveal the Father to those the Father takes the initiative to make it happen so that the person comes to Jesus. It's God's initiative and our 'yes' or 'YES!'—depending on how it happens. Either way, this is love in action. Love is God's activity towards us, through His Spirit, and His gift to us that He pours into our hearts (Romans 5: 5). John of the Cross says to us, *'That is what God does with us: He loves us, that we might love Him, through the love He has for us.'*[3] Our response to Him, though, is hardly a flicker compared to the flame that comes out of the heart of God.

If I were to summarise what I have just written, it might go a bit like this: We have to look to Jesus to know who God really is and who we are according to His will for us. Jesus is the full revelation of God. When you look to Jesus, you see the Father as He truly is, and it is only through Jesus's relationship with God the Father that you can know God as Father. Certainly, for most of us, anyway, we cannot truly know the heart of the Father through what was modelled to us by our earthly fathers, no matter how good a father and how loving we think they were (are). Because even the best of them could not show or express the love that God the Father has for us. It's unfathomable.

God would not be called the Father without having His Son, Jesus. The Son would not be the Son without His Father. And the Spirit is the one who shows us the relationship between Father and Son. The Spirit is also the one who unites us with the Father and the Son and brings us into fellowship with them. Faith is the channel through which this grace flows. God loves us first and calls us to Himself. Our 'yes' response to His call is the way in which we love Him back through the faith He has gifted to us by the power of that grace. Knowing God is the wisdom key that John Owen teaches about,[4] being all shut up in the Lord Jesus Christ. It is the essential key, found only in and by Jesus that unlocks the treasure chest and reveals the pearl of great price—God's eternal love for us. Look to Jesus because as the words of the hymn sing to us, *'You are my friend and you are my brother, even though You are a king. And I love you more than any other, so much more than anything.'*

Three Beacons

Sometimes we lost 'lock' on the stations. This usually occurred during electrical storms, poor atmospherics, or a power failure on the ship's electrical supply. When these events happened or whenever there was doubt in our position, we didn't need to go back to calibrate at each mark because we would deploy beacons around the survey area. These beacons were integral to help verify where we were because they were calibrated in with each known stations, so we could use them to help us verify whether we were still in right relationship with our known marks. The three essential beacons that God has provided to help us verify and validate our relationship with our known marks are our faith, hope, and love. They help us to verify that our hearts are in order and act as 'check-in' points. They are like the beacons of light that light the way and shine on the face of Jesus so that we can get glimpses of the glory to be revealed fully later.

Faith. John Eldredge wrote, *'Memory, imagination and a passion for glory—these we must keep close at hand if we are to see the journey to its end.'* Memory is where faith lies. *'Faith looks back and draws courage.'*[5] Jesus Himself exhorted the disciples (and us) to remember Him because He knew that our common union was in Him (Luke 22: 19) *'Do this in remembrance of me.'* Jesus knew that our faith relies on remembering Him, which we do when we receive the blessing cup and when we follow Him and stay on that narrow path that will take us home. Keep checking in with this beacon.

Hope. Our hearts cannot live without hope. Without hope, without vision for the future, we perish. Gabriel Marcel says that *'hope is for the soul what breathing is for our living organism'.*[6] Desire is kept alive by imagination. *'Hope looks ahead and keeps desire alive.'*[7] Jonathan Edwards once said that none of us move towards anything we don't desire. Or more clearly for me, we always move towards what we desire most! Sadly, we seem to be unaware of what our heart desires most. *'God has set eternity in our hearts'* (Eccles. 3: 11). We might 'groan' now, but if this (life) is as good as it gets, we have a real problem. But Paul assures us that this is not so. He said, *'If only for this life we have hope in Christ, we are to be pitied more than all men'* (1 Cor. 15: 19). C. S. Lewis wrote, *'If I find in myself desires which nothing in this world can satisfy, the only logical explanation is that I was made for another world.'* The crisis of hope that afflicts us is a crisis of imagination. Our 'online world' has reduced wonder and imagining to virtual realities. It is full of fantasy and futuristic, supernatural stories and heroes. But we Christians have much more—God's promises that are true. Instead of being mindless anthropoids, human beings are *'meaning-making people'.* We are made in the image of the living triune God. We search for answers. What's all this about? What does it mean for me? Do I matter? Does anybody care? The answer to these questions from God is a resounding 'yes'! Stay in touch with this beacon.

Love—as Jesus loves. We need to understand the larger story that God is telling us and imagine what it will be like. But 'self-preservation' seems to be the main theme of our smaller stories, mainly because we are driven by fear. But that narrative is so wrong because it violates who God is and whose image we bear, and it prevents us from having life to the full now. The persons of the triune God live for bringing glory to the others. This is our purpose also, to bring glory to God in the way we relate with Him first and then with others as we represent Christ to the world and reflect God's presence here on earth. To fulfil this purpose, we need His passion—His very nature. We need to relate with love—to love like Jesus loved—and not let it grow cold (Matthew 24: 12). We must stay married to this beacon.

So to move together, with eternity set in or hearts, we move towards the One we love and trust because we see our future with Him, living in the community of His people. This movement towards God together has two very important aspects for us: our future and being God's image bearers now. As human beings, we seem to have many ways of thinking about the future and what it means to us—we are meaning-making people. These two things—thinking about and imagining our future within the circle of love and relationship with God the Father, Jesus, and the Spirit and the meaning that has for us—are essential for us living life to the full now. Confident in our faith, strengthened with the assurance of hope in Christ, and motivated by love in the knowledge of who God is, we move towards Him together for His purpose and glory. These are our 'homing beacons'.

The Third Time

At seventeen, when I was lost, confused, and raging at the world through my contempt for everyone and everything that had contributed to, had neglected, ignored, and couldn't fix my shame and pain, I would not have heard God's voice even if He did speak to me. I was too consumed in my efforts at rebelling against the world and everyone in it to listen to anyone. And I was far too committed to my self-determined vows to look after myself, satisfying my wants and managing my self-centred needs to be concerned with what God might want of me. Still, now when I look back, I can see how He looked after me and provided for me through the safety net of the navy. I wonder whether or when I missed the first opportunity to hear His voice because I was too focused on loving me for my sake.

The second time I was aware of His voice, it was twenty years after joining the Navy, as I have already shared with you. At the time, I was jogging to the naval base to put in another day at the office as CO of HMAS *Flinders* when I heard God speak. It wasn't exactly the words *'Where are you?'* because He knew I wouldn't have been able to answer that question back then. But I believe God was making a similar point in words that I could understand at the time. I believe I heard Him clearly say, *'I could take you now,'* and I immediately stopped jogging and felt this huge pain in my chest. Then His voice again asked, *'What do you want?'* Suddenly, the images of the beautiful faces of my two daughters flashed before my eyes, and the words were out before I knew I was speaking. *'I want You, Lord.'* But I didn't know what that meant back then, although I was willing to love God for my sake.

Yes, the third time took about another twenty years before I understood the point that God was making. I had just suffered a microscopic stroke in my left eye and lost the majority of sight from that eye. I had always relied on my ability to quickly detect and size up life's challenges. This came at a time following some years of high performance and undue stress. I needed to recalibrate and settle on a wiser course and speed for the passage ahead. I had to come face-to-face with the layers of trauma that had impacted my life and relationships. And ever since, I detect His voice asking me, *'Where are you?'* He still asks, you know. He has many times since that third time. And He continues to ask, but now I know what He is doing as He guides me home. I hear His question whenever I am feeling confused, in some dark place and time, lonely, scared—you know what I mean. So I answer Him, 'Here I am, Father. I'm with Jesus because He picks me up when I fall. It's me your "fair-weather sailor" son, Jesus's walking companion—still surveying life, searching for You, reaching out (groping), comforted by Your presence within, stumbling along in the light that Your Word shines for me to place my next step on the narrow, sometimes rocky, steep, and difficult path.'

A lot of the time, I seem to think I need to love God for His sake because He is so good; but deeper down, I know He doesn't need that. So I'm on the way home, Father, guided by Your homing beacons. I am slowly learning to love myself for Your sake.[8] And I know that when You stop asking where I am, it will be because I am with You.

Chapter 9 Notes:

1. Dr Larry Crabb expands on this theme in his books *The Silence of Adam* (updated as *Men of Courage*) and *Fully Alive*.
2. Pascal's *Pensées* quote: *'When everything is moving at once, as on board a ship, nothing appears to be moving. When everybody is moving towards depravity no one appears to be moving. But, when somebody stops, he shows up the others by acting as a fixed point.'*
3. Cited in Matthews, *The Impact of God: Soundings from St John of the Cross*, 1995, page 110.
4. John Owen, *Communion with God*, 2007, Digression 2.1, pages 133–135.

5. Brent Curtis and John Eldredge, *The Sacred Romance: Drawing Closer to the Heart of God*, 1997, pages 157–158.
6. Ibid. page 178.
7. Ibid. page 158.
8. See the four stages of the spiritual journey as proposed by Bernard of Clairvaux cited in Crabb, *Real Church*, 2009, pages 26–29.

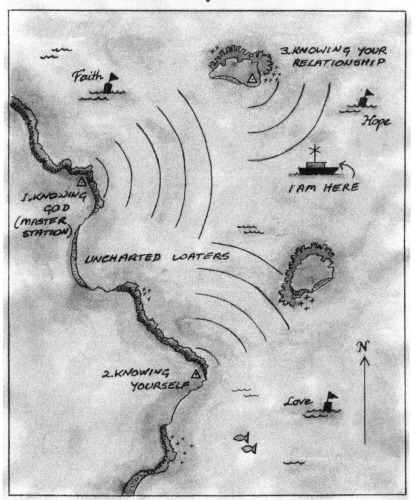

SURVEY GROUNDS

CONCLUSION

The glory of God is man fully alive, and the life of man is the vision of God.
—Irenaeus

There's more to me than what you see.
— Lindsay Duncan Lang

If you never never go, you will never never know.
—Author unknown[1]

WHEN WE ARE asked to describe where we are, we usually give our country, our state, town, city, suburb, street, and number as a reference. Whenever I have been overseas in other parts of the world, I let people know that I am from Australia—if they haven't already worked that out for themselves. Australia is my reference point. But for Australia to be 'known' as to where it is in this world, there has to be a datum point that locates it, a starting point from which we can make our other measurements, all the way down to the street where we live and even the house number. Because of the datum, all other marks that position us are integrated and can be known and located accurately with reference to Australia.

As a Christian, my reference point is God. He is both my Creator and the One to whom I was born. But I need a datum, a starting point so as to begin to describe where, what, and who He is and where I fit in. And then I need to describe other known marks that are accurately integrated with my datum that will describe where I am right down to the very place that I am positioned at this moment in time. Scripture—the Bible—gives me this starting point. From this known starting point, three essential marks are positioned from which I can measure where I am relative to each of the marks at any point in my life. These three marks that I have been referring to are knowing God, knowing yourself in accordance with God's will for you, and knowing how God and you are related right now. And for all our lives so far and until we know actually where we are when we are home with God, we need to keep searching and reaching for these marks. Not because they shift, but because as we get closer to them, we see them differently, and we see ourselves differently. This will be the case until we are with God, and we see things as they really are. Because the veil will be lifted, the mirror will no longer distort our image, and the gentle breeze of the Spirit will have blown away any fog.

The Search Really Matters

Cast your mind back to a time when you were sharing your faith with a safe and trusted 'someone' who was as curious about hearing your story as you were in hearing theirs. Can you recall noticing 'something' come alive in you as you shared together? Almost as if it was like your heart burning within. That's what it is like for me when I have conversations with men and women about the things of God and life—the things that really matter, the things of *'ultimate concern'* of which Paul Tillich wrote.[2] I feel a sense of the abundant life rise within me. And I wonder if this is something like what Irenaeus was saying in the quote at the beginning of this chapter. So it should be no surprise, really, that when we are fully alive, it is the presence of God that is being displayed.

If you have never experienced anything like this, then it is something to really look forward to, and I encourage you to take up God's invitation to search for Him until you do. If we don't experience this sense of aliveness, what is it that gets in the way, do you think? If you have read this book up to this point, I am hoping that you know what I think it is. But it's really only what God has been trying to tell us for thousands of years. And it is most likely our pride that keeps us from seeking God (Psalm 10: 4–6) and that causes us to turn away from Him (Hosea 4: 1–12) and undertake a search for life ourselves—somewhere 'out there'. It's pride along with all pride's hangers-on: the will to independence, vows of self-determination, wilfulness, and arrogance that yell out to others, 'Don't you tell me what to do!' We turn away from God because we have decided to seek our own happiness and pursue the 'good life' apart from God.

Knowingly or unknowingly, consciously or unconsciously—either way has a similar impact. We have exchanged or rejected our 'glory' for 'worthless idols' (Jeremiah 2: 11). Our one saving grace is that God knows us so well, and He also knows that apart from Him, our lives have and are of no value. Despite what the superior-sounding voices from our secularised societies try to convince us about what the 'good life' looks like, they are the desperate cries of lost and confused souls that are perishing, soon to be nothing but screams.

That will be one hell of a time because hell is the place where God isn't. So to keep us heading in the right direction, God has placed this desire for Him in our hearts—the spiritual wellsprings of our lives.

Out There or In Here?

Still, naively, in ignorance or self-reliance, we miss the marks that God gives us to be able to search for Him, reach out for Him, and find Him even though He is never far from us. Meanwhile, we are out there (in the never, never) searching in all the wrong places to identify and satisfy this desire that we sense is in us—consuming, tasting, and grabbing the counterfeits that promise satisfaction but that never deliver the real thing and delivering only momentary and fleeting pleasures. Before long, after what amounts to what seems to be much ado about nothing, if we are fortunate, we come to realise that our time, resources, and straining efforts were our attempts to seek entertainment and brief distraction so as to quash the pain and emptiness of unfulfilled desire—for just a moment, anyway.

If or when we come to our senses, we have an opportunity to seek out this desire more earnestly and purposefully. And when we find God, we come alive to know Him in the way that He longs to be known—and to live in a way that gives us life to the full. But if we don't seek Him or if we have moved too far away from Him and have lost a sense of His presence, we can forget about God altogether. And soon, there is no more room for Him in our thinking at all (Psalm 10: 4). This is the very place that human beings ought not to be. When dreams, visions, hopes, and plans for a future are shattered, where do we turn? Worse yet, we could come to accept that all life is only as we experience it—and it is not! But our worldly thinking gets conflicted, confused, and becomes fragmented as the different parts of us pull us this way and that and push us in directions we don't want to go until life is all mixed up and we no longer know which part of us is real. It's a life of sorts, but that is not the life that our hearts desire. Unable to help ourselves and disorientated as to where the door of hope is, life as we have been falsely promised by the world is revealed as a counterfeit to something real inside of us that is in danger of being quenched. The only way out seems to lead to a dead end—death, at least the death of man's personality, as Francis Schaeffer was describing in a culture that has turned away from God.

Look at the statistics that are being gathered around men's lives, and I include domestic violence and crime rates along with the suicide rates amongst the varying age groups of men. But wait—you may protest—those are not statistics. He/she was my husband/wife, mother/father, son/daughter, brother/sister, relative, friend—I loved them. Yes, that's the point. Each death and each person are important—it's personal and deeply meaningful. We all need to know who we are, that we belong, that we are loved, and that there is someone who would be curious enough to want to know me more intimately. A singer/songwriter friend of mine in the Northern Rivers, Luke Vassella, provides a deeply moving insight in his song 'In a North Coast Town.' In it, he sings that we (men) can be drowning and yet burning with desire at the same time. How do you save a drowning man who is on fire with desire? Luke asks. I believe the answer lies in assuring him to reach out his hand to the object of that desire—Jesus.

Humanism answers the question 'Who are we?' with *We are people with the capacity and the resources to make life work.'* It is your destiny to become fully yourself, to live out your dreams, to find yourself, and to discover who you are by what you do, who you relate with, and what you have. Do whatever it takes to get what you want so as to enjoy a good life now before you die because that's it, the lost voices of humanity tell us. But how do I know who I am? Lewis Sperry Chafer offers the hope found in the revealed truth of Scripture about human beings, from our datum. which include two core ideas: First, *we were created with the capacities necessary for relating with God* for desiring, knowing, loving, and enjoying Him. Second, *apart from community, we are not whole.*

Only in relationships do we derive our personality and enjoy the fullness of connecting and belonging. Broken connection lies at the root of all soul pathology—what's wrong with us. Then a familiar voice can be detected rising inside of us, demanding to be heard, and it seeks to drown out any other voice. 'I am your centre. I will look after you.' And we mistakenly think it is our voice, but it is not! It's the voice of the 'Other' I AM—the eternal I AM. It is not us. He is the 'something', the Someone who desires to be fully known, explored, and discovered. The One who wants us to be together forever with Him. The story that Christianity brings to us is the summation of it all, says C. S. Lewis. As every fairy tale, fantasy, never-ending love story, adventure epic, and drama gives promise to and attracts our heart, God longs to be known by us for who He truly is, for His name's sake, and for our ultimate good.

Susan was reading Buzz Aldrin's autobiographical book *Magnificent Desolation* and sharing some of the highlights with me. I was curious to hear her share how wonderful it was that Buzz took communion—the bread and the wine of the thanksgiving and remembrance sacrament—as a special thanksgiving before stepping onto the moon. Allow me to quote what he said: *'It was my hope that people would keep the whole event in their minds and see beyond minor details and technical achievements—a deeper meaning—a challenge, and the human need to explore whatever is above us, below us, or out there.'* [3] In that momentarily experience of reverent wonder, I can understand how he was captured by this hopeful desire. However, the remainder of Buzz's life seemed to be an unsettled searching for that something 'out there' that would finally provide the peace and assurance of what he was hoping for. Buzz doesn't appear to have found what he was looking for, and it seems he slipped away from his Christian faith in the process. His life seems to be a metaphor for searching in the wrong direction and perhaps a slight on how our Westernised Christianity has helped facilitate the search 'out there' rather than searching deep within us. What do you think?

Beyond Boundaries

One of the most popular books that has been around since 2004 and read by nearly anyone involved in understanding how to have healthy relationships is the bestseller from Dr Henry Cloud and Dr John Townsend, *Boundaries: When to Say Yes, When to Say No—To Take Control of Your Lives.* Now I agree that it is vitally important to be safe in relationships and to get all the help we can so as to do relationships well. But why was, and still is, this book so popular? Well, I think it is because of some of the issues I have written about. But allow me to put a simple proposition to you: we are made to enjoy great relationships, to love and to be loved, and to be known intimately, explored, discovered, and enjoyed. We are not made to be abandoned, rejected, hurt, and abused. We know that the major consequence of what happened back in that garden was broken relationships—with God, each other, and creation. There was always going to be fallout and collateral damage from humanity putting the 'self' first before the other because that was not what God intended. And we suffer greatly from damaging and destructive relationships. Some of the consequences include pain, abuse, trauma, separation, loneliness, grief, loss, depression, anxiety, violence, and even death.

For most of us, our relationships are not delivering the deep intimacy we are seeking. And they never will while we place the self ahead of the other. Self-centred needs that remain unmet turn into demands, and that does not work. Just have an honest look at what is going on around us, between us, and in us. If relationships were real ships, navigational charts would be littered with the symbol for shipwrecks. So it is not surprising that people are committed to their personal well-being and are reliant on our Western psychotherapeutic culture that aims at healing us, fixing the problem, and changing the circumstances—including changing the other person—so that we can feel better. Our personal goals seem to be aimed at making ourselves healthy enough so that we can be well enough to enjoy life as much as we can, for as long as we can. And we spare no expense at seeking all manner of ways to put back our fragmented selves and shattered lives, recover our lost souls, repair damaged hearts, and find our lost identities. Put me back together and make me whole—I'm so broken. Little wonder that *Boundaries* became a classic and still is the textbook for offering ways to be safe and protect yourself, teaching us how to be assertive and to stand up for our rights. Or is our real motive to be in control of our relationships so that the person who says they love me meets my needs so that I am happy and feel good?

While I do not read anywhere in Scripture that Jesus needed to assert Himself or demand that His rights be met, having a good understanding of where you end and where the other person begins is a respectful attitude because we all carry the dignity and the uniqueness of our personhood that God gives to us. I think that boundaries serve a useful purpose in certain circumstances and are necessary for a certain period of time during difficult life struggles in people's lives. For example, space and distance can create and strengthen desire—absence makes the heart grow fonder, we admit, especially when it puts us in touch with our God-given desire to connect. But what I want to emphasise is that having and setting personal boundaries was never the original intention in God's plan for relationships other than knowing where I end and where you start and are part of our flawed self-made human protective structures. We were not made for independence; we were made to be dependent on God and interdependent with others.

What is less known, and less popularly embraced, is Townsend's book written some seven years after *Boundaries*, which is titled *Beyond Boundaries*. In this follow-up book, Townsend is saying that we are drawn to seek out relationships with others. We have this internal drive that moves us towards some other. This drive is not something we can simply not choose to have; we are designed this way by God. And the thing that draws us is a God-given gift. So it is simply part of who we are as human beings made in the image of our relational God. While nearly all of us would seem to hope for good outcomes, Townsend cautions us that for this draw to work as it is meant to, any good and meaningful relationship must have trust at its core. And in our self-centred and needy condition, the draw can be self-deceptive because all of us have the potential to perceive things incorrectly. Not everything is as it seems.

So while the draw may feel good and the desire to connect can be strong, sometimes the choices we make are not so good for us and can produce painful outcomes. Pain produces a withdrawal response because we assume that pain is bad for us. Whoever told us that, by the way? We do whatever is necessary to avoid it, escape it, numb its effects, and get away from the perceived cause. Our goal is to protect ourselves from further discomfort and suffering. But we were not meant to live with self-protection; and the walls, structures, and barriers that we build to protect us not only keep others out—they also keep our real deep inner selves from trusting others to explore us, to know us, and also to stop us from presenting who we are to others.

To pursue someone, to offer yourself to another, and to open yourself to give and receive all from another present opportunities to be rejected; and we were not made to be rejected—that's why it hurts so much. Yet despite a measure of risk, the effort and courage to love is always worth it—love is life. We are meant to know love. Therefore, whatever your situation and circumstances, use appropriate boundaries for a time, give yourself some space to reflect in safety so as to develop the wisdom from learned experience, and proceed into the unchartered waters of relationships, beyond boundaries that prevent the unknown from being truly known. But it will always involve an element of risk, so do it wisely and well and stay relatively safe. [4]

A Friend's Legacy

My friend's life could have been a metaphor for loneliness. Let me tell you about his legacy. It's a good sad story. I first met my friend when he arrived in Lismore after separating from a long-term relationship. He had also cut himself off from his children and grandchildren, all of his own choosing. This is not an uncommon situation I have found in some men's stories. If you read between the lines of what I am saying, you might imagine some of the relational hurt and pain involved in such tragic circumstances.

My wife, Susan, and I lived fifteen kilometres out of town on five acres at the time. If you know the Northern Rivers region of New South Wales, you would be aware that five acres may as well be fifty, may as well be 500 acres in having to keep up with the fences, growth, and weeds. I was building a fence at the time, and my friend mentioned he had done some of that, so I invited him out to the farm. I soon found out that he was a painter and a carpenter who worked on fence lines and could do just about anything he said he could. He loved being out in the countryside, the peace and quiet, and he had a real interest in the bird life. I recall he counted over seventy different varieties of birds on the property. We also ran a few cows and kept a horse to manage the growth. He loved our red kelpie dog, although one time, when he was watching the property for us and had to introduce the dog to a tradesman, he seemed to have difficulty with the name Honey Bun! He wasn't so fond of the cat, though, and that appeared to be a mutual thing.

As Susan and I were travelling often for work, my friend would often spend a lot of his time on the farm, watching over it and the animals. He had a caravan on the property and would never sleep in the house. We would come home and find a well-kept, well-looked-after place, always freshly mown. And when we were home, he would be there mending fences, making the underneath of the house look like a Queenslander, building things, painting anything that didn't move, maintaining the ride-on mower, and whatever else took his fancy. He would refer to me as his Christian counsellor, but I wasn't really. Rather, we were mates; and for some reason, God had brought us together—an ex-Navy sea captain who couldn't change a tap washer and a jack of all trades who lived life like he was lost at sea.

However, my friend was a damaged and troubled man, and his personal relationships reflected that. The pain of early childhood abandonment and other traumas set him up to fail at relationships. The hurt and fear of rejection and of being hurt again were far too great for him to bear. The consequences were that it was much safer to keep people at a distance, and it was better to be independent so as to control life and people so that they didn't get too close. Deep down, the lies of *'I'm no good'*, *'nobody would like me if they really knew me'*, *'people aren't to be trusted'*, *'I'm unlovable'* and more were too powerful. So my friend adopted a life mantra that went 'I don't want to be any trouble.' This way, he didn't have to accept invitations. But this was an excuse so that people would not get to know him intimately. Deep down, my friend believed that he could not face the pain of rejection ever again, so he vowed to control things to ensure that he never had to.

But there's a problem when we keep others out, and we keep ourselves closed inwards. We never get to enjoy what we most long for: belonging, connecting, feeling part of a community, and enjoying close relationships—the deep way of relating that God means for us to have, with Himself first and with others. We are made in the image of a relationship; and our deepest desires are to be intimately known, loved, and enjoyed in a common union with God and with friends.

Although my friend had made a determined vow not to let anyone in, God had other plans. G. K. Chesterton once called it the *'furious love of God'*—the love that pursues us and never gives up. You see, God could see my friend's heart. Under all that bluff and cultural stuff, despite all his efforts to control his life, under all the self-managed strategies to make life go reasonably well, and down deeper than the mess we can make of life is where God is. And as he opened his heart to God, to Jesus, to the Spirit, to me a little bit, maybe, slowly, in little bits, to those who were willing to see Christ in him, his heart began to change. What God poured into my friend's heart he had to let out. Not through relating deeply because he never did heal in those places, but with what he did have to give. He gave his time, his skills, his efforts, and his resources in service to widows, single women in need of a handyman, or just anyone in need. He drove people around town or up the highway to the major airport. He even drove hundreds of miles to pick up someone he felt for but hardly knew when they were released from prison. He volunteered and gave his time to many organisations. And because of our friend's help, Susan and I enjoyed country farm life for nine years.

My friend gave of himself in a life of service, rendering himself to God. He gave of himself in the only way he knew how because he wanted to do good. He was certainly a doer. We built a boat together. Well, it required that someone read the instructions. To me, my friend was more like an older brother who showed me not only how to do things, but how to approach things. He taught me life lessons such as go at your own pace, work it through slowly, work hard but don't knock yourself out or get flustered, and to be patient. We had rather what was, for me, an awkward moment in what were the last few weeks of my friend's time on earth. Because his health was failing, I had called in to ensure that he was eating proper meals. I had tidied up his front lounge area a bit and folded his clothes and bedding, and then I went into his dimmed bedroom and read something from the Bible to him. As I stood to leave, he said, 'I love you.' And I awkwardly responded, 'I love you too,' and somehow made my way out the door.

My friend died shortly after that. As Susan and I have been cleaning out his unit, he is still teaching me things. And I proudly show off my newly acquired tool cupboard to my mates now—a gift from my friend. Look how organised I am now—everything in its place, although I still don't know how to use the tools properly. Since his passing, I have been able to reflect more about the good times in my friend's life. Of all the Scriptures that came to mind was Song of Songs 2: 8–17. I don't think my friend had ever read Song of Songs, but I know that this was God's heart for him. What struck me in this passage is how the bridegroom—Christ, our lover—pursues us, woos us, and then makes the wedding proposal. I saw that happen to my friend. A deeply wounded and lonely man who accepted God's proposal to him—and his heart changed forever.

Sadly, my friend's greatest desires—to be loved, to be accepted, and to belong—these vineyards were overrun by the foxes and darkened by the fear of shadows from his past. They ruined the goodness in his vineyard of life. Tragic during his life; but in the long run, in God's larger story, God had captured my friend's heart, and his heart desired God. God had promised to bring my friend to Himself, and so He did. The foxes are gone now. The fear shadows have fled, and my friend is free at last. And he's still teaching me stuff. Recently, he seemed to speak to me. I was saying to God, 'Is that all there is? Here today, gone tomorrow—ashes to ashes and dust to dust?' And I sensed my friend response, *'There's more to me than what you see.'* That's his legacy. Isn't that so with all of us? I will miss our Saturday conversations, and I will miss him.

There Is Something More

Have you noticed that the world always seems to be offering you more, and it's bigger and better than before? So this inherent desire within us that's never satisfied, but that draws us to seek something more really suits a world that feeds on sensualism, materialism, and our pursuit of happiness. Yes, indeed, there is 'something' more to me than what you see—and it wants to be fully known. The search for it becomes all-consuming and is critical to our spiritual journey and is especially dependent on the world view through which a person will look to carry out their search.

Mistakenly, human beings can think that what they are searching for is somewhere out there. Even people without any reference point who bother to take time to notice can see the wonders of our created universe(s). There is a sense that there must be 'something' out there; otherwise, we wouldn't spend so much on space exploration or produce an abundance of space fantasies to tantalise our imaginations. God gave us this sense of wonder so as to wonder about Him. It's a reverent wonder. It captures us (Psalm 8: 4). It gives a sense of knowledge of an immeasurable love that provokes our imagination (Ephesians 3: 18–20). And we are invited to build on this reverent wonder (the Message Bible, 2 Peter 1: 5–9). Chapters 1 and 2 of Romans provide a sense of God's immenseness and our smallness and need for Him. We glimpse His handiwork and where we fit in. And it's all from something that is *in* us.

Oswald Chambers in his book *My Utmost for His Highest* is pointing us in the right direction when he said, 'You will never cease to be the most amazed person on earth at what God has done for you on the inside.' And it's so amazing that it is indescribable—words cannot do it justice. And we would not know what it is or where or how to search for it if God did not reveal it to us. The full quote from Irenaeus is as follows: *'The glory of God is man fully alive, and the life of man is the vision of God. If the revelation of God through creation already brings life to all living beings on the earth, how much more will the manifestation of the Father by the Word bring life to those who see God.*[5] God has revealed as much as we need to know at this time until all is revealed in His perfect timing. Life is really all about knowing God, says Larry Crabb,[6] and so does John 17: 3.

There is a larger story that God is telling us about Himself and where we fit in. He gives us His Word and His promises so that we are able to search in the right direction, seek to know Him more intimately, reach out for Him, and find Him. But we need this datum, this starting point, to provide guidance and locate the three marks that are essential for us to know where we are at any point in our lives. And it has to be accurate to God's own determined standards; otherwise, we will miss the marks. God is our reference. Since He is the divine author of our lives, our datum is His revealed Word to us. We are able to search what is unknown to make it known from three marks that can be known with God-determined accuracy from our datum: knowing God, knowing ourselves according to His will for us, and knowing how we are related. Using these three marks, we are able to measure where we are in our journey of life as we relate in our communities, cultures, and societies—if we search for them with all our hearts and keep reaching for them.

Making Known What Is Unknown

Jesus did not come to establish a religion. He came to reveal the truth about our Father, that He is a relational God and that He desires to be known. We do not define God; rather, we discover who we are by starting with who God is. And we discover that we too are relational. Finding oneself, discovering 'who we are', is implicitly linked to who God is and being in relationship with Him first and then with others. God's great *purpose* in creating people is to reveal His glory (His perfect character of holy love) to people who can *desire* Him, *know* Him, *love* Him, and find *joy* in Him. Under God's plan, we undergo a process where we become more like Him (Galatians 4: 19) *until Christ is formed in (us) you* and therefore enjoy relationship with Him and community with others until we are invited into His community with Him—forever.

Jesus did come to show us a way to return to the Father and to make that way open to all who would enter in through Himself. In doing this, Jesus gave us a new start. He gave us a new identity, a new heart—His heart—and the power to live this life in relationship with God now and for eternity. This Christian biblical world view gives people a way of understanding 'who' God really is from His self-revelation, who we are as persons in relationship with Him, and what that relationship looks like with Him first and then with one another and the world around us. Any theology that seeks to understand our Christian faith must be looked at through relational glasses with the eyes of faith.

Everyone's life is a story, a narrative of their time spent on earth in relationship with their known universe and the people in it. Their smaller story will be defined by their responses to these things, through their attitude towards them, and by the personal choices they make. The story of our lives could be said to be made of two significant parts: the journey itself and the relationships involved. It seems to me that our part in the story is to go on our journey in relationship with one another and move forward together. For Christians, this smaller narrative of our life sits within a meta story—a larger story that God is telling about Himself and His relationship with His creation, including and foremost the crown of His creation—us. Christians see the pinnacle of His story being centred in Jesus, and our part is to follow in His footsteps, walking as He did and relating as He showed us.

I believe that each person is given a place in the larger story that God is telling. The essential stepping point at all times in our life journey is from where we are, and it is always the 'next step' that is the really important one. From this known position, we can figure out our purpose, direction, and destination and so be defined in our humanity by our courage, willingness, and choices to love. We know where we are going, why we are going there, and have been given the means to get there if we rely on God's Word *to* us and

His Spirit *in* us. As a navigator and surveyor, I learnt that it is essential to be able to define exactly where you are so that you can determine what direction to proceed with confidence to arrive at your chosen destination.

We know our purpose, we have our guidance, we've selected our datum, and we have moved onto the survey grounds to establish ourselves in relation to known marks. And we now know where we are. The survey preparations are complete. So we are ready now. We are able to go forward with hope, enjoying the experience and discovering new things as we search for what is unknown to make it known. Your life journey will also take you through uncharted waters. Do not be worried because you have the means to know where you are at all times, and as a Christian, you know that God is close by—and that He is *for* you, *with* you, and *in* you. And just think—if you never, never go, you will never, never know.

For this book, I have used hydrographic surveying as a metaphor for searching the unknown, unsurveyed, and uncharted waters of life—a little like being out on the survey grounds. While the analogy might have been useful for describing where you are under certain circumstances, it does not cover all of life's eventualities. There are times when we are on our journey through the sea of life that we find ourselves needing to set a course and make passage through unknown, unsurveyed, and uncharted waters that are not as clearly defined as like being on the survey grounds. What then? Well, that's for another story. I hope to make it the subject of a further opportunity for us to cast our eyes and minds over something together—when we find ourselves passaging through uncharted waters and when we need the strength and courage to be all we are meant to be.

But for now, as you set your course and get under way to continue on your journey, let go of everything that you are holding too tightly. Let it all go now—whatever you are hanging on to—because you might need to hang on firmly to the boat you are in as you go through stormy weather and rough seas. By the way, keep a close check on your speed. Jesus is at the helm, so relax as you set your face into the sea breeze and salt spray. Can you feel the warmth of the sun? Imagine yourself setting out into the unknown. Can you sense something inside of you getting excited and coming alive? You know who that is, don't you? You also know who you are according to His will for you. And you know, as every child knows his loving father, that you are His child and that you are safely on the way home.

We are all someone at some place journeying towards somewhere searching for something or someone other. It's been a privilege for me to share with you where I and some well known others have discovered some of the answers concerning our journeys. I hope my search has and will help you locate where you are in your journey. You'll have to excuse me now I think God might be trying to tell me something. I believe He is saying that I am not to call myself His 'fair-weather sailor son' anymore. He wants me to know that I *am* His adopted son, that He *loves* me, and that I give Him pleasure. He seems to be telling me that I am a fair sailor who enjoys good weather much more than bad weather and stormy seas. Yes, I believe that is true.

Bon voyage!

Conclusion Notes

1. This was an advertisement slogan for television and radio to promote tourism for the Northern Territory, Australia.
2. Paul Tillich, *Dynamics of Faith*, 1957, Harper & Row, New York. Review by JBH and SL: '*In the first chapter, Tillich succinctly delineates his own definition of faith. Put quite simply, faith is "the state of being ultimately concerned," the dynamics of which are, "the dynamics of man's ultimate concern."*' Accessed on Internet 8 December 2018, People. bu.edu/wwildman/Tillich/resources/review_tillich-paul-dynamics-of-faith.htm.
3. Buzz Aldrin, *Magnificent Desolation*, 2009, page 27.
4. John Townsend, *Beyond Boundaries*, 2011, pages 11–57.
5. Irenaeus quote from AH IV, 20, 7.
6. Larry Crabb continues to express this. It is throughout his book *Soul Talk* and in several other books.

READING LIST

Bailey, Kenneth, 2003, *Jacob & the Prodigal: How Jesus Retold Israel's Story*, InterVarsity Press, Downers Grove, Illinois.

Benner, David G., 2004, *The Gift of Being Yourself: The Sacred Call to Self-Discovery*, InterVarsity Press, Downers Grove, Illinois.

Bevere, John, 2017, *Killing Kryptonite: Destroy What Steals Your Strength*, Messenger International Inc., Palmer Lake Co.

Boyd, Gregory A., 2003, *Is God to Blame? Beyond Pat Answers to the Problem of Suffering*, InterVarsity Press, Downers Grove, Illinois.

Collins, Francis S., 2006, *The Language of God*, Free Press, New York, New York.

Crabb, Larry, 1988, *Inside Out*, NavPress, the Navigators.

Crabb, Larry, 1993, *Finding God*, Zondervan, Grand Rapids, Michigan.

Crabb, Larry, 1995, *The Silence of Adam*, Zondervan, Grand Rapids, Michigan.

Crabb, Larry, 2003, *Soul Talk: The Language God Longs for Us to Speak*, Thomas Nelson, Nashville, Tennessee.

Crabb, Larry, 2009, *Real Church: Does It Exist? Can I Find It?*, Thomas Nelson, Nashville, Tennessee.

Crabb, Larry, 2009, *66 Love Letters: A Conversation with God That Invites You into His Story*, Thomas Nelson, Nashville, Tennessee.

Crabb, Larry, 2013, *Fully Alive: A Biblical Vision of Gender That Frees Men and Women to Live Beyond Stereotypes*, Baker Books, Grand Rapids, Michigan.

Curtis, B., and Eldredge, John, 1997, *The Sacred Romance: Drawing Closer to the Heart of God*, Thomas Nelson, Nashville, Tennessee.

Dalbey, Gordon, 1988, 2003, *Healing the Masculine Soul: How God Restores Men to Real Manhood*, Thomas Nelson, Nashville, Tennessee.

Dreher, R., 2017, *The Benedict Option*, Penguin Random House, New York, New York.

Edwards, Dwight, 2002, *Revolution Within: A Fresh Look at Supernatural Living*, WaterBrook Press, Colorado Springs, Colorado.

Eldredge, John, 2000, 2007, *Desire: The Journey We Must Take to Find the Life God Offers*, Thomas Nelson, Nashville, Tennessee.

Jacobsen, Wayne, 2007, *He Loves Me! Learning to Live in the Father's Affection*, Windblown Media, Newbury Park, California.

Jennings, M. D., and Timothy, R., 2012, *Could It Be This Simple? A Biblical Model for Healing the Mind*, Lennox Publishing, Chattanooga, Tennessee.

Jennings, M. D., and Timothy, R., 2013, *The God-Shaped Brain: How Changing Your View of God Transforms Your Life*, InterVarsity Press, Downers Grove, Illinois.

Johnson, Darrell W., 2002, *Experiencing the Trinity*, Regent College Publishing, Vancouver, BC, Canada.

John Paul II, 1999, *Veritatis Splendor and the Renewal of Moral Theology*, Scepter Publishers, Princeton, New Jersey.

Jones, S. L., and Butman, R. E., 1991, *Modern Psychotherapies: A Comprehensive Christian Appraisal*, InterVarsity Press, Downers Grove, Illinois.

Letham, Robert, 2004, *The Holy Trinity: In Scripture, History, Theology and Worship*, P&R Publishing, Phillipsburg, New Jersey.

Manning, Brennan, 1990, 2000, 2005, *The Ragamuffin Gospel*, Multnomah Books, Colorado Springs, Colorado.

Manning, Brennan, 1994, 2002, *Abba's Child: The Cry of the Heart for Intimate Belonging*, NavPress, Colorado Springs, Colorado.

Manning, Brennan, 2009, *The Furious Longing of God*, David C. Cook, Colorado Springs, Colorado.

Matthew, Iain, 1995, *The Impact of God: Soundings from St John of the Cross*, Hodder and Stoughton, London, UK.

May, M. D., and Gerald, G., 2004, *The Dark Night of the Soul: A Psychiatrist Explores the Connection between Darkness and Spiritual Growth*, HarperCollins, New York, New York.

McClung, Floyd, 1985, 2008, *The Father Heart of God*, Kingsway Communications Ltd., Eastbourne, England.

McClung, Floyd, 2010, *Follow: A Simple and Profound Call to Live Like Jesus*, David Cook, Colorado Springs, Colorado.

Milne, Bruce, 1982, 1998, *Know the Truth: A Handbook of Christian Belief*, InterVarsity Press, Leicester, England.

Nouwen, Henri J. M., 1994, *The Return of the Prodigal Son: A Story of Homecoming*, Darton, Longman & Todd, GB.

Owen, John, 2007, 2012, *Communion with God: Fellowship with Father, Son and Holy Spirit*, Christian Focus Publications Ltd., Scotland.

Packer, J. I., 1973, *Knowing God*, Hodder and Stoughton, Kent, England.

Payne, Leanne, 1985, 1995, *Crisis in Masculinity*, Baker Books, Grand Rapids, Michigan.

Reeves, M., 2012, *Delighting in the Trinity: An Introduction to the Christian Faith*, InterVarsity Press, Downers Grove, Illinois.

Reno, R. R., 2002, *In the Ruins of the Church: Sustaining Faith in an Age of Diminished Christianity*, Brazos Press, Baker Books, Grand Rapids, Michigan.

Rohr, R., 2016, *The Divine Dance*, Whitaker House, New Kensington, Pennsylvania.

Sanders, Randolph K., 1997, *Christian Counseling Ethics: A Handbook for Therapists, Pastors, & Counselors*, InterVarsity Press, Downers Grove, Illinois.

Schaeffer, Francis, 1969, *Death in the City*, InterVarsity Press, London, UK.

Sitter, Gerald L., 2007, *Water from a Deep Well: Christian Spirituality from Early Martyrs to Modern Missionaries*, InterVarsity Press, Downers Grove, Illinois.

Stott, John R. W., 1990, *The Message of Acts*, InterVarsity Press, Leicester, England.

Thompson, Curt, 2010, *Anatomy of the Soul*, Tyndale House Publishers.

Townsend, John, 2011, *Beyond Boundaries*, Zondervan, Grand Rapids, Michigan.

Tozer, A. W., 1961, *The Knowledge of the Holy*, STL Books, Kent, England.

Wilbourne, Rankin, 2016, *Union with Christ*, David C. Cook, Colorado Springs, Colorado.

Willard, D., 1998, *The Divine Conspiracy: Rediscovering Our Hidden Life in God*, HarperCollins, London.

Willard, D., 2006, *The Great Omission*, Monarch Books, Oxford, UK.

Williams, R., 2015, *Post-God Nation*, HarperCollins Publishers, Sydney, Australia.

Zeller, Hubert van, 1985, *Spirituality Recharted*, St Bede's Publications, Petersham, Massachusetts.

ABOUT THE AUTHOR

J OHN IS A son, husband, father, grandfather, brother, and friend. He describes himself as an ordinary bloke but knows there is no such thing. He grew up as a country boy in coastal Whitsunday area of North Queensland, Australia where he gained his love for the ocean. At seventeen he ran away to sea. Closer to the truth he says that he joined the Navy to escape the confusion, anger and lostness he felt as a teenager. In the navy he specialised in hydrographic surveying and enjoyed a thirty year career carrying out surveys in mostly uncharted waters. In 2001 he believes he heard God calling him out from his security blanket and he left the Navy a year later to take up a new vocation as a counsellor.

Now he is sailing in a very different ship'- civilianship - and he is a self-confessed 'struggler', and pilgrim trying to navigate a different journey these last 17 years, re-learning life again, endeavouring to understand what it means to be a Christian man in our times. It's been a hard, messy, and sometimes lonely journey, he says. But he hasn't been alone, because he has been an avid searcher committed to his pilgrim journey alongside others as a counsellor and guide. With an inbuilt desire to know where he is on the journey, along the way he has read the spiritual classics, walked with, observed, witnessed, shared with, and learned from others who are an inspiration and encouragement for his own walk. Well, let's face it; we are never alone John says, yet each of us has our own journey to go on, and, since it is our journey, no one is going to walk it for us, though they may walk some of it with us.

CPSIA information can be obtained
at www.ICGtesting.com
Printed in the USA
LVHW041055010419
612520LV00004B/351

9 781796 000351